PHOTO
JOURNALISM
MANUAL

DAVID P. BERGIN

MORGAN & MORGAN, Inc., *Publishers*
HASTINGS-ON-HUDSON, N.Y.

The Fountain Press
London

First Edition 1967

Typographic Design and Layout
by John S. Carroll

Typesetting by Morgan Press
Hastings-on-Hudson, N.Y.

Contents

3

DEDICATED

To my mother, who bought me a $100
camera in the 1930 Depression, and
to Marion.

CHAPTER 1

Regulating Your Two Light Controls: Shutter & Aperture

The photographer can control light in two ways. One of these is the *speed* at which your shutter is set to open and close. A fast shutter speed of 1/400 second lets in very little light. A slow shutter speed of 1/25 second lets in a great deal of light. The second method of controlling the amount of light which is let into the camera and onto the film is the *size of the f/stop opening* or aperture. If the f/stop indicator is placed under f/4.5, a maximum opening results, letting in the most light. If the indicator is placed under f/32, the minimum opening and the least light results.

Now, how about these controls used in combination or in relation to one another? First, consider some generalizations. Then note the dicussion on regulating shutter speed and the size of the aperture.

In selecting shutter speeds, you must know which of three kinds of camera situations you will be facing: 1. Normal; 2. Action; 3. Depth of field.

A *normal camera situation* is one in which neither much action nor the maximum of depth of field is in the scene. Usually, 1/100 second is a good shutter speed for a normal situation.

An *action situation* would be photographing a football halfback breaking through a line or a field of racing horses rounding the track. If 1/100 second is used, the shutter will open, and the football runner will change his shape and position several times before the shutter closes. Each shift or change and position causes a blur. A sharp subject outline of action is obtained by using a very fast shutter speed. The shutter opens and closes before the subject (football player) can change his stance. This is freezing the action. So action usually requires a shutter speed of 1/400 to 1/1000 second to freeze the movement of your subject.

A *depth of field situation* is illustrated by the photo 1A. Objects are in the foreground, the midground, and the background. Many photos

7

TWO LIGHT CONTROLS: SPEED OF SHUTTER AND SIZE OF APERTURE

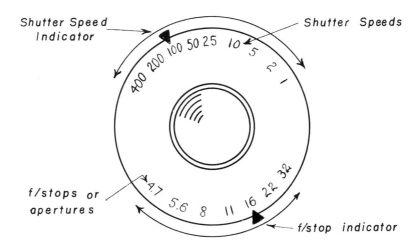

Shutter speeds range from 1 second up to 1/400 second. The faster the shutter opens and closes, the less light enters the camera. A shutter speed of 1/100 second freezes usual activity and movement: man rising from chair, person walking toward the camera. As the speed of the moving object increases, faster shutter speeds must be used to freeze the movement.

To change from one shutter speed to another, move the shutter speed indicator on your camera until it is either under the desired speed or until the desired speed shows in the shutter speed window when back shutter is used.

f/stop openings range from the maximum opening (f/4.7 lens) to the minimum opening of f/32. The bigger the opening in the shutter leaves, the greater is the amount of light which enters the camera.

Generally, big f/stop openings are used with fast shutter speeds. Small f/stops are used with slower shutter speeds. And small f/stops are required for depth of field shots (have objects near and far from the camera and all must be sharp).

have no depth of field. There is only one object in the foreground. Depth of field is defined as a situation in which the object nearest the camera (foreground) and farthest from the camera (background) are both in focus.

Best depth of field is obtained by using the smallest opening $f/32$, which lets in very little light. So a fairly slow shutter speed must be used.

In generalizing about the shutter speed and the f/stop openings, the following are true:

$f/4.7$ (big opening) (much light)	$+1/25$ second	(slow shutter speed) = (much light)	Too much light
$f/32$ (small opening) (little light)	$+1/400$ second	(fast shutter speed) = (little light)	Too little light

But the following combinations produce satisfactory exposures with certain films:

$f/4.7$ (big opening) (much light)	$+1/400$ second $1/1000$	(fast shutter speed) = (little light)	Action shot
$f/32$ (small opening) (little light)	$+1/25$ second	(slow shutter speed) = (much light)	Depth of Field shot

So the principle is to get your light as follows:

Action Fast shutter speed	Light must come from a big f/stop opening.
Depth of Field Small f/stop opening	Light must come from a slow shutter speed.
Normal $1/100$ at $f/$ 16 to 22	Some light comes from each of the controls.

Regulating Shutter Speed and Size of Aperture[1] for Changing Camera Situations

In the following discussion, assume that it is a normal day with good sunlight and that you are using a press-type film with an ASA rating[2] of 250. Further, basic data (BD) are $1/100$ second at $f/16$. Basic data is the exposure used in normal light for a normal camera situation.

---

1. f/stop opening and aperture are terms which are used interchangeably.
2. Every film has an ASA rating which is a measure of the sensitivity of the film. The numbers are proportional to the sensitivity of the film, often referred to as its speed. Thus a film having an ASA rating of 100 is twice as fast as one having a rating of 50, and half as fast (or sensitive) as one having a rating of 200. Generally, films rated from 12 to 80 are called "slow" films, from 100 to 400 are medium speed films, and over 400 are "fast" or high speed films.

PROBLEM: *Manipulating Basic Data for an Action Shot*

Your goal: To increase your shutter speed from 1/100 second to 1/200 second or faster to freeze a moving object which would blur at the slower shutter speed.

When the speed of the shutter is increased from 1/100 second to 1/200 second, it is opening and closing twice as fast as it did at the slower speed. So 1/200 second permits only 1/2 as much light to reach the film as did 1/100 second.

Unless the "lost light" is regained with your other light control, the f/stop, the film will be underexposed.

So you compensate or make adjustments with your f/stop opening to keep your exposure constant (the same amount of light as BD provided) by using bigger f/stops with faster shutter speeds. Bigger f/stop openings regain light lost by faster shutter speeds.

1/100 at f/16. *Basic Data are for a normal camera situation*

1/100 second is too slow a shutter speed to freeze much action.

So adjust your shutter speed indicator to 1/200 second.

When the shutter speed is doubled (from 1/100 second to 1/200 second), one-half of the light which BD let in the camera is lost. How can you get more light at your f/stop opening? Would you use a bigger f/stop or a smaller f/stop?

1/200 at f/11. Moving from f/16 to f/11, the next biggest stop regains the light lost when doubling the shutter from 1/100 second to 1/200.

If the action requires a faster shutter speed than 1/200, move up to 1/400, again doubling the shutter speed and losing one-half the light.

1/400 at f/8. Again, you must compensate for the lost light by regaining it at your f/stop opening by opening up from f/11 to the next largest opening, f/8.

The principle: Each time your shutter speed is doubled (cutting out one-half of the light reaching the film) to permit you to freeze action, you open up one full f/stop.

1/1000 at f/4.7 1/400 doubled is 1/800, but some cameras don't have such a speed. The shutter speed faster than 1/800 is 1/1000. This shutter speed calls for a little more light than f/5.6, which would have been used with 1/800.

PROBLEM: *Manipulating Basic Data for a Depth of Field Shot*

Your goal: When some objects are near the camera and some in the background and both sets of objects must be in focus, using your smallest aperture, f/32, helps make the shot possible.

10

So you must change from $f/16$ in BD to $f/32$.

Each time you decrease the size of the $f/$stop opening (moving from $f/16$ to $f/22$ to $f/32$) you cut out one-half of the light the bigger stop provided. So you have to regain the light by slowing your shutter speed.

1/100 at $f/16$. *Basic Data are for a normal situation.*

1/50 at $f/22$. Move the $f/$stop indicator to $f/22$, the next smaller opening, This cuts out one-half the light reaching the film, and regains the light by cutting your shutter speed in half.

1/25 at $f/32$. Set the $f/$stop indicator under $f/32$, your smallest opening. This cuts out one-half the light reaching the film. Regain the light by cutting your shutter speed in half.

In the two shutter and aperture problems just completed, you were adjusting your tool, the camera, from a normal situation to an *action* situation, and then to a DF (Depth of Field) situation. BD (1/100 at $f/16$) doesn't have a fast enough shutter to freeze action nor a small enough $f/$stop for the best depth of field. So you simply adjust your tool for a special situation, either action (a faster shutter speed) or DF (a small $f/$stop). In both action and DF adjustments, you compensate so that you keep your exposure constant—the same as in BD (Basic Data). Therefore, anyone of the adjusted sets of exposure data which result in either action or DF lets in the same amount of light as does BD. The following all let the same amount of light reach the film: 1/100 at $f/16$, 1/1000 at $f/4.7$, or 1/25 at $f/32$.

In making the changes above from a normal camera situation to either an action or a DF situation, neither your *light* nor *film* were problems because both remained unchanged.

The Three Variables in Photography

Photography's three variables are (1) camera situation, (2) light, and (3) film. We have seen how camera situations change, and how the camera must be adjusted. Basic data, used in a normal situation, do not have a fast enough shutter for action, nor a small enough $f/$stop for depth of field.

Light also changes throughout each day and in the four seasons. The light at sunrise, mid-morning, and high noon are different in both quantity and quality. And the light of summer and winter are quite different from that of fall and spring. On a "normal" day with good sunlight, BD work fine for a mid-morning exposure, but they would underexpose the film at sunrise and overexpose it at high noon. We have

11

3. THREE CAMERA SITUATIONS

SPRINGTIME ROMP: James Shaffeur, Dubuque, Telegraph Herald. Depth of field. Use a small f/stop to bring the near and the far objects into focus.

OUCH: Bob Hannah, St. Petersburg, Times. Real action. Use a fast shutter to freeze the action.

SOUNDING OUT HIS PETS: Maurice Johnson, UPI. Normal situation. Neither great depth of field nor action requiring a fast shutter speed is present here. About f/16 or 22 at 1/100 second would have done the job with a film with an ASA of 250.

a surplus of light in the summer and lack of light on many winter days. So we can't use BD for either of these extreme situations.

Photographic manufacturers make a variety of film. Fast film is very sensitive to light. Just a little light can produce a picture on such film. Some film is not nearly so sensitive to light. Such film requires either longer exposures or stronger light to produce good negatives. Between these two extremes is a medium kind of film. If you have been using moderately fast press film on which BD work very well, and you switch to either slow film, or a faster press film, you must expose differently for each of them. BD will underexpose the slow film and overexpose the fast film.

So a change in films means learning and using the ASA rating for the new film.

Fortunately, the light meter enables you to measure your light changes and to take them into account in adjusting your exposures. Veteran photographers who shoot pictures daily for years soon learn to judge light without using a meter. Is there any method to make certain of getting a properly exposed negative if a beginner doesn't have a light meter and his source of light is greater or less than normal light? Yes, the method is to bracket shots.

PROBLEM: It is a dark, winter day. You have much less light available than on a normal, sunny day when BD work well. Now, you can't use 1/100 at f/16 because these data won't get enough of the weak light on the film. BD will result in underexposed film. You must adjust the light controls to get more of the weak light onto the film.

4. THREE LIGHT SITUATIONS

FOG: B. G. Davis, president of B. G. Davis Publishing Company. Light is weaker than usual. More of the weak light (big f/stop opening or a slow shutter speed or a combination of both) must be permitted to reach the film.

CONTRASTY LIGHT: Sandy Seals, University of Oklahoma student. In this strong light situation, less light needs to reach the film. Excess light can be eliminated by either a smaller f/stop or by a faster shutter speed.

COLLEGE: Mary Fox McCall, University of Oklahoma student. Light is normal. Basic data of f/16 to 22 at 1/100 second will properly expose film with an ASA of 250.

The answer is to bracket your shot: Make three exposures of the same subject. In the first exposure, increase BD by two stops; in the second exposure, increase BD by four stops; and in the third exposure, increase BD by six stops. Develop all of the exposures the same. One of them will be a usable negative.

The logical question will arise as to which light control (shutter or aperture) to use for increasing your exposures. The answer: What is your camera situation, action or DF?

DF—Let light in at the shutter. Do not increase the size of your aperture from f/16.

ACTION—Let light in at the f/stop opening.
Do not slow down the shutter speed from 1/100.

BD = 1/100 at f/16
    1/50
1st exp. 1/25 at f/16
    1/10
2nd exp. 1/5 at f/16
    2/5

BD = 1/100 at f/16
    f/11
1st exp. 1/100 at f/8
    f/5.6
2nd exp. 1/100 at f/4.7

Unless you have a faster lens which can be interchanged with this one, you can't make the last shot.
    f/3.5

3rd exp. 1/2 at f/16

3rd exp. 1/100 at f/2.8

13

5. CONTRASTY SUBJECT MATTER

POLAR BEAR: George Koshollek Jr., Milwaukee Journal.

AFRICA: Ken Heyman from Meridian.

Photographs like these will catch your attention because of the tone contrast which is present. A white area in a photograph always draws your eye, especially when it is surrounded by or against a contrasting darker area, as is the bear in the water. Subject matter, rather than light, has resulted in these contrasting tones. In black and white photography, tone contrast is most important.

Now, you can also bracket shots in the summer, when light increases and BD would result in overexposed negatives. Use the same approach as on the last problem.

PROBLEM: It is a very bright summer day. You have too much light. You want to use less of this intense light. Bracket three exposures. Give them the same development. The kind of a camera situation will determine which light controls are used to cut out the excess light.

DF—Cut out light with the smaller f/stop.
Also cut out light with faster shutter.

BD = 1/100 at f/16
        f/22
1st exp. 1/100 f/32

Can't compensate farther with f/stop. Have reached smallest opening. So now use shutter speed to cut out light.

      1/200
2nd exp. 1/400 at f/32
3rd exp. 1/1000 at f/32

ACTION—Cut out light with faster shutter speed.
Also cut out light with smaller f/stops.

BD = 1/100 at f/16
      1/200
1st exp. 1/400 at f/16
      1/1000

Can't compensate farther with shutter speed. Switch to smaller f/stops to cut out light.

2nd exp. 1/1000 at f/22

3rd exp. 1/1000 at f/32

14

Lighting Affects Mood

Many factors determine whether a photograph will interest viewers: Does the photo have a message which will strike at the emotions of the viewer? Have techniques been used which would help (see Chapter 11)? How has the photo been lighted?

Psychologically, the use of light and shadow have much to do with the mood and message in a photograph. (See Chapter 4, page 59), Two Darkroom Methods of Creating Mood Photos.) Generalizing, high key (much light, light tones, and very little shadow), says liveliness, zest for life, joyousness, youth, happiness. Low key (emphasis on shadow caused by the absence of light, somber tones, and very few highlights) says dullness, retreat from life, despair, blight and age, sadness, tragedy, struggle, unwholesomeness, evil. Biblical writers spoke of the transformation of a mortal man into a spiritual reflection of God at the coming of light and joy and the departure from darkness and death. So the manner in which a scene is lighted is a prime factor in the emotional response which a photo will elicit.

Documentary or realistic photographs show all detail. They're razor sharp. They can be understood at a glance. They leave nothing to the imagination. Most mood photos show only a glimpse of the whole, shrouding most of the detail in darkness or blur. They hint without yielding details. And the viewer's mind quickly begins to work on the puzzle and to supply conclusions. When emphasizing feeling rather than subject matter, shadow rather than light is your approach. Before you begin to make photographs which successfully include these principles, you'll have to master the mechanics of handling your camera, light meter, flash and strobe, the reading of and application of light. You'll have to shoot a lot of pictures. You'll have to think about and look for and see around you, lighting situations. It takes a lot of patience and determination, as does any worthwhile accomplishment. But when you turn out a photo like any of these which illustrate this discussion, you'll taste the sweet nectar of achievement, and tap latent creative abilities which all possess.

Lens Facts: f/Stops

The f/number is the relation between the diameter of the diaphragm and the lens focal length. A diaphragm set at $f/8$ means the size of the opening is 1/8 of the focal length of the lens.

Lenses are identified and described by their maximum opening or fastest speed: an $f/4.7$ or 3.5 or 2.8 lens. In each example, the widest opening to let in light is the designation for the lens.

15

6. LIGHTING AFFECTS MOOD

SITTING PRETTY, Courtesy, MGM Studios. High key pictures like this one are often used in advertising. The radiance of light and the lack of shadow suggest the purity of a mother's love and the joy of life.

JUVNILE DELINQUENT from Ewing Galloway.

SEEK AND YE SHALL FIND from Ewing Galloway.

GOOD LIFE from Ewing Galloway. Usually, but not always, low key photographs with their shadows and black tones and lack of detail, suggest unhappiness.

SCALLOP BOAT: Gordon N. Converse, Christian Science Monitor. Lighting and shadow are everything in the appeal of this picture. If the same subject matter were photographed in noonday light, all that gives this picture its mood and impact would be lost.

WORKMEN: Allen Litten, Harrisonburg, Va., Daily News Record.

Light intensity doubles between each of the f/stop openings. f/4 is twice as fast as f/5.6 and gives twice as much light. This relation continues to your minimum f/stop opening.

Full stops   1.4   2   2.8   4   5.6   8   11   16   22   32   45   64
Half stops   3.5   4.5   6.3

Focal Length—After the camera has been focused for infinity (objects at 100 feet or more), the distance from an imaginary point (node) in the center of the lens to the film is the focal length of that particular lens. Manufacturers engrave the focal length of each lens on the front of the lens mount in terms of either millimeters or inches; 25.4 millimeters equal 1 inch. Suppose the following was on your lens mount: f/4.7, 133 millimeters. The widest opening or aperture of the lens is f/4.7. The focal length of the lens is 133 millimeters or 5¼ inches, approximately.

Size of the negative image is controlled by the lens focal length. Short focal lengths give a smaller image; longer focal lengths give larger images.

Selecting the Right Focal Length Lens

Still photographers may use an all-purpose standard lens, a wide angle lens, or a telephoto lens. Size of the negative influences the choice of the focal length of a standard lens. Generally, the diagonal distance of the negative is the focal length which is used with that particular size of film.

Size of Film	Diagonal Distance of the Film Also the Focal Length of the Lens Used	Press Prefers Shorter Focal Lengths
35mm	45mm or 1.8 inches	35mm or 1.5 inches
120 film	80mm or 3.1 inches	75mm or 3 inches
4x5 film	155mm or 6 inches	127mm or 5 inches

Press photographers prefer a bit shorter focal length lens than the standard size because they need a wider angle of view on many assignments where they are working in cramped quarters.

How Fast Should the Standard Lens Be?

Camera Size	Usual Speed Of Standard Lens
4 x 5 inches	f/4.7
120 Camera	f/3.5
35mm	f/2.8

17

The smaller the f/stop of a lens is, the bigger its aperture is, the greater its light gathering ability, and the faster the lens is.

A fast lens isn't necessarily the best lens, though usually it is the most expensive lens. Today's films are greatly improved and very sensitive to light. Because film is so sensitive to light, fast lenses aren't as essential as they once were. A fast lens is a useful tool in poor light conditions. But unless you are shooting 25 percent or more of your pictures in exceedingly bad light, you will be spending money foolishly to buy a faster lens than is indicated for your camera above. Fast lenses are complicated to construct, and they seldom give as good an image definition as slower lenses which present fewer construction problems.

Interchangeable Lenses

Your conventional, normal focal length lens has limitations. It is a middle-ground lens, between the wide angle lens and the telephoto lens. The standard lens has an angle of view of about 45 to 55 degrees, a relative aperture of from f/3.5 to f/6.8, and is sharpest when stopped to about f/11 to f/16.

When you need to cover a greater angle of view (65 to 140 degrees) you switch from the standard lens to the wide angle lens. And when you work a great distance from your subject matter and want big negative images, you switch from your standard lens to a telephoto lens.

Interchangeable Lenses For 35mm Camera

Wide Angle	*Other Sizes Used*
35mm	28, 25, and 21mm
Telephoto	up to 1,000mm
65 to 135mm	(Lenses beyond 135mm can't be focused with the coupled range finder.)

Short Focal Length Lenses

Advantages	*Disadvantages*
1. Great depth of field	1. Seeming distortions result if subject is too close to camera
2. Ideal for room interiors	2. Small image forces you to get close to subject
3. Easier to have subject in focus, hence good for news shots	3. May not completely cover negative and results in fuzziness at the edges of negative

18

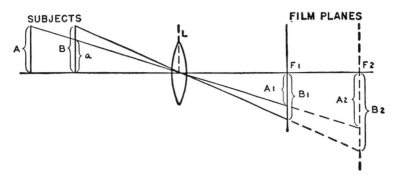

7. For a given subject distance, only the size of the image is affected by using lenses of different focal lengths. The relationships between sizes of objects at different distances do not change—note while A-2 and B-2 are bigger than A-1 and B-1 the ratio between A and B does not change.

Long Focal Length Lenses

Advantages	*Disadvantages*
1. Eliminates distortion. Excellent for portraits	1. Has a shallow depth of field and background may be out of focus
2. Good for close-ups of small objects	2. Difficult to keep in focus
3. Makes larger image of distant objects	3. Narrow angle of view makes it almost impossible to use on room interiors

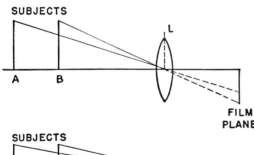

8. When the distance between camera and subject changes, then the perspective, which is actually the relationship between the sizes of objects at different distances also changes. Note that the images of A and B become more nearly alike as the distance from lens to subject increases.

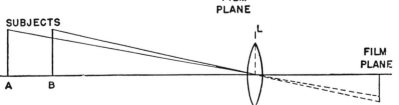

19

Seeming Distortions in Short and Long Focal Length Lenses

Perspective — the way things appear to you — depends on point of view. The same is true of lens perspective. Lens perspective is affected by how close or how far the lens is from the object as well as the lens angle in relation to the object. The same person at a distance of five feet and then of a half-block will appear to be different sizes. If you stand close to a wall of a long buiding and look down the wall, windows near you seem larger than those farther away.

Although the focal length of the lens has no true effect upon perspective, short focus lenses seem to distort foreground objects which are very near the lens. Such distortion results from the viewpoint of the lens and from the viewing distance of a print. A photo produced by a 50mm (2-inch) lens and enlarged five times has a viewing distance of 10 inches.

Long focal length lenses yield photos in which foreground and background objects seem much closer together than they really were in the scene. This illusion results because you shoot the photo at a greater distance from the scene than usual. The long lens brings the scene up to close viewing distance, but the perspective of the distant view is retained.

Circle of Confusion (Out of Focus Object)

In a depth of field picture, the objects nearest the camera and farthest from the camera appear to be in focus to the viewer's eye. One or both of the objects might not be in true focus, yet the human eye will not detect it. An object which is out of focus enough to be noticed results, because the reflected light rays from the subject have not been brought to a single point on the film plane. Light reflected from the subject should form an imaginary cone from the back of the lens and reach an apex on the film. When light rays do not do this, but strike the film in several separate spots, then circles of confusion exist.

CHAPTER 2

Action Photography

SEVEN FACTORS AFFECTING ACTION SHOTS

1. Speed of the moving object
2. Distance between the moving object and the camera
3. Angle between the camera and the moving object
4. Swing of the camera: panning
5. Quantity and quality of light
6. Depth of field
7. Speed of the shutter

1. Speed of the Moving Object

Different shutter speeds are required for a pedestrian, a halfback running an end sweep, and a speeding car on a race track. If 1/100 of a second, which is satisfactory for the pedestrian, were used on the halfback, what would happen? The shutter would open, the runner would change position before the shutter closed, and a blur would result. To freeze action, the shutter has to open and close before the object can change position.

RULE: As the speed of the moving object increases, the speed of the shutter must increase.
   Each time the speed of the moving object doubles, also double the speed of the shutter.

EXAMPLE: A man walking toward the camera might be frozen by 1/100 second.
   A man trotting (speed doubled) might be frozen by 1/200 second.
   A man running (speed doubled) might be frozen by 1/400 second.

2. Distance of the Moving Object from the Camera

RULE: The closer the moving object is to the camera, the faster the shutter speed has to be.

Each time the distance from the moving object to the camera is reduced by half, double the speed of the shutter.

EXAMPLE: Suppose a man was photographed walking toward the camera while he was 10 feet from the camera at 1/100 second. In a second picture, the man is at 5 feet. Now, use 1/200 second shutter speed.

In a third picture, the man is at 20 feet. Now, 1/50 second would work.

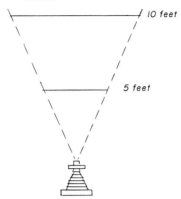

Possibly two more examples will help you understand how this rule works. The camera lens is similar to the eye in that each has a field of vision. Object A at 5 feet, crossing the camera's field of vision, would move in and out of vision more rapidly than object B at 10 feet. Obviously, a faster shutter speed is needed for A than for B.

For your second example, remember how the telephone poles along the train tracks seem to blur and run together as the train rushes past them? Those poles were fairly close to the train. If they were set back twice as far from the train, they wouldn't blur as much. Again, your eye is reacting like the shutter. The closer the moving object is to the camera, the faster the shutter speed has to be to freeze it. Telephone poles close to the train blur to your vision. Set farther back, the poles would not blur so much.

3. Angle Between the Camera and the Moving Object

An object moving toward or away from the camera in a straight line (no angle) can be frozen with a slow shutter speed. But if the object moves across the camera field of vision at a 45 degree angle, the speed of the shutter must be doubled. And if the moving object is at a right angle (90 degree angle) to the camera when photographed, again the speed of the shutter must be doubled to freeze the movement.

RULE: Each time the angle of the moving object is increased (no angle to 45 degrees to 90 degrees) double the speed of the shutter.

EXAMPLE: A man walks toward the camera. Use 1/100 second shutter speed.

A man walks at 45 degree angle to camera. Use 1/200 second shutter speed.

A man walks at 90 degree angle to camera. Use 1/400 second shutter speed.

Mixing and Applying Your Rules

Test your ability to use the rules by keeping speed constant but change angle and distance.

Angle of object to camera	10 feet from camera	5 feet from camera	20 feet from camera
No angle, man walks toward camera	1/100 second	1/200 second	1/50 second
45 degree angle	1/200 second	1/400 second	1/100 second
90 degree angle	1/400 second (may get some blur)	1/1000 second	1/200 second

The following chart is a crutch for you to use until you develop enough experience to judge what shutter speed to use for action shots. If you will remember only the following, you can fill in the table from memory:

a. Moving objects are in 1 of the 3 classifications: Pedestrians, Sports, Fast Cars.

b. Headings: Speed, Distance, and Angle (including the three divisions: no angle, 45 degree angle, and 90 degree angle).

c. A pedestrian at 25 feet, walking head-on can be frozen at 1/100 second.

d. Moving from Class 1 to Class 2, shutter is doubled to 1/200.

e. Moving from Class 2 to Class 3, shutter is doubled to 1/400.

STOP-ACTION GUIDE — CHART 1

SPEED	DISTANCE	ANGLE		
		No angle Head on	45 degree angle	90 degree angle
I. Pedestrian Construction work Ordinary activity 4-5 miles per hour	25 feet 1/50 *	1/100	1/200	1/400
	12 feet 1/100	1/200	1/400	1/1000
II. Sports, energetic activity Street traffic Boat races Football Sailboats Baseball 20 m.p.h	25 feet 1/100	1/200	1/400	1/1000
	12 feet 1/200	1/400	1/1000	—
III. Fast cars, planes Motorcycles Birds in flight 60 m.p.h.	25 feet 1/200	1/400	1/1000	—
	12 feet 1/400	1/1000	—	—

Auto races
Airplanes
100-400 m.p.h.

*These shutter speeds will freeze *most* of the moving objects

23

Data in the action stop guide will absolutely freeze. Experience will soon indicate to you that a man walking toward the camera at 1/100 second can be frozen with possibly the exception of his foot.

Further, 25 feet is a long way to work from your subject. The image on the negative will be small. Much of the negative is wasted. Blowing up a small negative image often results in grain in the print. Most of your good pictures will be shot about 10 feet from the subject.

General rule: Work as close as possible to the subject so that you will have a big negative image and so that you will eliminate unnecessary and distracting objects on either side of your subject.

4. Swing of the Camera: Panning

Suppose your moving object required a shutter speed of 1/1000 second. You have no curtain shutter. Your front shutter has a speed of only 1/400 second. Can you get a usable negative?

Yes. A bird hunter points his gun at a bird in flight, and pivots, keeping the gun barrel moving in the same direction that the bird flies. All the while the hunter is checking his sight on the bird. Then he fires when he believes he has the correct aim.

Panning is the same principle. Look through your view-finder, and swing the camera in the same direction that the object moves. Snap your picture. The background will be blurred. But your moving object will be pretty sharp—much sharper than if you had not used the panning technique.

And don't forget that you have two other techniques to help.

By changing camera position, so that the moving object moves toward the camera instead of at right angles, you improve your situation, and by doubling the distance between you and the moving object, you create a situation in which 1/400 is the correct shutter speed.

5. Quality and Quantity of Light

Action photography needs a lot of strong light. The shutter is usually so fast that very little light reaches the film when the shutter opens and closes unless a big *f*/stop opening is used. So fast shutter speeds require big *f*/stop openings, which decrease depth of field.

If you shoot action on a bright, sunny day when the light is strong, you can use smaller *f*/stop openings than are possible on a dull, gray day with two stops less of light. So good sunlight is a boon to action photography.

24

Good, Strong Normal Light | *Light is Two Stops Weaker Than Normal*

You can't begin now with $f/16$ at 1/100. Before calculating your changes for action, you must let in two extra stops of the weaker light. Adjust the light with the f/stop because you can't slow the shutter speed for action and still freeze the moving object.

Basic Data=1/100 at $f/16$ | Basic Data $= 1/100$ at $f/8$ (not $f/16$)

$f/11$	1/200	$f/5.6$ at 1/200
$f/8$	1/400	$f/4.7$ at 1/400
$f/5.6$	1/1000	

$f/4.7$ is a maximum lens opening unless your camera has interchangeable lens. Then you might switch to either an $f/3.5$ or an $f/2.8$ lens.

In good light, you can use $f/11$ at 1/200. But in bad light, you have to open up to f/5.6 at 1/200. This one comparison shows how poor light for action will demand a much bigger than normal f/stop opening, eliminating good depth of field possibilites.

Still worse is the fact that even with an $f/4.7$ opening, the biggest possible, the maximum speed in the bad light is 1/400 second. This shutter speed isn't fast enough for a lot of situations. Either you will have to change to a faster lens with a bigger opening ($f/3.5$, 2.8, or 1.5) or you will have to pan your shot. Bad light is truly a handicap to action photography!

6. Depth of Field

Action shots, requiring a fast shutter speed, seldom have good depth of field. As the shutter is speeded up to freeze the motion of the moving object, this light control (the shutter) lets in very little light on the film. So enough light for the exposure must be obtained at the second light control, the f/stop opening. RULE: Fast shutter speeds require big f/stop openings.

As indicated in discussing quantity and quality of light, good strong light helps you to have smaller f/stops when shooting action photography, improving the depth of field. But, generally speaking, action shots do not have much depth of field.

7. Speed of the Shutter

In action photography, you certainly realize by now that the speed of the shutter has to be adjusted to the speed of the moving object, or your subject will come out a blur instead of being frozen in one position when the picture is snapped. Your rule is to double the shutter speed each time the moving object doubles its speed. And you can rely on an action table as an aid until you get enough experience by trial and error to know when and how much to increase shutter speeds in relation to moving objects. The right adjustment of your shutter speed will determine whether your action pictures are good or bad.

When Should Action Be Frozen?

In all good action photos, the motion of the moving object is not completely frozen. Sometimes a more effective photo results when you purposely use a slightly slower shutter speed than is required to freeze the action, and your resulting picture is a bit blurred. This requires skill to use, and the knowledge of when to use it. You can't justify your bad, out-of-focus pictures by rationalizing that they are in this category!

Every trade has a few tricks which the professionals know and use. Knowledge of such techniques is what separates the pros from the amateurs. Any photographic subject has three dimensions: height, breadth, and depth. And your eyes see color in every scene. Yet in black and white photography, the best you can reproduce in your enlargement is a scene with only two dimensions, height and breadth. The third dimension, depth, has been lost as your scene is printed on a flat piece of paper. And the color you saw with your eyes — well, now it's different tones of black and white and gray. And in action photography, many subjects which are frozen look as if they were just standing still, not in action at all. So what does the pro do in these situations, to produce better pictures? He learns to use *symbols of action* which indicate to viewers of the photos that action is present. To add a third dimension to his photos, the pro learns to set up pictures that have depth of field, objects in the foreground, the middle ground, and the background.

What are some symbols of action which will help a photographer? Blur is one. Another is off-balance. And a third is diagonal lines. You have long associated blurring with speed. So, adopt it as a symbol of

26

action to communicate to your reader that he is seeing action in your picture.

The next obvious question is when should you blur a moving object and when should you freeze it. The two main considerations are (1) speed of the moving object and (2) whether the object is animate or inanimate.

GUIDE FOR FREEZING ACTION—CHART 2

Moving objects classified	Different shape in repose and in action?	Freeze or blur
1. Animate objects They live and breathe. People, animals, birds.	They change shape. In repose, look one way In action, appear another	Photographer's choice Depends on message you are trying to convey in the picture
2. Inanimate objects They do not live and breathe.	They do not change shape. They look the same in action or standing still.	Always use some symbol of action: blur, off-balance, diagonals. Frozen, they appear to be standing still, inactive.

Moving Objects	Freeze	Blur
1. Football player with ball. A tackle knocked him off his feet. He is standing on his head in the picture.	Because of a knowledge of gravity, readers know he won't remain long on his head.	
2. A track star at the finish line, has just set a world's record for the 100 yard dash.		A slight blur suggests that he's running faster than a human ever has before.
3. A boxer slugs his opponent with a thunderous blow.	Freezing the picture will catch what a human eye can't see: the misshapen head of the opponent under the impact of the blow, drops of perspiration flying out into space.	
4. A sailboat	It moves so slowly that blurring it would seem ridiculous. A series of photos would add a feeling of action.	

Five Ways To Suggest Action In Pictures

1. Composition

Gravity causes off-balance objects to fall.

Do not put your center of interest in the exact center of your print.

Balance is static and dull.

Place the center of interest above or below and to the right or the left of the exact center of the print.

Off-balance prints give the observer a feeling of unrest and motion. A hint of off-balance is better than too much of it.

Diagonal lines

SUBJECT: A fighter plane

Should it fly an even, horizontal line?

Or should it be zooming upward, in a diagonal line toward the corner of the photo?

SUBJECT: A TWA passenger plane. Theme of advertisement: Safety.

Should it fly in an even, horizontal line?

Or should it zoom upward in a diagonal line?

2. Controlled blurs: Slow the shutter so that the moving object isn't frozen.

3. A photo sequence of several pictures instead of just one picture gives the reader a psychological sense of moton as he moves his eye from one picture to the next.

9. THREE KINDS OF ACTION

CALF ROPER: (Upper right) Jack Kenward, Topeka Capital Journal.

Real action is a freezing situation which requires a fast shutter speed.

HEAVYWEIGHT CONTENDER: (Lower right) Ted Rozumalski, Houston Chronicle.

Peak action though slower than real action, is also a freezing situation which requires a fast shutter.

LARGEST LITTLE WEEKLY: (Below) Gordon N. Converse, Chief Photographer, Christian Science Monitor.

Simulated action often can be shot with basic data, f/16 or 22 at 1/100 second with a film rated at ASA 250.

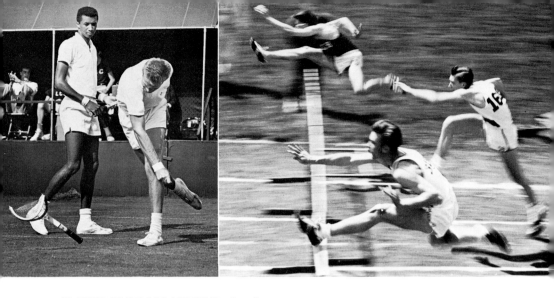

10. THREE SYMBOLS OF ACTION (Continued).

BEATEN: Jim Hughes, Christian Science Monitor.
The viewer looks at the left lower one-fourth of the picture because that's where the disappointed contestant flings his racket and that's where the other player is looking.

FLOWING MOTION: Arthur Uhlmann, World Book Encyclopedia Science Service. Panning can be used to emphasize action by blurring the background and to shoot action which requires a faster shutter speed than your camera has.

12. ACTION IN FACES

SHE HATES ELEPHANT JOKES: Clint Grant, Dallas News.
In both of these examples, the action in the face is dramatic. A twinkle in the eyes, or a quizzical raising of the eyebrows, or any show of emotion in a face will be action.

MY FRIEND, Don Brown: Jim Argo, Oklahoman & Times.

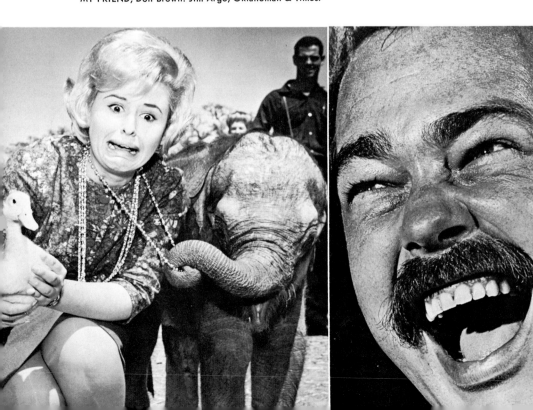

10. THREE SYMBOLS OF ACTION.

POLE VAULTER from Ewing Galloway.

Diagonals are formed by the athlete's body, the cross bar, and the vaulting pole. Also, this is another example of peak action, as the athlete pauses over the cross bar after his rapid rise and before his equally rapid descent.

GYMNASTIC CONTEST: Flip Schulke from Black Star.

Blur has been caused by purposely using a slow shutter speed.

11. REPEATED PATTERN

OLD WINDMILL: Gordon N. Converse, Chief Photogrpher, Christian Science Monitor.

GHANA: Gordon N. Converse, Chief Photographer, Christian Science Monitor.

Human figures indicate how huge these boats are.

13. SILHOUETTE
FATHER AND SON by Toby Massey, Miami News.

Silhouette blots out the details of clothing and facial expressions and emphasizes action of the boy and his father.

4. Freezing action and motion: a. Faster shutter; b. Panning; c. Speed light.

When the action is obvious, freezing it can promote more interest than blurring.

If the frozen action will reveal what the eye normally does not see, so much the better.

Example: Straining muscles in a horse jumping a hedge.

5. Time exposures at night which capture patterns made by moving lights have much action.

Some possible subjects for this technique:
   a. Fire works exploding against a black sky;
   b. the lighted Ferris wheel at night at the carnival;
   c. lighted boats on the river at night.

Three Kinds of Action

1. Real action
2. Simulated action
3. Peak action

Real action is the halfback with the ball under his arm sweeping an end, a batter slugging the ball or missing it, or a speeding car.

Simulated action is a person making no swift movements, yet obviously occupied with a task. Examples would be a person talking on a telephone, the President signing a piece of legislation, or the new

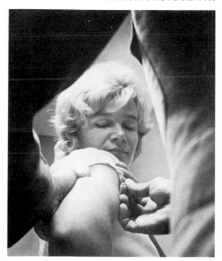

14. DRAMATIC ANGLE: It increases the feeling of action in photographs.
VACCINATION: Marvin Sussman, courtesy, Newsday.
Camera is lower than the subject, shooting up.

slate of club officers examining the book in which memberships are listed. A college girl drinking Coke or powdering her nose or the big man on campus lighting his pipe would be much more interesting to the viewer than a routine snapshot of either in which the student stands inactive and just looks into the camera with a silly, self-conscious grin. In photographing people, always have them doing something to introduce simulated action. Action makes a picture more interesting. A picture without action usually has little chance of publication.

Real action is a series of movements interspersed with *peak action,* for a split second when the real action slows.

Real action	*Peak action*
Boxer draws arm back to strike opponent	Arm is back, ready to shoot forward
Arm shoots forward	After blow lands and before arm is pulled back
Vaulter running toward the upright bar he must jump	Plants pole in box before beginning ascent into air
Ascent into air	Vaulter is horizontal with bar, before dropping back toward the sand pit

33

15. A SERIES OF PHOTOS: They aid action.
THE BASKETBALL COACH: Tom Blevins, Norman Transcript.

When the action pauses during its peak, you can get your picture with a slower shutter speed and a smaller f/stop (which permits greater depth of field). In bad light, late in the afternoon, being able to shoot action with the slower shutter speed at peak action can mean the difference between getting excellent pictures and bad pictures. Those who plan to shoot a lot of sports pictures should learn to anticipate peak action moments and expose their film at such times. Practice the technique when you have good light so when you encounter the bad light situation, you will be ready.

Other Ways to Increase a Feeling of Action in Your Pictures

1. The human face can be in repose, blank, or have action. Action is an unmistakable expression: Smile, quizzical expression, a puckish grin, anger, hate and defiance.

2. A dramatic camera angle: Shoot up or down on the subject.

3. A visually exciting pattern which is repeated in the photo, such as horizontal lines forming steps, outline of distant mountains, or human bodies on the football scrimmage line.

4. Silhouette shots in which the strongly contrasting tones of black and white strike the vision of the viewer with impact.

5. Good cropping (cutting away all unnecessary parts of a picture) so that the central object of interest will be emphasized.

6. Size is important. Both a big central object of interest and a big picture have more impact on the reader than a small image and a small picture.

7. Don't forget to use the series of pictures instead of just one to tell your story. This is a trend on the better picture papers. People like pictures. Giving customers what they want helps to sell more papers.

34

CHAPTER 3

Film: Selecting It and Developing It

Three Parts of Film

1. A *transparent, flexible* base of either sheet or roll acetate. Function:

   To provide the base upon which the light-sensitized emulsion can be spread.

2. *Light-sensitive emulsion.*

   Function: When exposed to light this part of the film records the latent scene.

   Emulsion is a mixture of gelatin and millions of crystals of silver bromide. The silver bromide crystals are the ingredient which is sensitive to light. Gelatin holds these crystals in suspension and binds them onto the acetate base.

3. A *dye,* similar to that used on cloth, is coated on the back of the acetate base.

   Function: To prevent light from passing through the film, hitting the back of the camera, and pouncing back through the film, causing halation or halos around your brightest highlight areas.

Four Characteristics Of Film

1. *Speed of the emulsion: Its sensitivity to light.*

   Every film has *an exposure index number* which tells you how sensitive the film is to light. The bigger the number, the faster the emulsion is. Slow to medium speed film index numbers range from 12 to 80. Fast film numbers range from 100 to 1250. Index numbers also are referred to as ASA film ratings. ASA is the abbreviation for the American Standards Association, which established the rating system.

2. *Color sensitivity*.

Films are classified three ways in relation to their ability to reproduce scene colors which the eye sees in varying tones of black, gray, and white in the positive.

a. *Color blind or blue sensitive films* are blind to all colors except blue and over-sensitive to blue. They are used for black-and-white copy work.

b. *Orthochromatic films* are sensitized to all colors except red. They can be developed by inspection under a red safelight. Portrait photographers use ortho for portraits of men because its insensitivity to red causes ortho film to render human skin darker.

c. *Panchromatic* or Pan film is sensitized for all colors, including red. Pan renders in black and white tones the nearest approximation to the colors which your eye sees in a scene.

The film was developed in three stages. Panchromatic A was the first film which was only moderately sensitive to red; Pan B was more sensitive to red; and Pan C is over-sensitive to red.

Most photographers select a Panchromatic film.

3. *Contrast or gradation of emulsion*

Some films (slow ones with low ASA numbers) yield the maximum contrast; others (those with medium ASA numbers) yield a normal contrast; and still others (those with big ASA numbers) yield a minimum of contrast.

4. *Grain of the emulsion*

Grain is no problem unless the silver crystals which form the negative image are so big they can be seen in your enlargement.

Films with the smallest grain are the slow films with the most contrast. Films with the biggest grain are the fast films used for press work (because a sensitive film can get a picture under the worst light conditions); they have the least amount of inherent contrast.

Selecting Your Film

It's really a simple matter. An all-purpose film should be panchromatic so filters can be used and so your prints will reproduce different tones for each of the different colors in the scene.

If you use a 35mm camera, you will want a fine grain film and a fine grain developer. The size of the 35mm negative is enlarged many times when it's blown up to an 8 x 10 or an 11 x 14 print.

If you use a 2¼ x 2¼ camera, either Kodak Plus-X roll film or Ansco All-Weather Pan film will fit your needs.

A person who does press-type work and who must get a photo, often in poor light, will choose a fast pan film with an ASA of 300 to 400. A

36

person who does salon work is much more interested in quality than in the speed of film and getting a picture in bad light. Quality films— low ASA films with more contrast and smaller grain—are for salon work.

Film manufacturers have made a break-through in their processes, and some of the old ideas no longer apply. For a great while, the following were true:

Fast films had big grain and poor contrast;

Slow films had small grain and better contrast. Probably these relations still hold to some extent today, in spite of the improved films which are available.

A real professional selects one all-purpose black-and-white film which is best adapted for the kind of work he does. Then he masters the film. He knows its capacity. He does not waste time jumping around from one film to another.

A newspaper or magazine photographer doesn't worry about his Tri-X roll film being lower in contrast because it is a fast film. Contrast can be affected by the way a scene is lighted, the way the film is exposed and developed, by the choice of the paper used in enlarging, and by using a condenser enlarger. Fast developers increase contrast. Cutting exposure by 50 per cent and doubling development increases contrast.

Handling Film

Don't touch the emulsion of a film with your fingers except on the edges. Skin oil will leave finger prints on the emulsion. The dye backing is not susceptible to finger prints.

Always handle film by its edges.

Don't load roll film in bright sun light. You could fog the film if it loosens. Change film in the shade.

Don't buy film which is out-dated. Every package of film is dated. Check the date on film before buying it.

Store film in a cool, dry place. Heat from a radiator or a steampipe, or moisture, will cause the emulsion to fog. Don't leave your camera or film in your car glove compartment on hot days; the thermometer often goes over 100 degrees in such places.

Don't tighten loosely wound film by pulling it tight. This scratches the emulsion and makes "cinch marks" across the pictures. Roll film should be wound tightly on its spool.

Don't squeeze a film pack or a cut film holder by holding either by its broad front and back. This fogs your film. Hold a pack or a film holder by its sides.

Take care not to let the sharp corners of cut film nick the emulsion side of other negatives during development.

37

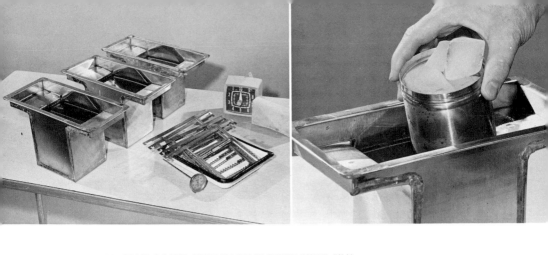

16. SOME OF THE STEPS IN DEVELOPING SHEET FILM.

(Above, Left) Sheet film tanks, film hangers, thermometer, timer.

(Above, Right) If developer is too warm, it can be cooled by immersing a can of ice cubes or chilled water in the tank. Do not simply put ice in the developer; water from melting ice will dilute the solution.

(Below, Left) Loading sheet film into hangers is done in total darkness.

(Below, Right) Put entire batch of hangers in the developer at one time, to secure uniform development.

(Opposite Page, Left) Agitate by lifting entire group of hangers from tank, allow to drain, and return to solution.

(Opposite page, Right) After films have been developed, fixed and washed, rinse shortly in running water to remove any surface grit or sediment, then dip in Photo Flo and hang to dry.

Photos by Dick Cobb.

DEVELOPING CUT FILM IN AN OPEN TANK BY
TIME AND TEMPERATURE—CHART 3

Equipment needed: Timer clock, cut film hangers, thermometer, tanks, and developing solutions.

LIGHT

1. Use thermometer to take temperature of solutions: Developer, short-stop, quick fix, and wash water.
2. Consult time-temperature chart to find how long films remains in DEVELOPER, first solution.
3. Shut door to dark room and lock it. This prevents anyone from opening the door by accident and fogging your film as it develops.
4. Check your timer to be sure it is wound. Set the timer hand for the length of time the negative must remain in the developer. CAUTION: Turn hand to left.
5. Place your empty cut film hangers to the left of you on the loading shelf. Place your holders with the exposed film in front of you.

DARK

6. Cut off the light.
7. Transfer exposed film from the cut film holders to hangers. As each empty hanger is loaded with an exposed film, place hanger and film to the right of you on the loading shelf.

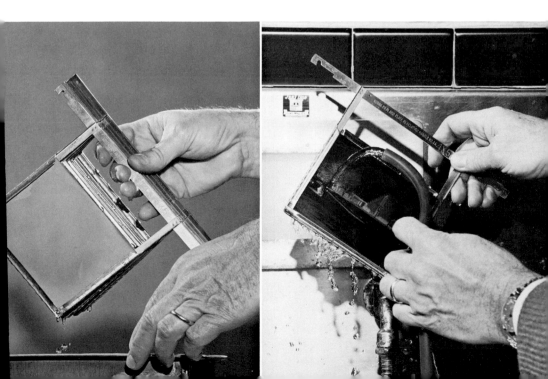

8. After all the film is transferred to the hangers, put the hangers into the developer.

9. Pull down the timer arm (switch) so that the clock will begin to tick off the seconds. An alarm will sound when the negatives should be transferred from the developer to the next solution, the short-stop.

10. The negatives should be agitated for 10-15 seconds of every minute they are in the developer. You can't see the clock. So estimate the time. Count slowly from 1 to 60, each count approximitating a second of time. As you count, hold the hangers and film over the developing tank so that the developer on the film will drain off of it diagonally. Immerse the film in the developer again, draw it out and permit the developer to drain from the film diagonally from the opposite corners of the film. Continue this agitation for 10-15 counts of every minute the film develops.

CAUTION: Films must be agitated. This action keeps fresh developer in contact with the negative. If the films are not agitated, your negatives may have a streaky appearance.

11. When the timer alarm sounds, pull the film out of the developer, carefully drain off the developer on the film into the developer tank, and then place the film in the second solution, the short-stop.

12. Film should remain in the short-stop at least 30 seconds with constant agitation.

13. After 30 to 60 seconds, drain the film and transfer it to the third solution, the quick fix. Agitate films continuously for one minute, than turn on the light.

LIGHT

If you can see traces of a milky coating on the back of the film where the dye backing was, note how long is required for the quick fix to remove the milky coating. If the coating disappears in 1½ minutes, leave the film in the quick fix for a total of three minutes. RULE: Leave the film in the quick fix twice as long as is required for the quick fix to remove the milky coating.

Generally, if the coating is gone when you turn on the light (quick fix is fresh and at the right temperature), leave the film in the fix a total of two minutes.

CAUTION: All photographers are eager to inspect the developed film as soon as the light is turned on.

Quick fix will damage clothes, even eat holes in them. To avoid dripping it on either the floor or your clothes, place a tray under negatives as you view them. Many professionals take the precaution of diluting the quick fix on the negatives by dipping the negatives into running water and draining them before viewing the negatives with the protective tray under them.

14. Wash your negatives in RUNNING WATER for at least 30 minutes if you want them to be permanent. Newspapers cut time by washing a negative for only 3-5 minutes and then making a wet print of the negative.

15. Newspapers hasten the drying of negatives by placing them in a closed cabinet and blowing hot air over them.
    Hanging them up to dry or using an electric fan is slower but just as effective.

After a negative has been washed, make certain that all excess water is drained off of the negative. A clean wet sponge (or cotton) which has been squeezed out is excellent to get the scattered drops of water still on the negative.

If a few scattered drops of water are allowed to dry on the negative, one of them almost always causes a water spot—a discolored area the size of the drop of water. This spot will show up on your finished enlargement, unless it is an area that you can crop out in enlarging the picture. Too often, the spot will be in a part of the picture which can't be cropped!

DEVELOPING ROLL FILM IN A ROUND, CLOSED TANK—CHART 4

Equipment needed: Developing solutions, closed tank and reel, two measuring beakers or graduates, timer clock, thermometer.

LIGHT

1. Assemble your equipment in the sink where you intend to work.
2. Check the developing tank and the reel inside of it on which you will wind your roll film. Both tank and reel should be dry.
3. Find the temperature of your developing solutions with a thermometer. Ideal temperature for *all* solutions is 68 to 72 degrees. If solution temperatures range more than 5 degrees, you are inviting reticulation and graininess.
4. Check time-temperature chart to find how long film should be developed.

DARK

5. Lock the door. Cut off the light.
6. Holding your film by the edges, unroll it and remove the protective paper cover from the back of it. In pulling the paper cover

from the back of the film where the two are glued together with adhesive tape, pull them apart gently. A quick jerk will generate enough static electricity to cause a flash of light which you can see.

7. Holding your film by the edges, wind the film onto the reel, taking taking care to *keep your hands off the emulsion.* You should practice this maneuver in the light and in the dark before you attempt to put film on the reel for development. In your practice, use a developed roll. If you have trouble in the light, go back to the dealer who sold you your tank and get him to show you how it's done. Then practice.

8. Place the wound film and the reel inside the tank. Place the top on the tank. This tank is light tight. You can turn on the light. Do not remove the top of the tank until the film has been fixed in quick fix.

LIGHT

9. Run tap water in the vented top of the tank. Pre-wetting your film will speed the time of the developer in getting into the emulsion and reaching the silver bromide crystals. Agitate the tank and tap water continuously for about 30 seconds. Pour out the water.

10. Pour *developer* into vented top of tank. *Start timer.* Agitate tank about 5-10 seconds of every minute. Develop film for recommended time depending on how film was exposed, and what temperature of solutions is. Pour out developer.

11. Pour *short stop* into top of vented tank. Agitate continuously for 30-60 seconds. Pour out.

12. Pour in quick fix into top of vented tank. Agitate continuously for 60 seconds. Let tank sit for another minute. Remove top. Check back of film. The milky substance on the back where the dye was should have disappeared. If the back of the film shows any traces of the milky substance, leave the film in the hypo another couple of minutes. Pour out quick fix.

13. Leave film wound on reel while it washes under a stream of tap water for 10 to 30 minutes, depending on whether you want the film for permanent storage.

14. Put a few drops of a wetting agent into the tank of water after washing is complete. Let the film sit in the water and the wetting agent for about 30 seconds. The wetting agent causes the water to drain off of the film evenly when it is removed from the tank.

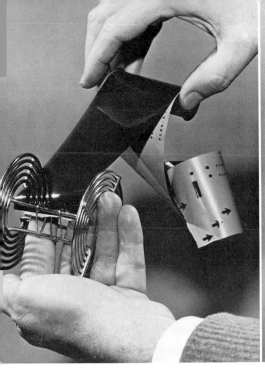

17. SOME STEPS IN DEVELOPING ROLL FILM

A. Loading film onto the reel.

B. Place the reel and film in the tank.

C. Pour developer into the tank.

D. Remove cover for washing the film while it is still on the reel.

Photos by Dick Cobb.

15. With a clean damp photo sponge or cotton, carefully wipe the front of the film, from one end of the roll to the other. This pulls away tiny particles of grit and any isolated drops of water which didn't drain away, preventing water spots.

    Wash sponge, squeeze it out. Now repeat the wiping process on the back of your film.

16. Hang film up to dry. Attach a film clip or clothes pin to the free, dangling end of the film to make it hang taut.

17. Wash tank and reel and dry it. Put up your other equipment.

Time and Temperature Charts

Films can be developed by either of two methods, in a tray by hand or in a tank. For tanks single sheets of cut film require metal hangers to hold the film suspended in the developing solutions. Roll film is wound into a reel and then placed in a tank.

Manufacturers make many different kinds of films and developing solutions. The photographer seeking the best results will use the developer which the manufacturer recommends for a particular film. The manufacturer of the film has spent time and money freely and used the best possible technical brains to find the formula that is right for his film.

The instruction sheet with the film tells which formula should be used for developing the exposed films. Manufacturers also publish time and temperature charts to show how long to leave the film in the developer. Charts are readily available on the information sheet with each roll or box of film.

Because manufacturer's recommendations for processing films are frequently changed, often reflecting changes and improvements in the film emulsions themselves, it is not practical to give any useful charts in this book. Manufacturer's data books, if up-to-date are good sources of such information, where only a few films are used. For the worker who has to develop many different kinds of film, the PHOTO-LAB-INDEX (Morgan & Morgan, Inc. Hastings-on-Hudson, N.Y. 10706) contains hundreds of charts covering almost all the useful combinations of film and developers.

Ideal developing temperature is 68 to 72 degrees. If the developing solution is warmer than 68 degrees, you shorten the development; if it is colder than 68 degrees, you lengthen the development. Increasing agitation also shortens development, and decreasing agitation lengthens the development required.

Because the temperature of a developing formula determines how long development will continue, you can see how the term, time and temperature, arose.

FUNCTION OF NEGATIVE DEVELOPING BATHS—CHART 5

DEVELOPER DK-50	SHORT-STOP Water+diluted (28%) glacial acetic acid	QUICK FIX (Hypo)	WASH Running water
Alkaline	Acid	Acid	
Time required: About 4-6 minutes Thermometer and temperature tell how long	10 to 30 seconds	About 1-3 minutes, depends on age, temperature.	30 minutes if all quick fix is to be removed. Use a wetting agent.
Agitate 10-15 seconds of each minute. Drain negatives in alternate diagonals, then back into developer, etc.	Continuous agitation	Continuous agitation for one minute.	Sponge off water drops before hanging up negatives to dry to avoid water marks.
Drain off developer carefully after clock rings before moving to next bath.	Drain negatives carefully before moving to next bath.	Turn on light Look at back of negatives. Do you see a milky substance where dye backing was?	
Function: To bring out latent image Chemical reaction between solution and silver bromide crystals releases the bromide. Remaining metallic silver forms negative image.	1. To stop the action of the developer quickly, uniformly. 2. To catch and prevent developer from being carried into the quick fix. Quick fix is more expensive than short-stop	1. To fix the silver image permanently. 2. To remove the unexposed silver crystals[1] from the negative emulsion so the light can be turned on without fogging the film.	To remove hypo from emulsion so negative won't fade.

Five Ingredients Used In Most Developers

Manufacturers have packaged chemicals for processing films and positives so conveniently that even professionals no longer mix their own ingredients. So no effort will be made to make a chemist out of you. However, any intelligent person with an interest in photography

---

[1] A note of explanation may be needed in relation to unexposed silver salts. Scene highlights reflect the most light onto a film. Scene shadows often do not reflect enough light onto the film to affect the silver crystals. So crystals in shadow areas are not affected by development. Unless these live crystals are removed by the quick fix, the film would fog when the light is turned on.

should understand how his developer functions. What magic permits the developer to turn an invisible latent image into the metallic negative image of the scene which was photographed? How does one select the right developer?

DEVELOPER INGREDIENTS—CHART 6

Solvent: Water

Reducer: Releases the bromide from the exposed silver crystals so they turn into black metal and form the negative image.

Chemicals:
Eastman: Elon, Hydroquinone, Amidol, Pyro
Ansco: Metol, Hydroquinone, Glycin

Activator: Must be added to give the solution the energy to act. It's like the starter on a car. Without this activator, water and a reducer do not make any changes in the latent image.

Chemicals: Sodium carbonate, borax, Kodalk Balanced Alkali

Preservative: When the first three ingredients are mixed, they have a great affinity for oxygen in the air. As the solution absorbs oxygen, it turns brown (oxidizes) and loses its power to develop properly. This can happen in 24 hours. Having to mix a developer each time you have dark room work is inconvenient. So a preservative is added to the developer, to make it resist oxygen. Now, with care, a developer can be mixed and stored for about two weeks before oxidation is noticeable.

Chemical: Sodium sulfite

Restrainer: A developer must be selective and attack only *exposed* silver crystals. To keep the developer from attacking unexposed silver crystals, a restrainer is added.

Chemical: Potassium bromide

By using different chemicals for reducing agents and by varying the proportions of the above ingredients, skilled researchers concoct the many different developers which are available today. Generally, most professionals select *one* developer most suited to their kind of photography. Then the pros stick to the *one* developer. They get professional results because they know how to use their tools.

Selecting A Developer—Chart 7

Camera Size	Developer Selected	Qualities
4 x 5, 5 x 7, larger	Permadol (Ansco) DK-50 (Eastman)	Ordinary developers 4-6 minutes development time No grain problem under average conditions Average contrast Satisfactory for salon work with this size negative
	DK-60a (Eastman) D-19 (Eastman)	Fast, press-type developer 3½ minutes developing time Rapid developers increase negative contrast They also increase size of grain Shadow detail suffers
	Ansco 17 (Ansco)	10-15 minutes at 68 degrees
	D-76 (Eastman)	A moderately fine grain developer 6 to 8 minutes full strength; longer 1-1 Lower contrast than DK-50 Better shadow detail
2¼ x 2¼	Ansco 17 (Ansco)	10-15 minutes at 68 degrees
	D-76 (Eastman)	1:1 about 9-11 minutes development time depending on **tempera-ture** and agitation
	Normadol (Ansco) Microdol-X (Eastman)	32 minutes at 68 degrees 6-8 minutes at 68 degrees Maximum fine grain as size of enlargements increase Slight reduction in contrast Greater detail in shadows
35mm A negative this size makes grain a paramount consideration	Finex-L (Ansco) Microdol-X (Eastman)	15 minutes at 68 degrees 14 minutes developing time

47

Underexposed and underdeveloped:

All-over—density extremely low

Contrasts—much too low

Shadow detail—completely lacking

Highlights—much too weak

Remedy: None. Such negatives are total losses

Correctly exposed but underdeveloped:

All-over—density too low

Contrasts—too low

Shadow detail—present but thin

Highlights—too weak

Remedy: Print on paper of hard gradation

Overexposed and underdeveloped:

All-over—density almost normal

Contrasts—too low

Shadow detail—abnormally strong, highlights not strong enough

Remedy: Print on paper of extra-hard gradation

Underexposed but normally developed:

All-over—density too low

Contrasts—too great

Shadow detail—practically lacking

Highlights—rather transparent

Remedy: None. No intensifier can produce shadow detail that is not there

---

Correctly exposed and correctly developed:

All-over—density normal

Shadow detail—is present

Highlights—strong but still transparent

Negatives intended for enlarging should generally be slightly thinner, more transparent, than those intended for contact printing

The **ideal** negative

Overexposed but normally developed:

All-over—density too high

Contrasts—too low
Shadow detail—abnormally strong

Highlights—too dense, graininess rather pronounced

Remedy: If negative is very dense, reduce in Kodak R-15 reducer

Print on paper of hard gradation

Underexposed and overdeveloped:

All over—density about normal

Contrasts—much too high

Shadow detail—too weak
Highlights—rather dense and black

Remedy: If extremely dense, reduce carefully with ammonium persulfate; print on paper of soft or extra-soft gradation

---

Correctly exposed but overdeveloped:

All-over—density too high

Contrasts—somewhat higher than normally desirable

Shadow detail—strong

Highlights—very black and blocked, pronounced graininess

Remedy: Reduce in ammonium persulfate; print on paper of soft gradation

---

Overexposed and overdeveloped:

All-over—density extremely high, negative appears practically black

Contrasts—about normal
Shadow detail—much too strong
Highlights—perfectly black and detailless, graininess extremely pronounced
Remedy: Reduce in Kodak R-15; print on normal paper.

EXPOSURE

Too Short	Correct	Too Long

Too Short

DEVELOPMENT
Normal

Too Long

49

No one developer is flexible enough to meet all the varied needs of photography. Generally, size of camera and negative size, and one's assignment influence the selection of a developer. A press photographer with a 4 x 5 camera could save a minute or two in meeting deadlines by using DK-60a. But if he used a 2¼ x 2¼ camera and D-76, he'd have to spend 9-11 minutes developing his negatives. Generally, fine grain developers require longer developing time.

A salon photographer isn't concerned with time and deadlines. He is conscious of quality. He will want a developer which will minimize grain and get good shadow detail and fair contrast. His prints will be blown up to 11 x 14 or 16 x 20, and they must be technically almost perfect.

Developer Terms And Procedures

Before films were improved and made so sensitive to light, photographers developed them by inspection. A safe light filter permitted the photographer to look at his film in very weak light and see the density of his negatives.

Developing films in a completely dark room by time and temperature is much more scientific and satisfactory than the old method.

Reticulation

Ideal temperature of baths is 68 to 72 degrees. Temperatures in all of the baths must be within five degrees of the same temperature or reticulation can result. The emulsion on the front of your film is gelatin and silver bromide crystals. This emulsion is spread on the acetate base while warm. The cooled gelatin hardens and holds in suspension the light-sensitive silver crystals, which light affects to form a latent image.

The reason why developing bath temperatures should be almost constant becomes apparent when you realize that warm solutions swell the gelatin and cool baths cause it to contract. Think of gelatin as a rubber band. The rubber band has a limit beyond which it cannot be stretched without breaking. If a film is placed in an 80 degree developing bath and later washed in 60 degree water, the gelatin cannot adjust to such great temperature differences. First the gelatin is swelled by the heat; suddenly the cold demands that it contract. The gelatin, originally in one smooth, continuous body on the acetate sheet, pulls apart and breaks. Now, many lines appear all over the acetate sheet, indicating places where the emulsion no longer covers the acetate. In enlarging, light goes through these emulsion breaks readily, producing this pattern on your enlargement.

Where developing temperatures are not kept constant, you risk both reticulation and big, objectionable grain.

50

Agitation

Agitation is necessary to care for the liberated bromide (chemical reaction frees the bromide from the silver crystals). The liberated bromide tends to concentrate on the denser parts of the negative and spread into the transparent areas. And it acts as a restrainer on the developer, causing unevenness and streaks in the film, if it isn't agitated. But proper agitation keeps fresh developer in contact with the emulsion and prevents the bromide from causing streaks.

Drying Film Rapidly with Hot Air

This practice makes the grain larger. Newspapers find it practical to use dryers. But newspapers don't have to worry about grain. If you use 2¼ x 2¼ or 35mm film which will have to be blown up larger than 8 x 10, allow your film to dry slowly without help from a hot-air film dryer.

Negative Density

The right amount of blackness or density in negatives is important. A negative which is too dense takes longer to enlarge and it will have other faults. A negative which is not dense enough, but which is thin and transparent, allows too much enlarger light to pass through it and register on the enlarging paper. When the overexposed paper is placed in the developer, the image appears quickly, then gets darker and darker. A "burned up" print is fit only for the wastebasket unless you are striving for some special effect or mood picture.

Density or the lack of it depends on one of two factors: exposure or development. Examine the chart below to see the three classifications of light values in any scene, and the relation of each light value to negative density or the lack of it.

RELATION OF SCENE LIGHT TO DENSITY AND TRANSPARENCY—CHART 8

Three Light Values in Any Scene	*How the Three Light Values of One Scene Affect the Density or Transparency of an Exposed Film (After Development)*

1. Highlights = areas with either
  a. The most light OR
  b. Surfaces/objects which reflect the most light
  Highlight areas reflect more light than they absorb.
	Highlights are the blackest areas on the negative
	
	All parts of the negative are equally sensitive to light but the highlight areas received the most reflected light, so they are the blackest.

2. Shadows = areas with either

a. The least light in the scene OR

b. Surfaces/objects which reflect the least light
Shadows absorb more light than they reflect.

Shadow areas are the thinnest and most transparent parts of the negative.

They receive the smallest amount of reflected light.

3. "Normal" light value areas

a. Not so bright as highlights; reflect less light

b. Not so dark as shadows; reflect more light

c. A middle value area between the two extremes of highlight and shadow

Normal areas are denser than shadows and less dense than highlight.

They receive less light than highlight areas.

They receive more light than shadow areas.

Effect Of Exposure And Development Upon Negative Density—Chart 9

Two Factors Which Affect Density Have Three Possibilities	Density Which Results	Density Changes Affect Enlarger Exposures
1. EXPOSURE—snapping the picture		
a. Right amount of light=	Correct density IF negative is properly developed.	Normal exposure time produces a good print (10 to 20 seconds).
b. Too much light=	Too much density if developed normally.	The very black negative holds light back from the print paper during enlargement.

Quality of negative: Not a good one.
Overexposure reduced the contrast.
Negative is flat and lacking contrast.

Correction: Some compensation and improvement can be made by selecting print paper which has higher contrast, #3, 4, or 5, depending on how flat the negative is.

c. Too little light=	Too little density A thin, transparent negative.	Enlarger light registers heavily on paper, overexposing it.

Quality of negative: So bad it should be thrown away. Beginners believe that by lengthening development, they compensate for lack of the light which should have reached the film but didn't. This idea won't work. Shadow areas are completely transparent without any detail!

Correction: None. Re-shoot scene. Developing the negative for a week will not put light on film. Only a long enough exposure will permit enough of the weak light from shadow areas to affect the film enough to result in details.

Two Factors Which Affect Density Have Three Possibilities	*Density Which Results*	*Density Changes Affect Enlarger Exposures*
2. DEVELOPMENT		Normal exposure time
a. Right length of time	Correct density.	produces a good print (10 to 20 seconds).
b. Too long a time	Too much density. Film is too black.	In enlarging, a longer exposure time must be used. A larger f /stop helps.

    Quality of negative: Too much contrast.
    Correction: Select an enlarging paper which is
      lower in contrast, say #1

c. Too short a time	Not enough density. Too much transparency. A thin negative.	In enlarging, negative will permit too much light to reach enlarging paper and burn it up.

    Quality of negative: Not good, but it can be corrected.
      Shadow areas have a little more detail
      than underexposed negatives.

    Correction: Bleach negative (chemical removes
      underdeveloped image) then re-develop for the
      the proper length of time. See manufacturer's
      handbook for formulas.

PAPER GRADATION

	Too Soft	Correct	Too Hard

EXPOSURE

Too Short

Paper too soft—
print underexposed

Paper right—
print underexposed

Paper too hard—
print underexposed

Correct

Paper too soft—
exposure correct

Paper right—
exposure correct

Paper too hard—
exposure correct

Too Long

Paper too soft—
print overexposed

Paper right—
print overexposed

Paper too hard—
print overexposed

54

CHAPTER 4

Enlarging and Developing the Print

Knowledge gained from Chapters 1 and 3 enabled you to shoot and develop a negative. Information in this chapter will deal with matching your negatives to the right grade or contrast of enlarging paper, operation of the enlarger and use of the test strip, and processing enlargements.

Before you begin absorbing facts on matching the right grade of enlarging paper to a negative with specific characteristics, you need to understand what is meant by *contrast in photography*. A white sheet of your enlarging paper has no picture on it because there are no contrasting tones of black and gray, forming images. So in black and white photography, contrast results from a difference in tones: black, gray, and white.

MATCHING NEGATIVE CONTRAST WITH THE RIGHT ENLARGING PAPER

CONTRAST—CHART 10

Three Factors Affecting Negative Contrast

1. *LIGHT*

Situation	Kind of negative contrast produced	Paper contrast which will improve negative
a. Dull, gray, rainy day	Lacking in contrast	Need a paper with more than normal contrast, #3 or 4
b. Night scene Black apartment buildings White (light) windows in buildings Black and white are the ultimate in tone contrast	Ultimate in contrast	Here great contrast is desired so use #3 paper to dramatize

Day scene Summer at 12 noon Intense shadows Glaring high lights	Great contrast	Need a paper with less than normal con- trast, #1 or perhaps #2 normal paper. Try both. Which looks best?
c. 9-10 a.m. Spring, Fall Good sun light	Normal contrast	Need normal contrast #2

2. EXPOSURE

a. Overexposure	Too much light, dense negative Cuts contrast	Need an increase of contrast, #3, 4, 5
b. Underexposure	Not enough light, transparent nega- tive, no detail in shadows	Use a hard, contrasty paper, not to improve contrast, but because it is less sensitive to light than #1, 2 papers. Stop down enlarger diaphragm.

Contrast is not the main problem. Negative is so thin and lacking in density, it is difficult to print without burning up the print. With no detail in shadow areas, negative isn't worth fooling with. Throw it away.

3. DEVELOPMENT

a. Overdevelopment	Increases contrast Too long develop- ment, dense nega- tive	Need less than normal contrast, #1
b. Underdevelopment	Too short a de- velopment, thin negative, a little detail in shadow areas	Use contrasty paper. Less sensitive to light than #1, 2 and hence less likely to burn up

Again, lack of density rather than contrast is the problem in printing this negative. A print may be obtained with great difficulty on a hard contrasty paper.

A thin negative which has adequate shadow detail (that is, one which has been underdeveloped, not underexposed) can sometimes be improved by intensification. A number of methods are commonly used; in general the negative is bleached in a bath containing chromium. It is then redeveloped fully. The result is to add a certain amount of chromium to the original silver image, and thus produce a somewhat denser negative. Intensified negatives are usually grainier than normal, the image contrast tends to be harsh, and in general, the

56

| Flat | Soft | Normal | Hard | Chalky |

18. CONTRAST IN PHOTOGRAPHIC TONES
Photos by Andreas Feininger

method is suitable mainly to salvage a picture which cannot be re-taken. It should not be considered a routine method of improving underdeveloped negatives.

Six Characteristics of Enlarging Paper—Chart 11

1. *Gradation or Contrast*[1]
   #1: Less than normal contrast
   　　Widest range of middle grays
   #2: *Normal paper*
   #3: More contrast than normal
   　　Fewer midde grays than normal
   　#4, 5: Increasing contrast
   　　Fewer middle grays than normal
2. *Emulsion Sensitivity To Light*
   Like film, paper can be fast, medium, or slow
   a. Very slow *Chloride paper*
   　　Contact printing only
   　　Won't work with enlarger
   b. Very fast *Bromide paper*
   　　Enlarging only
   　　Too sensitive for contact printing. Burns up
   √ c. Medium speed *Chloro-bromide paper*[1]
3. *Surface Texture*
   Is it smooth or rough: Is it dull or glossy?
   √ a. Glossy: Smooth and brilliant
   　　Yields maximum range of tones
   　　Many favor it for photos which will be printed in
   　　　publications.

[1]Checks √ indicate the characteristics which are present in the kind of enlarging paper most press photographers use.

      b. Matte: Smooth and duller
          Used by portrait photographers
          Used for some salon exhibition photos
      c. Special surfaces for portrait photographers
          Paper with a rough surface finish
          Resembles silk, tapestry.

4. *Weight Of Paper Stock*
√ Single weight paper is thinner, costs less
    Double weight paper is thicker, costs more

5. *Image Tone Of Print*
    Blue blacks: Velox, Azo—Contact papers
√ Neutral blacks: Kodabromide, Medalist—Enlarging
    Warm blacks: Platino—matte enlarging paper
    Brown-black: Opal, Ilustrator's Special and portrait proofing
       paper—Enlarging

6. *Tint of Stock can* be √ white, cream, old ivory, buff.

[1]Checks (√) indicate the characteristics which are present in the kind of enlarging paper most press photographers use.

    Chart 11 indicates that you have five different contrasts of enlarging paper with which to work, numbered 1 through 5. Has it occurred to you that photography might be simpler if there were only one grade of enlarging paper? But such a situation would seriously limit the quality and flexibility of photography. Suppose you had only normal Number 2 paper with which to work. You have two negatives to be enlarged. One lacks contrast because it was shot on a dull, rainy day. The other has too much contrast. It was shot at 2 p.m. in the summer. On Number 2 paper, neither of these negatives will produce a good print. Your first negative needs a paper with greater than average contrast (No. 3-5) to supply this quality which is absent from the negative. And your second negative would look best on a soft paper which has less than a normal amount of contrast (No. 1). Now, you begin to see the wisdom of having different gradations of paper. It's up to you to learn quickly what the following kinds of negatives look like: a contrasty negative, a normal negative, and a flat negative. Study the negatives in Figure 20, page 60. Then you'll be set to match the correct contrast of paper to the specific characteristics of your negative. Chart 10 indicates how scene light, exposure, and development affect negative contrast, and what gradation of paper should be used in each situation.

    Of the six characteristics of enlarging paper set forth in Chart 11, only the first one, gradation or contrast, is considered in matching enlarging paper to a negative's specific characteristics. Paper Number 1, soft and lacking contrast, has four shades of gray separating

19. TWO DARKROOM METHODS OF CREATING MOOD PHOTOS.   Andreas Feininger.

A. PURPOSELY OVEREXPOSING PRINT. Above left, a normal daytime interior in New York's Pennsylvania Station. Above right, by "printing down" or overexposing print, the effect of night, gloom or foreboding is attained.

B. CHANGING PRINT CONTRAST. Below, left. Soft paper gives the effect of an early morning, misty scene. Below, right: Printing same negative on hard paper gives the effect of a sunset scene.

pure black and pure white. The farther apart black and white are separated by increasing numbers of gray tones, the less contrast a paper has. Remember, your ultimate in contrast is black against white, without intervening gray tones. Only two tones of gray separate black from white in number 4 paper. The closer black is to white, the fewer the gray tones which separate the two contrasting tones, the greater the contrast of the paper. Soft papers lacking in contrast (long scale) record the greatest amount of detail. Hard papers with contrast (short scale) record the least amount of detail but are the most dramatic papers.

As is indicated by Chart 10, in matching negatives with the right contrast of enlarging paper, you generally choose a paper which supplies what the negative lacks.

Summary

Negative Fault	*Correction*	*Paper Contrast to Select*

Lacks contrast
  Overexposed or
  underdeveloped or
  flat scene light
	Get needed contrast
	in your choice
	of paper
		#3, 4, 5, depending on
		how flat and lacking in
		contrast the negative is

Has too much contrast
  overdeveloped or
  scene light too harsh
  and contrasty
	Decrease negative
	contrast by using
	a paper with less
	than the normal
	amount of contrast
		#1 paper

Normal negative	No correction needed	#2 paper

However, some other factors should be considered in the selection of the contrast of paper to be used. Suppose you set out to do a mood picture. You want a print which says it's a cold, gray, winter day, and it's raining. Your scene light is flat. Your negative will be flat. Try both #1 and #2 paper. You wouldn't want a contrasty paper like #3, 4 because this would defeat the mood you are trying to create.

Suppose you want a picture to suggest the threat of trouble, an approaching storm. Photo A is a peaceful, cheerful scene. By purposely overexposing your print and getting it too black, the black tones change the scene into one which holds the hint of trouble. Another way to change mood is to print the same negative on #1 paper and then on #4 paper. Hard, contrasty papers, with rich blacks clashing with whites, are dramatic. Soft paper suggests mist and fog.

20. NEGATIVE AND PRINT CONTRASTS: Contrasty, Normal, Flat. Andreas Feininger.
    A. NEGATIVE: Short exposure, long development, great contrast.
        PRINT: Normal paper.
    B. NEGATIVE: Normal exposure, development, and contrast.
        PRINT: Normal paper.
        Good detail in highlights and shadows.
    C. NEGATIVE: Long exposure, short development, low contrast.
        PRINT: Normal paper.
        Shadow definition is excellent; contrast is flat.

Discussion: Negative Contrasts

A photographer can increase and decrease the *inherent* contrast in a film by manipulating exposure and development.

To Increase Contrast	*To Decrease Contrast*
Cut exposure 50 percent (A ½ meter) Or one f/ stop	Double your exposure (2 x meter) Or one f/ stop
Double development If normal development is 5 minutes, develop for 10 minutes.	Cut development in half From 5 minutes to 2½ minutes

Conclusion:

Contrast is built by long development

When long development is used to increase contrast, you must shorten the exposure. Otherwise, normal exposure/increased development will yield a negative which is too dense or black. And contrast will also be lessened.

Use: On a dull day, your assignment is to photograph a new building. Cutting exposure, doubling development and #3 paper will improve contrast.

Contrast is decreased by shortening development + overexposure.

To obtain a satisfactory negative when development is shortened, you must increase (double) your exposure.

Use: In any scene in which contrast is objectionable.

Negative A is more contrasty and C is flatter than is practical in films exposed for reproduction. Extreme contrast (A) and flatness (C) are presented so that you can study their characteristics and then recognize these same characteristics in your own negatives.

Contrasty Negative—Often a large part of the negative is thin and lacks normal density.

It will have a few black dense areas caused by scene highlights (parts of the scene which reflect the greatest amount of light):
　white blouse
　woman's legs
　boy's light slacks and white socks.

It will have large areas of thin, tranparency (parts of the scene which reflect very little light onto the negative emulsion):
　tree trunk
　edge of the dark skirt against the trunk
　boy in the shadow.

Normal Negative—The whole negative has a better overall density than A.

Scene highlights are the blackest parts of the negative.

Scene shadows have enough density to show details, rather than being transparent. Look at the details in the

    tree trunk

    edge of the black skirt against the tree trunk

    boy in the shadow.

Flat Negative—The whole negative is a monotonous gray. True, shadow details are denser than those in B. But the needed contrast of B is also missing!

SCENE CONTRAST AFFECTS NEGATIVE DENSITY AND PRINT CONTRAST

A scene in which there are highlights, shadows, and middle-light value areas has contrast. The eye can see this contrast. Some parts of the scene which (1) have the most light or (2) which are brightest and reflect the most light are the highlight areas. Other parts which are (1) poorly lighted or (2) which absorb more light than they reflect are the shadow areas. Between the two extremes, are the normal areas.

Scene contrast is transferred to a negative in terms of density. Examine the scene which will be photographed. The same amount of light hits all parts of the subject. But the black skirt absorbs more light than it reflects (shadow area). The white blouse reflects the most light, more than it absorbs (highlight). Between these two extremes are the "normal" areas (hair and skin). The variation in the ability of the different parts of this subject to reflect light creates scene contrast. Besides the *reflecting ability* of the different parts of a subject, scene contrast results when one part of a subject/scene gets stronger light than another part.

TRANSLATING SCENE CONTRAST INTO DENSITY AND TRANSPARENCY—CHART 12

Scene	Contrast	Reflecting Ability	Negative Density and Transparency	Tone Contrast in Enlargement
Black skirt	Dark	Poor	Transparent	Black
White blouse	White	Excellent	Very dense and black	White
Skin	Light	Good	Dense	Light
Hair	Almost light	Fair	Some density	Gray

A light meter can measure the units of light which different parts of a scene reflect. To find the shadow-highlight ratio or the difference in the extremes of light values, note the darkest and the brightest part of any scene. The dark skirt reflects 25 units of light; the blouse reflects 200 units.

$$25 \quad : \quad 200 = 1:8 \text{ is the scene contrast}$$

$$\text{shadow} \qquad\qquad \text{highlight}$$

If a scene has an equal amount of light in what should be the shadow area and in what should be the highlight area (1:1), there is no contrast or difference in the light values. But if a scene has 1 unit of light in the shadow area for 4 units of light in the highlight area, contrast exists. It follows that the bigger the gap between the units of light in shadow and highlight areas, then the greater the contrast in the scene. For example, 1:8 is more contrasty than 1:4, which in turn is more contrasty than 1:2.

Some contrast is desirable. But too much contrast in the scene and the negative (great density in highlights and none in shadows) can increase problems when you enlarge a negative. Ideal contrast is from 1:4 to 1:8. A film can record much more contrast than a piece of enlarging paper. Enlarging paper can not record contrast greater than 1:30. And such contrast would be difficult to print, requiring a lot of dodging and burning in.

Information Needed for Purchasing Photographic Paper

What contrast: #1, 2, 3, 4, 5?

What weight: Single or double?

What size: 4 x 5, 5 x 7, 8 x 10, 11 x 14, 16 x 20?

How much: 25, 50, 100, or 500 sheets?

Emulsion sensitivity

Whether a paper is glossy or matte

Image tone of print

Tint of stock.

Many newspapers prefer a hard, glossy finish for reproduction. Some magazines which have photos retouched prefer a semi-matte paper which has a better tooth for retouching. Portrait photographers use a dull, matte paper for portraits. Point in mentioning that papers are either glossy or matte or a special classification is for you to know that each kind of paper should be developed in its own recommended developer.

Kind of Paper	Kind of Developer	
SW glossy	Vividol (Ansco) Dektol (Kodak)	Dektol has an activator which enhances contrast.
DW matte	Miradol (Ansco) Selectol (Kodak)	Selectol has a slower, softer working activator which produces less contrasty prints.

Enlarging and Developing the Print

Like the camera, the enlarger is a tool for controlling light. The top three-fourths of the enlarger is called the head. It contains a light bulb, and the light rays shine down through the enlarger and onto the light-sensitive paper below. Very little light escapes the enlarger except through the lens opening when you switch on the enlarger light. You control enlarger light two ways: 1. By the size of the f/stop opening you set on the lens; 2. And by the length of time you let the enlarger light remain on.

Operating the Enlarger

1. Note the *lever* on the left side of the enlarger head. Pull the lever forward and catch it on a latch. Note that an opening appears between the head and the shoulders of the lens box.
Caution: Your enlarger light shouldn't be on when you raise the head. Do not have your enlarger paper uncovered.

2. Your *negative carrier* is lying on top of the lens box, and projecting out all around the box, in an overhang. Take your carrier out and examine it. It is two pieces of square metal, with a cutout for the negative, fit together like two pieces of bread forming a sandwich. The negative, carefully dusted, is placed on top of the metal frame with the male plugs, emulsion side (dull) facing down.[1] Then the metal frame with the holes is placed on top of the negative edges and the bottom frame. Obviously, the holes in the sides of the top frame have to fit around the male plugs, extending up from the bottom frame. Now, the negative is held securely between the two metal frames. The negative can't curl with heat from the enlarger light or slip or turn.

---

[1] To make certain of getting the negative emulsion (down) facing the enlarger paper emulsion (up), find the notch on your piece of cut film. Hold the film so that the notch is at the top, right-hand side of the negative as it faces you. Now, the emulsion side of the negative faces you. Place the bottom of the negative on the far end of the negative carrier and the notched end on the near end of the negative holder. Now, the emulsion side is down, as it should be.
   If the negative is not positioned as instructed, newspaper identifications in cutlines will identify the sheriff as the criminal, and a libel suit could result.

65

3. Place the negative in the carrier on top of the lens box.

    a. Make sure the emulsion side of the negative remains down toward the enlarging paper emulsion.

    b. When light passes through glass the light is bent or refracted. A person on a camera ground glass seems to be standing on his head.

        Refraction works on the enlarger, too. If your negative contains the image of one person, the feet or the waist (bust shot) should point away from you, with the person's head nearest to you, as you position the negative in the carrier. This position is standing the person on his head. Then refraction turns the person around, so that on the enlarging paper he is positioned correctly, feet on the ground and head near the top of the paper.

        If your negative image is standing on his head, upside down, on the enlarging paper, you have positioned the negative carrier wrong (assuming that the negative was put in the carrier correctly).

4. Release the lever, so that the enlarger head rests on the negative carrier, closing the gap. Now, when the enlarger light is snapped on, light will be forced through the negative and lens, and not come out the sides of the lens box and fog your paper.

5. Snap on your enlarger light. The negative image is projected down onto the white background of your easel.

6. Check your lens opening. It should be opened to your biggest opening, probably $f/4.5$, to let as much light as possible shine down on your easel background while you focus.

7. Focus the enlarger. Note the focusing knob on the right side of the enlarger, near the bellows-lens box area. Twist the knob back and forth and watch how it raises and lowers your lens mount. After getting a sharp focus, ask: Is the projected image filling most of my enlarging paper? Have I cropped out unwanted parts of the negative image? Is my negative image big enough? Remember that readers like BIG image outlines!

8. To get a bigger image outline, place your hands on the two enlarger head grips at the back of the enlarger and push up. The higher and farther the enlarger head is away from the easel, the bigger the negative image that can be projected. And pulling the enlarger head down, closer to the easel, diminishes the size of the negative image. You will have to re-focus the enlarger after changing the size of the negative image by raising or lowering the enlarger head. Some enlargers focus automatically as you raise or lower the head. Naturally, an automatic focusing enlarger costs considerably more than

one without this feature. You may have to adjust the size of the image outline two or three times on the easel background and focus after each adjustment before you get the effect which you want.

9. Close down on your lens. The question is, how much? A good rule of thumb: Find a shadow area in the projected image on the easel (dark part of the picture, but transparent part of the film) like the hair of a person. Slowly stop down until you can barely see the detail in the hair.

10. Snap off your enlarger light. Your enlarger is set up for the projection.

Exposing an Enlargement and Developing the Print

11. Open your enlarger paper. Take out the top sheet. Close the paper. The shiny side of the paper is the one with the emulsion on it. This is the side that's senitive to light. Get in the habit of keeping this side down, away from even the dim light of your safelight, if you have to put the paper down for a minute or two before using it.

12. Cut your test strips from the sheet of enlarging paper. Some people cut test strips which are about 2 inches wide and 4 inches long. Others like bigger strips. Cut them to suit your preference.

IDEA: It's a lot less expensive to use 4 or 5 small test strips to get some idea of how long a time light must shine on the enlarging paper to properly expose it than it is to use a sheet 5 x 7 or 8 x 10 paper each time. Don't forget that these test strips are sensitive to light and can be fogged. Emulsion side of the paper should be down so light won't affect it as you cut the strips. If you put the strips down near the enlarger, turn the emulsion side down. And cover the strips with your box of paper, or shove the strips under the raised base of your enlarger (the board on which the easel rests).

13. Using test strips. If you have an "average/normal" negative and you have stopped down the enlarger correctly, probably your exposure time will be from 10 to 15 seconds. But don't worry if 30 seconds are required.

    a. Select three of the strips. Mark a different exposure time on the back of each strip with a soft pencil: 5 seconds; 10 seconds; 20 seconds. Note that the exposure times double from one strip to the next.

    b. Hold your 5 second strip in your hand, behind you out of range of the enlarger light, and snap on the light. Study the negative image on the easel. Where is a strong high-light and a shadow which are close together that will fit on your test strip? Having located such an area, snap off the light, position the strip, and expose for 5 seconds. Expose your 10 and your 20 second strips.

14. Develop all of your strips simultaneously for the same length of time. The manufacturer's recommended length of development is on an information sheet in every package of paper. Use the time recommended for your particular paper. Suppose the developing time recommended is 1 minute.

When the minute is up, drain developer off of the three strips and move them to the short stop for 30 seconds (continuous agitation), and then to the quick fix for 1 minute (continuous agitation). Keep your strips submerged in solution. Do not try to study the strips critically until the fixing is completed. Then hold all three strips together near the safelight and compare them.

Possibly the 20-second exposed strip looks ripe in the developer in 10 seconds and in 15 seconds it is getting darker and in 20 seconds it is burned up. This strip got too much enlarger light and is overexposed. Do not pull the strip out of the developer until the full minute has passed, even though it is turning black.

The 5-second strip is probably rather pale and anemic in appearance even with full development. This strip didn't get enough enlarger light.

The 10-second strip looks best to your eye. If the model is smiling, look at the black tone of the lips and the white of the teeth. Is the black tone just a gray, and are the teeth a little chalky, instead of being a clean white, showing in detail, each tooth clearly? Then even your best exposure at 10-seconds is underexposed. Why not try one more test strip at 15 seconds? If it's a little hot—slightly overexposed, the esimated exposure time for your first try at any enlargement might be about 12½ seconds.

15. Place a sheet of paper in the easel. Make a straight print (no dodging or burning) using the exposure time suggested by your test strips.

16. Develop the print for the full minute. Drain off developer before moving to short-stop.

17. Drain off short-stop and move print to quick fix. When the print is fixed, study it to see if the highlights are a little chalky and need more enlarger time and if your shadow areas are so black that the details are blocked up. To correct for chalky, weak tones, increase exposure; to improve black, burned areas, hold back enlarger light. Return your exploratory first print to the quick fix.

Your study shows: 12½ second over-all is a good exposure.

Two highlights are chalky. They need burning in. You estimate that an extra 5 seconds of light on each of these areas will be about right.

One shadow area is burned black. You estimate that probably 6-seconds of light on this area will be enough. So for the remaining 6½ seconds of the 12½ second exposure, hold back light from the one shadow area.

68

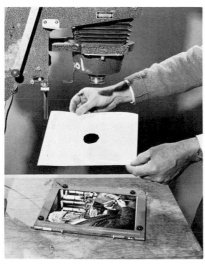

21. DODGING AND BURNING-IN AIDS. Photos by Dick Cobb.

(Upper left) The hand may be used to hold back odd-shaped areas, but must be kept in motion during exposure. (Upper right) Large areas may be held back with a card or piece of paper, also kept in motion. (Lower left) Small areas may be burned in by using a piece of paper with a ragged hole in it. (Lower right) Small areas may be held back by the use of dodging aids on a wire handle.

18. Place a second piece of enlarging paper in the easel and make the second print as you planned above.

During the full 12½ second exposure, use a finger, your hand, or a prepared dodging aid to hold back enlarger light from the shadow area every other second.

At the end of the full 12½ seconds, use an enlarging aid (8 x 10 discarded print with a small hole cut in the center of it) to hold back light from all of the print except one of the chalky highlights which needs another 5 seconds of light. Enlarger light can pass through the hole in the enlarger aid. By raising and lowering this enlarger aid you can let a bigger or a smaller circle of light hit the highlight area. After giving one area an extra 5 second exposure, move the enlarger aid so that light is now directed through the hole onto the second highlight area needing extra exposure. Give it 5 seconds, too.

Now develop your print. If your estimates were correct, you will have a good print. If your estimates were off, the highlights can be either chalky or too dark and your shadow area can be either too black or a weak gray (needs more exposure). Make new estimates and try a third print.

19. Prints should remain in the quick fix from 3 to 10 minutes. During this time, turn every print each time you put another one in this bath.

Otherwise, one print will lie on another, keeping fresh quick fix from replacing worn out quick fix, and the prints will not be properly fixed. When the quick fix doesn't remove all of the unexposed silver crystals, after the print is washed and exposed to light, it will turn yellow. Now, your work is lost. Another print will have to be made. So turn prints frequently while they're in the quick fix!

20. Wash your prints in running water at least 30 minutes to remove the quick fix.

21. Dry your print
   a. On a ferrotype plate;
   b. On a dryer;
   c. Between blotters weighted with a heavy object to keep them pressed flat.

Tips on Developing the Print

1. Learn to use print tongs. Professionals do. Have two pair, one for the alkaline developer, and a second for the acid short-stop and the acid quick fix.

2. Even with tongs, your hands will get wet with developer. Dip the hand in stop bath, then rinse it in a beaker of standing water or under running faucet water. Then dry your hands.

22. PRINT CONTROL BY DODGING AND BURNING-IN. Andreas Feininger.

Print at left is a straight one from a back-lighted negative on soft paper. It is a good rendition but lacking in drama. The picture at right is a print from the same negative on hard paper, dodged to hold back the middle distance and give a foggy appearance, while the sky and distant buildings have been burned in for emphasis. The result is much more dramatic.

Working with wet hands causes all sorts of waste and trouble. You leave finger prints on your enlargements, the tell-tale signs of a sloppy dark room worker. You leave fingerprints on your negatives. Soon your negative carrier and the focusing knob of you enlarger will show signs (white powdery spots) of wet hands.

3. Submerge your enlargement in the developer with one quick downward thrust so that the print is covered with the developer as quickly as possible.

4. Rock the tray gently, so that the motion of the developing solution will agitate the print.

Keep your hands out of the developer, and off of the print!

Do not rub the print.

Do not pull the print out of the developer to examine it and then return it to the developer. Developing prints which are exposed to air oxidize and turn yellow.

After the print is in the developer, leave it there the full development time.

5. After the full minute of development (or whatever your paper manufacturer recommends) if your print is not done, extending the development time of the print for one-half of the recommended time (½ minute in this case) won't harm the print. But leaving a print in the developer for 3 to 5 minutes and trying to force an underexposed print is a losing game. The forced print will often turn yellow when exposed to light. Correct exposure and the right development time are the steps for avoiding forced prints.

6. Suppose your print is done in 30 seconds, and you jerk it out of the developer and drop it into the short-stop. Chances are your blacks will be muddy and not the full, rich blacks the paper is capable of

71

yielding when properly exposed and developed. You are settling for only half a loaf.

7. Many professionals work with a small container of full strength Dektol beside the tray of developer. In it are cotton swabs of different sizes on round wooden splints.

Applying full strength developer to a stubborn highlight that has been burned in and still needs aid can be a life saver.

This aid cannot replace the proper amount of burning in!

Do not rub the print with the swab. Just apply some full strength developer and let it do the work.

Probably your first effort may be a disappointment because the full strength developer runs and shows by the path it leaves exactly where it has been. By trial and error, you will learn to keep running water in a hose handy and dry cotton to wash away and blot areas which the concentrated developer threatens.

8. Standardize length of development. In transferring the negative image on to the enlarging paper, your goal is to get a print which has a pleasing range of contrasting tone values from blacks (shadows) to many different grays to a few clean whites (highlight). You have two controls over your product (1) exposure and (2) development.

So that you can recognize any error committed in making prints, you will be wise to standardize one of these controls. The control to keep the same is your print development time. Always leave your prints in the developer for the full time the manufacturer recommends. Now, with one control standardized, you can quickly pin-point errors and correct them. A print that is too dark got too much enlarger light. And a print which is too chalky and light didn't get enough light. But if both of your controls are constantly varied, you will have no basis for figuring out which control you goofed on.

Standardized Development Helps To Find Print Errors

Error	Cause	Correction
Print gets done too quickly, burns up	Too much enlarger exposure on print.	Shorten your exposure time.
At end of recommended development time, print is still pale, weak. Blacks are gray. Whites are chalky and without texture, detail.	Not enough enlarger exposure on the print.	Lengthen your exposure time.

9. Always dust your negative before placing it in the negative holder. A camel's hair brush is best for this. A rubber hand blower works well, too.

IS YOUR PRINT A GOOD ONE?

J. P. Smith, Norman, Okla.

(Upper left) Good print on correct ~~grade~~ de of paper. (Upper center) ~~Paper~~ per is too soft. (Upper right) ~~Paper~~ per is too hard. (Lower left) Paper correct, print underexposed. (Lower ~~right~~ ht) Paper correct, print overex~~pos~~ed.

10. Before you place your negative in the carrier, hold the negative in front of a safe light and study two characteristics:

A. DENSITY (overall blackness and blackness of highlight areas) controls the length of exposure time required for the print.

    1) A normal negative is usually exposed for 10 to 15 seconds.

    2) A very black negative can be stubborn and require from 30 to 60 seconds, even with the f/stop wide open.

    3) A thin negative will require a shorter than normal enlargement, and the f/stop may have to be stopped down all the way to f/32.

Which kind of a negative do you have? Try to estimate the right exposure time. Half this time for a second test strip and double it for the third test strip.

Soon you should develop the ability to judge exposure time required for a negative fairly accurately.

73

B. CONTRAST of a negative (difference in density between highlights and shadows) determines which grade of paper is chosen for the enlargement.

1) Normal negative requires #2 paper.

2) A negative with both intense highlights (black areas) and deep shadows (transparent areas) which contrast sharply to the eye will usually require a paper low in contrast, say a #1 paper or a #2.

3) A negative which is black and lacks contrast (flat) needs a paper with more contrast than normal to improve it, say #3, 4, 5 paper, depending on just how flat the negative is.

Learning to detect the amount of contrast in a negative and select the right grade of paper requires time and patience, but work to achieve this skill. The sooner you master this technique, the quicker your prints will look professional.

FUNCTION OF PRINT DEVELOPING BATHS—CHART 13

Developer	Short Stop	Quick Fix	Wash
Dektol (Eastman) Mix 1 part developer 2 parts water	64 oz. water + 3 oz. of 28% glacial acetic acid	Use full strength as mixed.	Need running water
Time: Manuf. recommends 1 to 3 minutes	30 to 60 seconds	2 to 10 minutes	30 minutes to 1 hour Depends on 1. Need permanent print?
Rock tray gently Constant agitation	Constant agitation	Turn prints to keep fresh fix working	2. Single wt. or double wt. paper
Function: Brings out latent image on print	To stop development. To catch excess developer.	Fixes print image. Removes unexposed silver salts to prevent fogging.	Remove quick fix. It will fade print, cause print to turn yellow in time.
Discard after each work session.	Discard.	Discard.	

Many photographers soak prints in Pakosol before drying them on ferrotype plates or on a commercial dryer. The solution helps to keep prints from sticking to the hot metal plate when it is dry, and Pakosol helps dry prints to remain flat instead of curling up.

Buying, Mixing and Storing Photographic Chemicals

Your photo supplier will help you. Keep in mind that in buying a negative developer, the size of your film is a consideration. The smaller the film, the more likely you are to need a fine grain formula. The manufacturer's information sheet with your film recommends a developer.

With your enlarging paper you also get an information sheet which recommends the developer for the paper.

Developers, quick fix and hypo are all packaged in a wide range of sizes. Instructions are simple and clear. Just follow them. It is no trouble to mix up the chemicals one needs to either develop film or enlarge prints.

A small bottle of concentrated acetic acid will serve the home worker in preparing the short stop. In mixing all your chemicals you will need a glass or enamel beaker with ounces marked on it. In diluting your concentrated acetic acid to a 28 per cent solution, use 3 parts acid to 8 parts of water.

After you mix up a gallon of negative developer, a gallon of 28 per cent acetic acid, a gallon of quick fix and a gallon of printer developer, you'll need bottles for storing these solutions. Your druggist will sell you brown, 1-gallon bottles with good, screw-on caps.

KINDS OF ENLARGERS
Which Should You Buy?

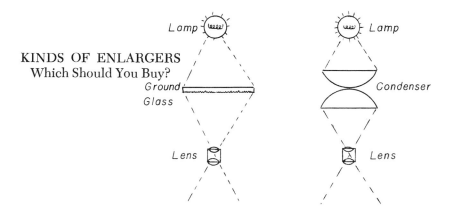

25. ENLARGER TYPES.(Left) Diffusian type uses ground glass to soften light. (Right) Condenser type with lenses results in harsh light and brilliant prints.

The two enlargers above are alike except in one respect. The diffusion type has a ground glass between the light and the negative. And the condenser type has two clear glass condensers, back to back, 'in exactly the shape shown in the diagram.

This one difference in the two enlargers is very important, for the diffusion enlarger emits a soft light while the condenser yields a harsh light. The ground glass on the diffusion enlarger is semi-transparent. It appears slightly frosted because sand has been blown against it with great force. When a long ray of light hits the ground glass, two changes occur in the light. 1) It is refracted. 2) A long ray of light is broken

75

up into many shorter and less brilliant rays. So because of the ground glass, which diffuses and breaks up the long rays of light from the enlarger bulb, a diffusion enlarger delivers only soft light to shine through the negative and transpose the image down onto the print paper in the form of a latent image.

By contrast, on the condenser enlarger, a ray of light is only refracted. No breaking up of long rays into short rays of light occurs. Light from the enlarger lamp has no interference in penetrating the two clear condenser discs. So this type enlarger delivers only harsh light to the negative.

Diffusion	*Condenser*
1. Gives a soft, diffused light.	Gives a hard brilliant light
2. Produces a duller print which lacks brilliance of tone.	Produces a brilliant print.
3. Does *not* emphasize skin blemishes: wrinkles, pock marks, ec.	*Does* emphasize skin texture and blemishes.
4. Does *not* emphasize negative defects: dust, scratches, grain.	*Does* emphasize negative defects
5. Used by portrait photographers who wish to make prints which flatter subjects.	Used by news photographers and commercial photographers who want brilliant prints with plenty of contrast in tone values.
6. No attachment can be placed on this enlarger to convert the "soft" light to the kind of light a condenser produced.	A *diffusion disc* held under the lens for about one half of the required exposure time will soften and diffuse the enlarger light so that the print will have the appearance of one produced on a diffusion enlarger.

Both types of enlargers can be bought with automatic focusing if preferred.

Many who want an all-purpose enlarger which will do almost everything will buy the condenser enlarger and diffusion disc.

Some manufacturers produce an enlarger which is called a diffusion-condenser enlarger. As the name indicates, it tries to be one-half fish and one-half fowl. It is a compromise between the two basic kinds of enlargers already discussed.

CHAPTER 5

Using the Weston Light Meter

A meter reading can be taken by either the overall or the range of brightness method. Most photographers prefer the second method because it is more acurate.

Overall Method

1. Check the number in the *red cutout* and make certain that it is the same as the ASA rating of the film you are using.[1]

2. In measuring light for a scenic view: Point the meter at the horizon (back toward scene), and tilt it down slightly toward the earth. Make certain to hold it by the right end so that your hand does not cover the *photo electric cell.*

   Light reflected from the scene to be photographed will strike the *cell.* The *needle* will jump back and forth, as the light affects the cell. Finally, the needle will rest on only one of the numbers on the *vertical scale.* Suppose the number is 200.

3. Note the 200 on the *circular scale.* Turn the *dial with the Normal Arrow* on it so that the normal arrow points at 200.

   Now the light in the scene has been measured. The meter has been set so that you can choose the data you need for a good exposure: the right shutter speed and the right f/stop opening.

4. Note all of the different *f/stop openings* listed on the Normal Arrow dial, under the red cutout.

---

[1] All film manufacturers make films of varying sensitivity to light. Fast films, medium films, and slow films are available. A slow film will have an ASA rating of 40 to 100. Fast films range from an ASA of 125 to 1250. Note that the faster the film is, the bigger the ASA rating number assigned to it. An information sheet available for every film indicates the ASA rating of that particular film.

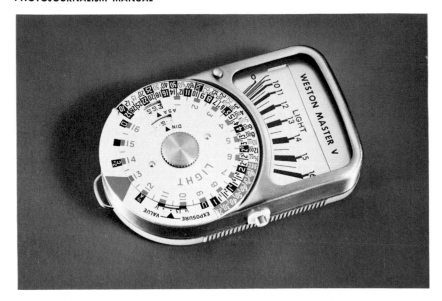

25. WESTON MASTER V EXPOSURE METER. Calculator dial at right with window for setting ASA speed; inner section of dial rotates to set light value against normal, A.C.U. or O markers. Number shown through window automatically change to high or low range when baffle on back of meter is opened or closed.

Also note that on the luminous dial, under the f/stop openings, are many different shutter speeds.

Measuring the light and setting the Normal Arrow on 200 has aligned the f/stop openings opposite the correct shutter speeds which will yield the proper exposures for this particular scene. Any one of combinations of f/stops and shutter speeds which are opposite one another will be a correct exposure. All of the various combinations result in the same exposures.

Some possibilities: (all yield the same amount of light)

f/32	1/60	Depth of field camera situation
f/12	1/400	Fair depth of field, medium action
f/8	1/1000	Less depth of field, maximum action

Range of Brightness Method

Range of brightness method gives a much more accurate measurement of light in a scene than the overall approach.

An overall reading on the scene in Figure 18 would result in a bad negative. The biggest and brightest object is the white wall, reflecting 800 units of light. Your goal is to get a good picture of the person in front of the white wall. The great amount of light reflected by the wall is much brighter than any part of the person. So the overpowering

78

light reflected by the wall would influence the photo electric cell, if an overall reading were used. Such a reading would result in badly under-exposing the person and the shrub (shadow area).

A more accurate measurement of the scene would be *close-up* readings of several parts of the scene, as you seek to find the highlight (brightest part) and the shadow areas (darkest part). All scenes are not as obvious as this one, in which your extremes are the shrub (shadow) and the wall (highlight). As the scene indicates, the shrub reflects 6.5 units of light while the white wall reflects 800 units of light. Now, instead of exposing for either extreme, you compromise and expose half way beween the extremes. No involved math is needed. Hold the meter with your left thumb on the square indicating 6.5 and your right thumb on the square indicating 800. Move the left thumb to the next square, 13; the right thumb to the next square, 400. Finally, the left thumb will end up on 50, the right thumb on 100. Set the Normal Arrow on 75. Depth of field data would be $f/32$ at $1/25$; maximum action data would be $f/4.5$ at $1/1000$.

If there were no wall and no shrub, and only the person to be considered, your scene contrast range (the darkest versus the brightest area) would be 25:100 or 1:4. In this situation, your normal arrow would end up on 50.

Exposure possibilities- —Right selection depends on camera situation:

$f/25$	$1/25$ DF	$f/6.3$	$1/400$ Medium Action
$f/12$	$1/100$ Normal Shot	$f/4.$	$1/1000$ Maximum Action

A Close-up Meter Measurement

You could stand several feet from the wall and get an accurate measurement of the light it reflects. But in measuring only the light reflected by the shrub, without getting any of the light reflected by the wall, you would need to be close to the shrub. A side of the shrub would be better than either the front or back of the shrub. Take some care in getting exactly the right angle of the meter in relation to the shrub, so that the photo electric cell will not be affected by light reflected from the wall.

In measuring the light reflected by the person, again you have the problem of excluding the brighter light from the wall. Keep the person between the meter and the wall, taking care to hold the meter at the right angle to exclude light reflected by the wall. Also take care that the meter and your hand do not cast a shadow on the person, and that your light measurement is not of that shadow. Probably your meter will be within 8 inches or so of the person.

When a person is backlighted (has his back to the sun) and his face away from it, you have the same problem of the white wall again. Take

26. ATTACHING THE WESTON INVERCONE. For incident light measurement the Invercone is inserted into the recess to cover the photo-cell. When the light is bright, the
baffle is first closed and the Invercone is attached over the baffle as shown here.

care to get close enough to the person and to keep the person between
the meter and the sun, so that the direct sun rays do not affect the
electric cell. You want to measure only reflected light from the person.

Use of A and C Instead of the Normal Arrow

The inherent contrast of film is controlled by the manufacturer, who
can make films on the flat side, films with a normal amount of contrast, or films with more than normal contrast.

Generally, films which are very sensitive to light are low in contrast
and have coarse grain. Films less sensitive to light have more contrast
and finer grain.

You can influence the inherent contrast which the manufacturer puts
into his film by the way you expose and develop. You can increase the
contrast of the film, and you can also decrease the contrast, within
limits.

Situation: Suppose you are using a film lacking in contrast—a fast
emulsion. The light of the winter day is dull and flat. Your assignment:
A new building being dedicated on the State University campus. You
want to expose and develop the negative so that it will have more con-

trast than the manufacturer intended. Old photographic idiom: Expose for shadow; develop for contrast.

    Your formula: Cut your exposure 50%   )   Developing
                 Increase your development 100% (for Contrast

After taking range of brightness readings and determining the mid-point between the extremes, do *not* set the normal arrow on the mid-point. Instead, set A on the mid-point. This means you are using one stop of light less than normally, or that you have cut exposure by 50%.

If your thermometer says to develop 4 minutes, you should develop for 8 minutes.

In using this formula, you purposely shortened exposure so that you can lengthen development. *The increased development builds contrast.* If you exposed normally, and then lengthened the development, your density would be too great. So to keep density in check, cut exposure so that you can use the lengthened development to increase contrast.

If you wish to continue to build your contrast, select a #3 or #4 paper instead of a normal #2 paper. Expose your enlarging paper so that it will require an extra minute of development.

Situation: You are using the press-type film, low contrast. Your assignment: Another new building at State University surrounded by an acre of concrete, for parking cars. It is 2 p.m. on a very hot summer day. The front of the building is in shadows because of extremely wide overhanging eaves at every floor of the 3-story building. You want to decrease the scene contrast so the white concrete won't be disproportionately denser than the building details in shadows.

    Your formula: Increase your exposure 100%   )   Exposing for
                 Cut your development 50%   (Shadow

Set C (2X) on the mid-point between the scene shadow and highlight areas. You will be overexposing the negative one full f/stop.

27. When light is dim and in-cident-light reading is to be taken, open the perforated baffle before attaching the In-vercone.

If your temperature indicates a 4 minute development, use only 2 minutes.

Try your negative on #2 paper and #1. If #1 isn't too flat, it will subtract contrast which was in the scene and on the negative.

Use U and O Instead of the Normal Arrow

If *U* is set on the midpoint between scene shadow and highlight, you will underexpose four full *f*/stops of light. This is the maximum underexposure which can be given to black and white film which will then be given a longer development than normally. A little experimenting on your part will find how much longer you should increase your development. The increased time will be longer than that used for only a 1-stop underexposure, when development was increased from 4 to 8 minutes.

If *O* is set at the midpoint on the meter after a range of brightness reading, you will overexpose your film four full stops. This, too, is the maximum everexposure which will still yield a usable negative.

Photographing Dimly Lighted Objects

In dark buildings—cathedrals or large auditoriums—where your red needle won't move much even with the baffle open, try this:

a. Take a reading of the brightest part of the object you want to photograph
b. Note the number indicated on the vertical scale by the red needle and find the same number on the circular scale.
c. Place O (not the normal arrow) opposite the number on the circular scale
d. Use normal development

For the Minimum Correct Exposure and Thin Negatives:
Darkest Object Method

a. Take a reading on the *darkest object* in the scene
b. Note the number indicated on the vertical scale (red arrow) and locate the same number on the circular scale.
c. Place U opposite the circular scale
d. Use normal development

Occasionally a backlighted or very contrasty scene exceeds even the wide acceptance range of black and white film. In this event the exposure can be keyed to that portion of the scene, (either the shadows or the highlights) whichever is of most importance, by placing the U or O opposite the darkest or brightest reading respectively.

Film Latitude

Ideal exposure is best most of the time. For special situations (Expose for shadow; develop for contrast) exposure and development should be manipulated. A film which will permit an overexposure or an underexposure of four stops has a wide latitude for error. Black and white film has a much wider latitude for error than color films, which look best when given ideal exposure. Color films have very little latitude for error.

Three Kinds of Light Meters

The three kinds of meters include:

1. Meters which measure *reflected* light: Weston

2. Meters which measure *incident* light: Gossen Pilot
General Electric
Golden Crown

3. Meters which measure either kind of light: Gossen Luna 6
Weston

Light which falls upon objects is incident light. A light ray, traveling in a straight line, strikes an object. Some of the light ray is absorbed; some of it is reflected. Light reflected from objects is reflected light.

Many photographers use an incident light meter because they believe it is a more accurate instrument. Many other photographers prefer a reflected light meter, and they can make a strong case for such a meter. More important than arguing the merits of either type of meter is the knowledge that you do have a choice of a basic reflected light meter, a basic incident light meter, or a meter which can measure either kind of light. Further, the Weston Master IV and later models can be converted into an incident light meter.

The Weston meter has been discussed here and used in teaching photography students for over 15 years for several reasons. The first is that as a precision instrument, receiving rough treatment from students, the Weston is rugged. Its manufacturer maintains an excellent repair service. And now the Weston, basically a reflected light meter, can be converted into an incident light meter.

Using the Invercone for Incident Light Readings

With the Invercone attached, stand at the subject which you are going to photograph and point the meter at the spot where the camera will be when the picture is taken. The exposure meter settings are then selected the same as when taking reflected light readings. If the subject is inaccessible, a substitute reading can be taken at the camera position (take a reading of the back of your hand) providing the illumination is the same as on the subject.

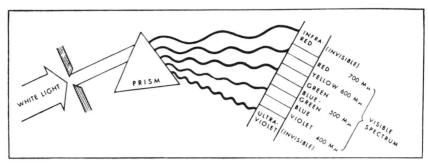

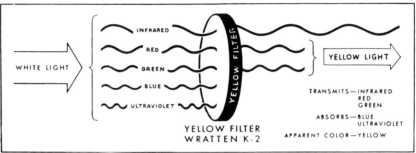

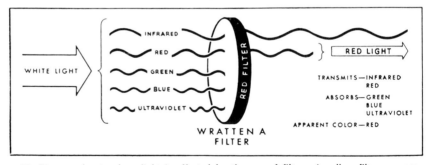

28. Diagram showing how light is affected by the use of filters. A yellow filter appears yellow because it subtracts blue from the white light, leaving the red and green, which combined, produce the sensation of yellow. A red filter appears red because it subtracts both blue and green from the white light, leaving only the red.

CHAPTER 6

Using Filters

What Are Filters?

Filters are made of two round pieces of glass, placed together like a sandwich with a colored sheet of gelatin cemented between them. A metal rim binds the whole unit together. The various colors of filters are listed in manufacturer's tables.

Filters can be held in front of the lens by metal adapter rings or by lens hoods. Two situations in which filters are used most often are (1) to obtain greater tone contrast in a black and white print when two scene colors like red and yellow are exactly the same tone; (2) to improve the sky area in outdoor shots.

A few facts about film and light will help you understand why filters can improve tone contrast and help immeasurably with outdoor pictures which include the sky.

Film and Filters

One of the characteristics of film is its ability to see and reproduce color in varying tones of black, gray, and white. The first films were blind to all colors except blue hence, they were over-sensitive to blue. Such a film would yield the same dark tone for colors red and yellow, and almost white tones for blue. The blue would register heavily on the negative, causing dense areas. When enlarged, the dense parts of the negative representing blue colors would hold light back from the print paper, so print tones representing blue would be quite light.

A color-blind film simply was not satisfactory. One needed a film which would not be so sensitive to blue, and which would be more sensitive to other colors; that is, a film which would yield different tones of gray for contrasting scene colors like red and yellow.

Orthochromatic film was the next step. Ortho film was sensitive to most colors except red. The next advance was Panchromatic film, which was fully color sensitive to all colors, including red. Such a

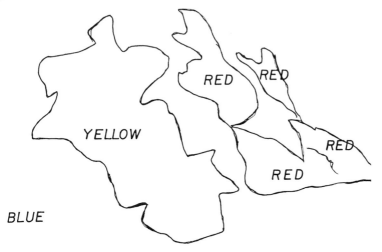

YELLOW

RED RED

RED

RED

BLUE

29. COLOR SENSITIVITY OF TWO TYPES OF FILM.
Andreas Feininger.

This sketch shows the colors of the principal parts of the picture below. Yellow and red flowers on a background of blue cloth.

30. COLOR SENSITIVITY OF TWO FILMS SHOWN.
Andreas Feininger.

Photographed on orthochromatic film, the red flowers are black, the yellow flowers are gray, and the blue background cloth is quite light.

31. COLOR SENSITIVITY OF TWO FILMS SHOWN.
Andreas Feininger.

Photographed on panchromatic film, the red flowers are gray, the yellow flowers nearly white, and the blue background is quite dark.

film would photograph colors as the eye saw them and show different colors as contrasting rays, whites, and blacks.

Yet, even with Pan film colors like green and red may be represented in a black and white print by the same tone of gray (see 31. Color Sensitivity of Two Films Shown). The way to improve the ability of the film to render different tones for different colors is by using filters.

Light Characteristics

Incident light, which appears colorless, travels in straight lines. When it strikes an object, some of the light is absorbed and some of it is reflected. How much light is absorbed or reflected depends on the color of the reflecting object and whether it has a high or low reflecting ability. If a ray of "colorless" light is shot through a prism, the spectrum (all the different colors making up light) emerges. Roughly, the colors in the spectrum are purple, blue, green, yellow, orange and red.

CHOOSING THE RIGHT FILTER—CHART 14

Color of Object	Filters Make Color Lighter	Filters Make Color Darker
Red	F, A, G	G-5, B
Orange	G, A	C-5
Yellow	G, A	C-5
Green	B, G, X-1, X-2	C-5, A
Blue-green	C-5, B	F, A
Blue	C-5	F, A, G, B
Purple	C-5	B

Why is grass green, a red car red, and a blue dress blue to your eye?

Incident light		Reason
↓	= green to vision	All colors except green are
green grass		absorbed.
		Green is reflected.
Incident light		
↓	= red to vision	All colors except red are
red car		absorbed.
		Red is reflected.

An object appears to be a certain color to the eye because it reflects its own color and absorbs other colors.

How can a filter make an object lighter or darker in tone?

Red car + red filter = very light tone

Red filter transmits its own color to the film.

Red color registers heavily on the negative, so car is dense.

87

32. EFFECT OF CORRECTION FILTER ON SKY.
Modern panchromatic film without filter produces effect similar to that seen by the eye.

33. EFFECT OF CORRECTION FILTER ON SKY.
Pan film with K-2 Yellow filter darkens sky slightly, also lightens foliage to some extent.

34. EFFECT OF CORRECTION FILTER ON SKY.
Pan film with A (Red) filter, darkens sky even further, lightens foliage to a slightly greater extent.

In enlarging: Negative density of car holds light back from print paper.

In print: Car appears light in tone because little light reached print.

Red car + green filter = darker in tone

Green filter transmits less of the red light to the film.

Now red color does not register so heavily on negative, and car is less dense.

In enlarging: A more transparent car outline transmits more light to print paper.

In print: Car appears darker in tone because more light affected paper.

Conclusion: To make an object a lighter tone, use a filter of the same color as the object. To make the object a darker tone, use a filter which is complementary or different from that of the object.

Two Uses of Filters

A filter used to improve contrast, as just discussed, is called a *contrast* filter. If the same filter were used in a scenic shot to improve the sky, the filter would be called a *correction* filter.

Films are still over-sensitive to blue. If no filter is used with an outdoor shot with a lot of sky, the blue of the sky registers heavily on the film, making the sky area dense. In enlarging, the dense sky area of the negative holds back light from the print, so that the picture has a washed-out, pallid sky. A yellow filter holds back some of the blue light from the sky, so that in the negative the sky area is less dense. When enlarged the negative permits more enlarger light to reach the print in the sky area. Now, the picture has a better contrast between the blue sky (dark gray in print) and the white clouds. As more enlarger light gets through the negative sky area, and affects the print emulsion, the sky tone is much darker. A red filter yields almost a transparent sky in the negative, permitting greater amounts of light to reach the print and turn the sky still darker. For effective skies in which there is a good contrast with white clouds, use a dark yellow filter, a K-2. For dramatic skies with greater tone contrast between the sky and the clouds, use a light red filter, an A.

What Is a Filter Factor?

When a filter is placed in front of the camera lens, some of the available light does not reach the film. To prevent underexposing film when filters are used, more exposure must be used. The extra light, to compensate for that which is held back from the negative by the filter, can be gained at either light control, depending on camera situation.

How much more light has to be used with a filter? This depends on your filter factor, a number indicating how exposure should be corrected. If your filter factor were 1.4 you should open up ½ stop larger than normal. If your factor were 2, open up a full $f/stop$. A factor of 4 would require a compensation of two extra stops of light.

The following formula works if you want to correct your exposure with your shutter.

Filter factor $= 2$
Meter reading $= 1/100$ second $2/X \times 1/100 = 2/100X = 1/50$ second.

FILTER FACTORS — CHART 15

Color	Filter	Verichrome	Panatomic X Plus-X Super Panchro-B		Tri-X Pan	
Yellow	K-1	2 1.5)*	1.5	(1.5)*	1.5	(1.5)*
Dark Yellow	K-2	2.5 (2)	2	(1.5)	2	(1.5)
Orange	G	5 (3)	3	(2)	2.5	(2)
Green	X-1	- (-)	3	(2)	4	(3)
Dark Green	X-2	- (-)	8	(8)	8	(6)
Red	A	- (-)	8	(4)	4	(6)
Dark Red	F	- (-)	16	(8)	8	(4)
Blue	C-5	3 (4)	5	(10)	5	(10)

*Tungsten light

Copying Photos

Thumbtack your photo to your copy board on the wall.

Set your two copy lights (reflectors with Number 2 photofloods) on either side of the photo so that the light is even on it without shaded areas or hotspots.

Adjust your camera so that the subject will fill the negative. Focus.

Take a meter reading. Use overall method, holding the meter over the camera, above the film area.

If your copy camera is closer to the photo being copied than eight times the focal length of the lens, $f/values$ are changed. Negatives will be underexposed unless exposure is increased.

A 5-inch lens which is closer than 40 inches would be affected as would a 6-inch lens which is closer than 48 inches. In copying a 5x7 print onto a 4x5 negative, you should open up about 1½ $f/stops$. Extreme close-ups call for increased exposure of 6 to 8 stops.

A revolving calculator, the Effective Lens Aperture Kodaguide, will supply data on how to compensate in copy work.

With *continuous tone photos*, correct your exposure and develop normally. Your copy will tend to be a bit more contrasty than the original because some of the very light grays in highlight areas will drop out.

With *black and white line drawings*, correct your exposure if the camera is farther away than eight times the focal length of the lens.

90

Then increase exposure by at least one more stop. Then double your development.

Reason: You want the white of the paper containing the line drawing to be very black and dense on your negative. Then little or no enlarger light can go through it. On your positive, the white paper background will be a clean white.

If the paper background on the negative is not dense enough, some enlarger light will get through and the paper background on the print will be gray instead of a clean white.

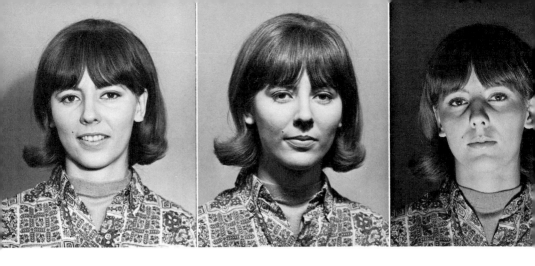

35. SIX BASIC POSITIONS FOR LIGHTS. Photos by Dick Cobb.

(Left) One light beside camera yields flat front lighting. (center) Raising the front light slightly creates the "butterfly shadow beneath the nose. (right) Underneath light for "spooky" lighting as for Hallowe'en pictures; not suitable for normal portraiture.

35. SIX BASIC POSITIONS FOR LIGHTS (Continued)

(Left) Light above subject's head at a 45 degree angle; the most common placement of the main light for normal portraits. (center) Full side light is not suitable for anything except very special effects; it tends to chop the face in half. (right) Putting all light on background and slight underexposure produces a silhouette effect.

CHAPTER 7

Lighting the Portrait

You don't have to be a professional photographer to turn out a good portrait. And learning to make a good portrait is not wasted time. In shooting portraits, and working with incandescent lighting first, you learn to judge light quickly and less expensively than with flashlamps. With incandescent lights you learn where to position lights by observing the actual effect of the light, and what combination of lights give pleasing results. Later, when you do multiflash work, you will know from this experience, where to place your flashlamps.

Six Basic Positions for One Light

A. A front light on the camera, about even with the subject's head is called *flat lighting* because both sides of the face get the same amount of light. Great tone contrast of highlight and shadow is not here, as it is in either narrow or broad lighting. Flat lighting is the easiest to reproduce for printing purposes, but it is not as interesting as either narrow or broad light, which have more contrast of highlight and shadow. This is the most used of the six positions by beginners.

B. A front light, held higher (off the camera) than the subject's head has been called both butterfly lighting (because of the nose shadow) and glamour lighting. *Rule*: Do not permit the nose shadow to extend past the top half of the space between the subject's upper lip and his nose. And never permit the shadow to cross the lips! The higher your light is, the longer your shadow will be.

C. A low front light (off the camera) which shoots up at the subject is used only for special effects. This light produces the effect of stage footlights. Since the sun and room lighting are both overhead, you are used to top lighting. When a subject is lighted with a low light, it appears unnatural to your eye. Somehow, it tends to make the subject appear unwholesome. This kind of lighting is excellent for a Hallowe'en subject.

93

36. LIGHTING THE PORTRAIT. Photo by Dick Cobb.

Bread and butter lighting; a 45° main light plus a fill light alongside the camera. Learn to recognize the triangle of light on the cheek and the 45 degree slope of the shadow under the nose as keys to this lighting.

D. A light held at a 45 degree angle (off the camera), a bit higher than the subject's head is the most used of the six positions by news photographers. The reason is obvious. You have stronger contrasts between highlight and shadows so that the print will have better contrast of tones than is possible with front lighting. This 45 degree light has been called Rembrandt lighting because the painter used it often. Your subject should have a perfect triangle highlight under the eye on the shadow side of the face. The narrow tip of the inverted triangle should not merge with a highlight near the lips. Keep the lips in shadow.

This effect can be obtained with flash or strobe by removing your flash gun and holding it at arm's length from the camera, so that the light will strike your subject from his side. Make sure the light is a little higher than the subject's head.

E. About the only place you will see 90 degree lighting (at a right angle to subject) is in the "before" advertisement for aspirin. Such lighting shows how terrible you feel before you swallow the magic pill! In the "after" picture, the subject is out of the shadows into sunlight, smiling broadly, and feeling great—so the advertisement says.

F. Silhouette lighting is an important technique which you should master. In any series of 4 or 5 photos, one of them should be a silhouette. It will lend contrast of tone to the layout, giving it a change of pace. The whole trick in silhouette is underexposure.

Light behind the subject should be much stronger than the light which the subject itself reflects. The main subject, then, is underexposed. It will be thin on the negative, permitting a lot of enlarger light to register on the print paper, turning the outline of the subject black.

94

Out of doors, place objects to be silhouetted between the camera and the sun and underexpose.

Bread and Butter Lighting

This is the approach which most portrait photographers master first. It is their stock lighting, the basic light which accounts for over 50 percent of the portraits which have been made in the past — the bread and butter light.

Subject is positioned in front of the camera. Camera is about the same height as the subject's head. Position your key or #1 light first. The light should be 3-5 feet from the subject at a 45 degree angle, higher than the subject's head. The triangle of light on the shadow side of the face will tell you when the light is properly placed.

This light places a strong highlight on the side of the face nearest the light. The far side of the face, in shadow, gives a pleasing, interesting contrast to the highlight.

Your fill or #2 light is placed beside the camera, about the same height as the camera. The purpose of this light is to fill in the shadow side of the face with some light, not enough to eliminate the shadow, but enough to light up the shadows so details will not block up and be black.

Do not pull the fill light away from the camera, so that the light will be at an angle to the subject. Your key light is at a 45 degree angle, causing shadows on the far side of the face. Now, if you place the fill light at an angle to the subject, the result is cross shadows on what should be the highlight side of the face. The result is not pleasing.

How far should your fill light and camera be from the subject? Assuming that both lights are the same size, if your key light is 3 feet from the subject, the fill light should be 6 feet away. If the key light is 4 feet from the subject, the fill light should be 8 feet away. *Rule*: The fill light should be twice as far from the subject as the key light. This proportion will yield a 4:1 ratio between highlight and shadow.

As light travels away from its source, its strength and intensity diminish rapidly. The inverse square law is at work here. Refer to Chapter VIII or Flash Lamp Lighting for the explanation of this law.

Using a Third Light in Bread and Butter Lighting

A useful third light in portrait work is a small spotlight on a boom. Generally, this spot is placed overhead, so the subject's hair will be bathed in light. A brunette's head tends to merge with dark background if extra light isn't used on the dark hair. And the extra light will put some highlights into the hair of a blonde! Caution: Don't get this spot too far forward, so that it spills light on the front of the face. If this occurs, the light will put a highlight on the nose of your subject, flattening it out.

95

Producing Either a Light or a Dark Background

Your background will be influenced by its color and by the amount of light you place on it.

In front of a white background, if you work close to it, your key and fill light will yield a gray background. To get a black background, simply move the lighting set-up and subject farther away from the background. Now, your light has so far to travel, and it falls off so rapidly as it gets farther from its source, that you will get either a darker gray or black background. If you want a white background, just put a lot of light on the white background. This would call for a fourth light, which would be to the side of or behind the subject. The light would point upward on the background.

Narrow and Broad Lighting

Yousuf Karsh, the famous Armenian photographer who works in Ottawa, Canada, is one of the most skilled users of the following lighting effects.

Narrow refers to a small highlight, meaning that the greater part of the subject's face is in shadow. *Broad*, then, would mean that the greater part of the subject's face is in highlight. The idea is to use your light to flatter your subject. If the subject has a round face, narrow lighting would give it a more slender appearance. If your subject has a long,

37. LIGHTING FOR THE PORTRAIT. Photos by Dick Cobb.

(Left) "Narrow" lighting; the main light is on the side of the face away from the camera and illuminates about ⅓ of the visible face area. (right) "Broad" lighting; the main light is brought around to the front and illuminates about two-thirds of the visible face area.

96

38. TEXTURE LIGHTING. (Upper left) head on shadowless lighting kills texture. (Upper right) Low skimming light from "soft" source such as frosted photoflood lamp in large reflector brings out some texture, but it is slightly mushy because of excessive diffusion of light. (Below left) Low skimming light from "hard" spotlight source exaggerates the texture; it is dramatic but not natural. (below right) Low skimming light from spot as at left, but shadows softened slightly with a second lamp, a diffused flood. Most natural result.

thin face, broad lighting would give the face the illusion of being less thin and long. When in doubt about which approach to use, narrow lighting seems to flatter more people than broad lighting.

One way to get a broad lighting is to place your key and fill lights, as in a bread and butter situation. Then move your camera and shoot the picture from the same side of your subject as the key light. About three-fourths of the face now is in highlight. For narrow light, move the camera to the other side of the subject, away from the key light. Now about three-fourths of the face is in shadow, and one-fourth is in highlight. The narrow part of the face is in highlight. With these ideas as a beginning, some experimenting on your part should result in other ways to get broad or narrow lighting.

Texture and Lighting

Two factors will affect texture. One is the kind of light you use. A broad light (wide beam of light) is less intense and concentrated than the narrow beam of a spotlight. A spotlight, with its narrow beam of light is easier to place and control than a broad beam of light. And a

39. JO-JO GOLDWATER. Photograph by Billy Ray, courtesy Life Magazine. Strong texture lighting which is unsuitable for younger women, often not objected to by older ones.

40. TEX BROWN ROLLS HIS OWN. Photograph by Albert Moldavy, National Geographic Magazine. Even stronger texture lighting can be used for character portraits of men.

spotlight, because it is intense and concentrated, will yield better texture than a broad beam.

A second factor influencing texture is the position of the light in relation to the object. Light which falls upon an object without any angle kills texture. Light which falls on an object at an angle increases texture. The greater the angle between the subject and the light, the more the texture will show.

Generally, women over 25 don't want texture to show in a portrait. So flat lighting will be the most flattering. The youthful skin of some girls from 16 to 20 can stand texture lighting if there are no blemishes or pock-marks. Texture lighting is excellent for men. Skin texture in a male's photograph suggests that he is rugged, manly, a 100-percent, redblooded individual.

A few women, when very old, forget vanity. If your assignment were to photograph a 90-year-old woman, you might include a few texture exposures along with some which are flat-lighted. Send one of each to your editor. Probably he will select the one which emphasizes the wrinkles and the character of the woman.

What Kinds of Light Should You Use?

Photographic lights include the spotlight, the broad light, and the boom light. The spotlight gives a narrow, concentrated beam of light.

98

which is easy to place. The broad light has a wide, less concentrated beam, which is difficult to place on a small portion of the subject without spilling over into an area where you don't want extra light. A boom is a long metal arm which holds a spot or a broad light over the head of the scene or the subject.

POSSIBLE COMBINATIONS OF PORTRAIT LIGHTS—CHART 16

Key Light		Fill Light	Subject
1. Spot	+	Spot	Men; subjects where texture is desirable.
			Subjects that demand exact placement of the narrow beams of light.
2. Broad	+	Broad	Women over 22
			Younger women with skin blemishes
			Children who cry in harsh, bright light
3. Spot	+	Broad	A compromise
			Key light (spot) at 45 degree angle gives texture.
			Men; Women with no skin problems: blemishes, wrinkles, crow's feet, etc.

Lights you see in a professional's studio are expensive. One light can cost $100 or more. You don't need expensive lights to make good portraits. Two broad reflectors, stands to support them, and a couple of #2 photofloods are enough equipment for mastering lighting techniques. Equipment doesn't make good pictures. Good pictures are the result of a photographer's skill.

Posing Your Subject

Turn your subject at an angle to the camera, so that one shoulder is nearer the camera than the other. When both shoulders are at a right angle to the camera, the subject is static and suggests less action than turned as suggested. Getting a pleasing, spontaneous expression is trial, error, luck, and skill.

CORRECTIVE PORTRAIT LIGHTING—CHART 17

1. *Nose Faults*

Uneven noses—have the subject look directly at the camera. Avoid profiles.

Nose curves to one side—try a low angle, include ¾ of the face, with the nose curving toward the camera.

Pug-noses—use slightly higher than normal camera angle. Also raise the key light to give a longer nose shadow.

2. *Eye Faults*

Deep-set eyes—don't get the main light too high. Don't use too great

99

a lighting ratio; stick pretty close to 4 to 1. Camera angle should be at eye level or slightly lower.

One eye is weaker or smaller than other—keep shadow on the far side of the face. Use a ¾ view with best eye closest to camera.

Eyes which are too large—have subject lower gaze a trifle and use a high #1 light so the eye sockets will get less light than usual.

3. *Facial Faults*

Round faces—use ¾ view and narrow lighting.
  Don't have subject smile. It broadens the face.
  Keep the sides of the face in heavy shadow by feathering the light.
    Increase the shadow-light ratio.

Sunken cheeks or protruding cheek bones—avoid ¾ view. Subject should face camera and flat light should be used.
Narrow faces—Use broad light and ¾ view. Lower #1 light somewhat.
Wide mouth—use ¾ view so part of the mouth doesn't show.
Thin lips—thicken by a heavy shadow underneath bottom lip. Use #1 light at a higher angle than usual. Or without changing light, have subject tilt head slowly up and down and watch the shape of the mouth.
Have all moisten lips to aid the highlight.

4. *Double Chins*—use a higher than usual camera angle. Subject should tilt head backward slightly to take up some slack. Light subject so that there is a heavy black shadow under the chin.

5. *Square Chin*—helped by a higher than usual camera angle.

6. *Forehead Is Too Large*—Keep it in shadow and use a low camera angle. Tilting the camera stand or easel in enlarging will help to reduce the size of the forehead in relation to the rest of the face.

7. *Narrow Forehead*—broaden by using a high angle and by tilting the plane of the camera back in proper direction.

8. *Long Neck, Prominent Ears, and Bald Head*—keep light off these areas by proper placement of lights and with assistance of head screens. A high camera angle shortens a long neck. A low camera angle shows less of the bald head.

9. *Wrinkles* in a man's face are character lines. Accentuate them. In a woman's face, they are undesirable. Use flat light or diffused lights. Keep the key light lower than usual. Retouching helps. Make the enlargement with a diffusion type enlarger or use a diffusion disc with a condenser enlarger.

100

10. *Glasses*

    a. reflection of lights in glasses—use a high key light and a fill-in with more angle than is normal.

    b. rim shadows on face and small hot spots of light on subject's face due to thick lens will require retouching.

Exceptions exist for all rules. Use your common sense and the powers of observation and consider the feeling of the subject in deciding when to use the rules and when to break them.

11. *Eye Catchlights*

Tiny reflections—something no portrait should be without. If lacking--portrait has a dull, blind appearance.

Many photographers prefer only one catch-light in each eye for the psychological reason that man is used to viewing objects by only one source of light, the sun.

Eyes with more than one catch light indicate more than one source of light.

Extra catch-lights may be removed by retouching the negative.

12. *Placing the Camera*

Shooting from a low angle elongates. If a person is stout, the double chin may appear too prominent. Nostrils become prominent, and the mouth slopes downward. Top part of head appears smaller because of perspective.

Bird's eye view has the opposite effect upon the subject. The neck is shortened, the forehead is given prominence, the body is shortened and made to appear broader.

Generally, the camera should be on the same level as the face. The eyes should be in sharpest focus. Allow some space on negative above the head.

If a person stands, height of the camera is about five feet. If a person is seated, height of the camera is about 3½ to 4 feet.

13. *Posing the body*

If the subject is either heavy or thin, turn the body so that it doesn't face the camera squarely and leave doubt as to the build of the subject.

Avoid parallel arms. They make the body look too solid.

Seated stout people should lean forward to cover the paunch. If the chair has arms, place one elbow only on the chair arm.

Check: Badly tied ties, wrinkes in man's coat, hike of coat behind neck.

101

Hands, unless very small, should rarely be fully shown. If turned sideways, they will attract less attention from the face. Be cautious about placing hands together to avoid shapeless masses or a large bright spot which will conflict with the face for interest.

Turning the head strongly to one side produces on the neck a series of accordion pleats. They are unpleasant photographically. The easiest way to hide the pleats is to raise the shoulder nearest the camera until it hides them.

When the background is light, try to avoid arm and leg traps. If they occur darken them.

Avoid extreme foreshortening of the arms. Even without the emphasis which short focal lengths give arms, such distortion is unpleasant.

Avoid stumps in which the forearm is hidden.

CHAPTER 8

Lighting with Flash Lamps and Strobe

Light is controlled in flash photography just like it is normal, outdoor sunlight. Your two light controls are still the (1) speed with which your shutter opens and closes and (2) the size of your f/stop openings. Fast shutter speeds let little light reach the film; and small f/stop openings let little light into the camera. Generally, a fast shutter speed requires a big f/stop opening. And a slow shutter speed requires a small f/stop opening. A fast shutter speed is used to freeze action and the big f/stop opening supplies the light for the exposure. A small f/stop opening is used for depth of field, and a slow shutter speed supplies the light for the exposure. These principles are discussed in detail in Chapter I.

GUIDE NUMBER TABLE FOR PRESS 25 FLASH LAMPS—CHART 18

Shutter Speeds	ASA Film Speed Ratings						
	10-16	20-32	40-64	80-125	160-250	320-500	650-1000
1/30	95	140	200	280	400	550	800
1/60	90	130	180	260	360	500	750
1/125	75	110	160	220	320	440	650
1/250	60	85	120	180	240	360	500
1/500	46	65	95	130	190	260	380
1/750	34	50	70	100	140	200	280

Steps in Computing Flash Exposure

1. *Select your shutter speed.* In Chart 18 note that shutter speeds are on the left, presented vertically, one above the other. Suppose you decide to select a shutter speed of 1/125 of a second. Selecting the shutter speed completes one-half of your exposure problem with flash. Next step is to figure out what size f/stop opening to use with 1/125 second shutter speed.

2. *Select a guide number.* The shutter speed selected (in this case 1/125 second) and the ASA rating of your film determine the guide number you should select from the table. Note that in Chart 18 ASA

103

film ratings are grouped horizontally across the top. The first of the ASA film ratings on the far left are 10 to 16, which indicate slow films that are comparatively insensitive to light and require long exposures. Each succeeding grouping of the ASA numbers will be faster films, as the ASA numbers get larger.

Suppose that the ASA rating of your film is 250 (fifth column). Since you selected 1/125 second for your shutter speed, your guide number must be one of the seven numbers to the right of 1/125 in the table. And since your ASA film rating is 250, the guide number must come from the fifth column. So, your guide number will be 320.

3. *Divide the distance from the flash to your subject (10 feet) into your guide number (320) to find your f/stop opening.* In this instance, the f/stop would be 32.

Now suppose you want to work five feet from your subject. Use the same formula discussed above to find your f/stop with 1/125 of a second shutter speed.

$$
\text{(Distance from flash to subject) 5 feet} \mid \frac{\begin{array}{r} 64 \\ \overline{320} \\ 30 \\ \overline{20} \\ 20 \end{array}}{} = f/\text{stop opening}
$$

Hmmm. f/64 won't work. Probably the smallest f/stop on your lens is 32. The f/32 opening won't cut out enough of the light at five feet from the subject to prevent overexposure. Another way will have to be found to control the excessive amount of light so near the subject.

One way to control the light would be to *remove the reflector* from behind the flash lamp. When the reflector is removed, the flashlight is only about one half as brilliant as when a reflector is assisting it. With your reflector removed, try one shot at f/32. Try another at f/22. One of them should produce a good negative.

Another method of controlling excessive flashlight when working close to your subject is *bounce light.*

Generally, your flash gun and lamps are pointed directly at your subject. Bounce light requires the flash gun to be removed from the side of the camera so that the reflector can be pointed at the ceiling. The light will hit the ceiling and bounce back onto the subject. As light rays get farther from their source, they become weaker. In bounce lighting, a lot of the original light is lost as it travels up to the ceiling, and bounces back down to light the subject.

To use bounce light:

1. Compute your exposure according to the suggested formula. In computing it for an f/stop with the flash only 5 feet from the subject, you found that f/64 was required.

2. Open up your diaphragm 4 stops: 64—32—22—16—11
   (1) (2) (3) (4)

Exposure data = 1/125 at $f/11$

Flash lamps are packaged in lots of 12. On the back of the sleeve or lamp container will be a Guide Number Table. Number 5's made by GE are quite similar to the Press 25 made by Sylvania. Many photographers use these lamps interchangeably.

A change in any of the following requires a new guide number:

1. You decide to use a faster or a slower *film* than the one you have been using.
2. You decide to use a smaller or a larger *flash lamp* than the one you have been using.
3. You decide to use a slower or a faster *shutter speed* than the one you have been using.

Number 5's and Press 25's are ideal for working close to your subject (5 to 20 feet) in a building or outside for a fill light.[1] Other flash lamps which are larger in size give more light than the number 5 or Press 25.

Your formula for computing flash exposure can't be used blindly. It is for the "average" situation indoors. You must think and adapt your exposure to changes in your photo situation, when it isn't "average." The formula works fine in a room of "normal" size. But the following conditions would require some adjustments in your formula for correct exposure:

1. A bigger or a smaller room than is normal;
2. white walls or dark walls which reflect or absorb light affect exposure;
3. a black dog or a college beauty queen in a white dress.

The walls of a smaller than normal room will reflect some of the light back onto the subject. So in this situation, compute your exposure for a normal situation, then close down 1/2 stop to compensate for light reflected from the walls of the small room, especially if the walls are white.[2] In a very large room, where the walls are far apart, you might open up 1/2 stop to 1 full stop. Now the black dog — it's hard to get enough light on such an object! He absorbs more light than he reflects. Compute your exposure for a normal situation, then open up a full stop. And the beauty queen is the reverse of the black dog. The queen's white dress will reflect so much light onto the film, that the dress will be very dense on the negative, holding light

---

[1]Discussed under the topic, Synchro-Sun Flash, later in the chapter.
[2]Reflecting ability of colors: White—80 percent of light; ivory, 70 percent; buff 65 percent; light green, 40 percent; sky blue, 35 percent; deep green, 20 percent.

105

back from the enlarging paper. The dense white dress on the negative would require extra long exposure — burning in. To prevent such a situation, compute flash exposure for a normal situation, then close down a 1/2 to a full stop.

Out of doors, if flash is used at 10 feet, try opening up 1/2 stop larger than the formula indicates. If you're working 15 feet or farther from the subject, open up a full stop larger than the formula indicates.

Seven Problems in Flash

1. You will have a hard time comprehending how much concentrated light is packed into a single flash lamp. Even with the guide number formula for computing flash lamp f/stop sizes, some who are new to flash overexpose the subject. If your negatives are too black and dense, especially in the highlight areas (parts of a scene which reflect the most light onto the film), you are having this difficulty. It is a simple matter to cure overexposure by flash. Try stopping down 1/4 stop to a full stop smaller than the formula calls for. A small stop lets less light reach your negative. Or cut your development 30 to 60 seconds.

One Press 40 flash lamp (smaller than a 100 watt electric light bulb) releases the same amount of light as 1,500 100-watt lamps all burning simultaneously.

2. You may have difficulty in understanding *how rapidly light diminishes in strength as it gets farther from its source.*

In Figure 41, you have an object at 5 feet and another at 10 feet. Suppose your flash is set to expose perfectly the object at 5 feet.

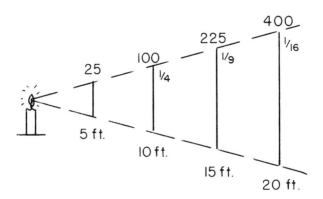

41. INVERSE SQUARE LAW. The brightness of an object falls off in proportion to the square of the distance between the light source and the object.

106

How much of your light will you lose before the rays reach the object at 10 feet? You might guess that perhaps one-half of your light would be lost. Such would be a logical guess because of the mathematical relation of 5 feet to 10 feet. But your logical guess is wrong. You would lose 3/4 of the original light, and only 1/4 of it would reach and illuminate the object at 10 feet, which would be badly underexposed.

Your rule (inverse square law) says that the light falls off in proportion to the *square* of the distance between the light source and the object. Note in the diagram that both 5 feet and 10 feet have been squared, and the mathematical relationship between 25 and $100 = 1/4$.

This rule has a *practical application.* Every time you double the distance between the flash and the subject, open up your diaphragm *two* full f/stops. If you compute exposure for 10 feet, and have a second shot at 20 feet, just open up two full f/stops. If the second shot is at 15 feet (instead of 20 feet), open up only one f/stop. And if the second shot is at 5 feet (now you've moved closer) close down two full f/stops.

How would you plan your exposure for a depth of field shot with one object at 5 feet and the second at 10 feet? The situation might be handled with either one flash or two synchronized flash lamps.

Single flash lamp. Compute exposure for 5 feet. Open up 1/4 stop larger. Set your adjustable flash reflector for a narrow, spotlight beam. Object at 5 feet will be slightly overexposed; object at 10 feet will be underexposed. In printing, burn in the 5 foot object and hold light back from the 10 foot object. A straight, undodged print of this situation will not be satisfactory.

Multiflash: One lamp will be at or near the camera, 5 feet from the near object. A second flash in an extension, and out of the lens range, will be 5 feet from the second object. Now both objects get about the same amount of light. Compute exposure for one light at 5 feet. A straight, undodged print should be possible from the negative.

3. *Flat lighting is uninteresting.* Such lighting results when the flashgun is on the camera, and the reflector/lamp point directly at the subject. Both sides of the face get an equal amount of light. To avoid flat lighting, and to add interest to the resulting photograph, most cameramen will take the flashgun off the camera. By holding the gun a little higher than the subject's head and at a 45 degree angle, you can approximate the effect of a Number 1/key light, which yields Rembrandt lighting. Now, part of the face will be a highlight and part of the face will be in shadow. Resulting contrast of tone is more interesting than flat lighting.

107

42. HOT SPOT ON BACKGROUND. Reflections of lights are seen, not only in mirrors as in this picture, but in glossy painted walls, and in the glass of windows. Moving the light off to about a 45 degree angle usually prevents the formation of a hot spot. Photo by Dick Cobb.

4. A flash photo of a person in front of a glass window or door will probably have a *hot-spot* — an area on the glass where much of the light hit and was reflected back onto the film, leaving a round, dense area. The resulting print will have a big chalky white area where the hot-spot is on the negative. Such a chalky area in a print is bad. The reader's eye is pulled away from the central object of interest by the white hot-spot. Any time the reader's interest is divided between two objects, much of the punch of the photograph is lost. Try to avoid hot-spots or anything else which puts a big white area in a photo. White areas are like a magnet. They catch a reader's eye. And the central object of interest is neglected!

A flash on the camera which puts a hot-spot directly behind a subject can't be cropped out of the resulting print. But if the flash is removed from the camera, and placed at a 45 degree angle to the subject, the hot-spot will be formed to the side of the subject. When the negative is enlarged, the hot-spot can be cropped out.

To avoid hot-spots in your prints, light your subjects from an angle when any shiny surface is behind the subject — glass or highly polished wood, or a white wall.

5. *A background shadow in a flash picture is distracting.* When your subject is close to a light wall in a flash picture, the subject usually casts a shadow on the background. The shadow results from strong, concentrated flashlight striking your subject, between the light and the wall. The strong flashlight causes your subject to cast a shadow on the wall.

One of two solutions can be used. Pulling the subject farther away from the wall is one way to kill the shadow. Another way to lose the shadow is to take the flash gun off the camera, and hold the gun

108

higher than the subject's head. Now, the shadow will be much lower on the wall, and directly behind the subject instead of to the side of him. It is possible to crop out the shadow in an enlargement.

6. *Illogical use of flash* happens every day, but it still isn't good. Too often unthinking photographers destroy a mood or an atmosphere with too much light from a little flash lamp.

Suppose your assignment is a sleeping baby. What kind of light does a baby usually sleep in, diffused light or crisp, bright daylight? Probably soft, subdued light. But you pop a flash light on the sleeping child, who will be shown in brilliant light in the resulting enlargement. The mood of your shot is not true reporting. You have used your light illogically. It would be better to use a soft, diffused light for the shot, just like the light which surrounds the sleeping baby. Try a time exposure, then a bounce-light shot, and finally one without your reflector.

Consider another example. A man sits near a window. You're going to photograph him with flash. Look at the man. The side which is nearest the window is a highlight area. The side away from the window is less strongly lit. How can you use your flashlight to maintain the true light which is in the scene? It will have to be a multiflash shot.

7. *Use the correct reflector with your flash lamp.* A reflector designed for Press 25 or Number 5 lamps won't be effective with a Press 40 lamp.

43. SHADOW ON BACKGROUND. Black shadow on wall behind subject's head is annoying; note also shadow alongside body on right of picture. Such shadows are avoided by placing light very high and directly over the lens of the camera; it helps to pose subject away from the background, rather than right up against it as shown here. Photon by Tony Wood.

109

If you decide to use a different kind of a flash lamp, make certain you have the right reflector behind the lamp. Otherwise, you may get less light from a bigger flash lamp with the wrong reflector than you would from a Press 25 lamp with the right reflector.

A flat reflector behind a lamp increases light from 2 to 5 times. A reflector for a midget lamp increases light from 6 to 15 times. When the lamp and the reflector are not properly matched, hot-spots can also result.

In buying a reflector, insist on one which is adjustable. Such a reflector can give a spotlight effect, a broad light effect, or light for the average shot.

Multiflash

The user of multiflash has two problems: 1) How to place lights so that they will work together for a pleasing result; and 2) how to calculate exposure with either two or three flashes directed on the subject.

Thanks to two pioneer users of flash — Don Mohler of General Electric and Rus Arnold, a Chicago commercial photographer — multiflash today is a relatively simple photographic tool, quickly understood and mastered.

The basic placement of two photographic lights was discussed in Chapter 7, "Lighting for Portraits." You learned that a key light

44. MULTIFLASH PORTRAITS. Photos by Dick Cobb.

(Left) Main light at 45 degrees, fill light near camera, produces balanced but slightly flat lighting. Background is dark and blends with the hair. (Right) Bringing in main light to get a stronger highlight and shadow pattern on girl's face, plus addition of a background light improves picture.

45.WHEN NOT TO USE FLASH. The natural lighting of this picture is very dramatic; using a flash on the foreground would destroy the mood of the picture. Photo by Rex Lyons, Courtesy "Newsday".

at a 45 degree angle to the subject and a fill light beside the camera yielded a pleasing result, with no cross shadows. These principles of bread-and-butter portrait lighting are good in multiflash work.

The Don Mohler Triangle Method of Calculating Exposure for Multiflash

In the diagram, your subject is 15 feet from the camera, Line A is the camera-subject axis. Lines B-C, which are imaginary, complete a triangle. If you were using one flash with your subject 15 feet away, you would calculate your exposure as follows:

$$\frac{\text{shutter speed}}{1/500} \qquad \frac{\text{ASA of film (320-450)}}{\text{Flash factor} = 260} \qquad \frac{f/\text{stop opening}}{260 \div 15 = f/17}$$

One seldom adds a second flash, X, on the left side of the camera. But if this were done, to keep the added light from overexposing the film, close down your diaphragm one full f/stop, from $f/17$ to about $f/23$. You are closing down from a larger opening to a smaller opening to cut out a part of the added light. This is compensating for the added light.

Principle for Arriving at Exposure for the Second Light

Divide imaginary line C into three equal parts, C1, C2, and C3. When flash X remains on the side of the camera:

111

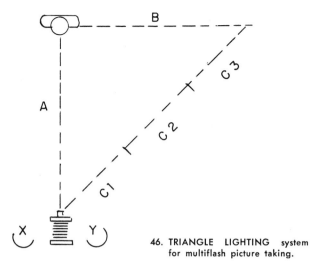

46. TRIANGLE LIGHTING system for multiflash picture taking.

If flash Y is anywhere in area C1, close down your lens opening 1 full *f*/stop;

If flash Y is anywhere in area C2, close down your lens opening 1/2 *f*/stop;

If flash Y is in area C3 or behind the subject, no compensation is necessary.

SUMMARY: If your second flash, Y, is

either beside the camera or at no greater angle to the camera than 60 degrees, close 1 *f*/stop;

at about a 45 degree angle, close 1/2 *f*/stop;

at more than a 45 degree angle or behind the subject, no compensation is necessary.

Suppose flash X is beside the camera and flash Y is in area C2. You readily recognize this as bread and butter portrait lighting. In portrait lighting, you would carefully measure with a meter the amount of light Y (key light) places on the subject.

In multiflash, your approach is different. Here, you calculate your exposure for the light on the camera (fill light), then compensate for the addition of the second flash, depending on its placement.

In the diagram under consideration:

Exposure for one flash, X, on the camera at 15 feet would be *f*/17 at 1/500 second.

If the second flash, Y, is added at a 45 degree angle, exposure for the two would be *f*/20, a compensation of 1/2 stop smaller than with one light.

112

If a third flash, Z, were added behind the subject, no further compensation would be made unless you were shooting the photograph in a small room with white walls. In such a room it might be necessary to close down an additional full stop, to $f/30$, not because of the amount of light which originally strikes the subjects, but because of reflected light from the white walls which are close together in the small room.

In Fgure 46 flash X yields a strong highlight on the near-side of the subject and a shadow on the far side. Y, the back flash, will keep the subject from blending into an inky black background. And a reflector on the left will help the shadow side of the face.

To figure your exposure:

shutter speed	ASA of film (320-450)	f/stop opening
1/500	Flash factor = 260	$260 \div 10 = f/26$

The Rus Arnold Method of Flash Placement

Arnold[*] envisions eight possibilities for flashlight placement. If the first placement is 1, an odd number, the second light selected should be an even number, 2 (and vice versa). Then the third light should be an odd one, etc.

Selection of 2 (fill light), 3 (key light), and 5 (back light) would yield a typical bread and butter setup. If only two lights were to be used, 3 and 6 (or 4 and 5) could be selected.

Synchro-Sun Flash

Flash in daylight is primarily for use inside a building as the *main* source of light. Outside, in sunlight, flash should be used as a fill light and not as the main source.

[*]*Advanced Flash Photography*, Crown Pub. Co., 1964.

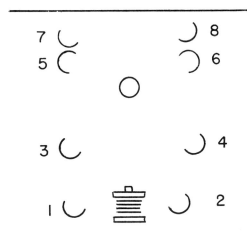

47. LIGHTING BY THE NUMBERS.
The Rus Arnold system of light placement.

113

48. SYNCHRO-SUN FLASH LIGHTING. Photos by Dick Cobb.

(Left) Sunlight alone produces hard shadows on face and excessive contrast. (Center) Flash used too close to subject overpowers sunlight completely, and gives the effect of a night shot; this is unnatural and undesirable. (Right) Flash properly balanced to sunlight exposure merely softens shadows without eliminating them, producing effect which is both natural and flattering.

You can use flash out of doors in daylight in the usual way. However, if the camera-flash is 10 feet or closer to the subject, the resulting picture will look as if it were taken at night. In the print, your main object will be well illuminated. But your background will be an inky black because your flashlight diminishes quickly as it travels farther from its source.

When should flash be used on an outdoor subject? As has already been indicated, the proper use of flash in sunlight is as a fill light, to put more light into shadow areas. Look at your subject. Suppose it is a hot summer day. The subject wears a hat. The brim of the hat casts a shadow over the upper part of the face — the eyes and the nose. If only raw sunlight is used for the exposure, and if a straight print of the negative is made, the resulting enlargement will block up or be black in the eyes and nose area. But if flash is used to get light into this shadow area, then the negative will have sufficient density in the eyes and nose area to prevent the blocking shadow in the enlargement.

If the sun is used as the main source of light, and the flash as a fill-in, you will need a long extension wire for your flashlight. And you need to get the powerful flash far enough away from the subject, so that the flashlight won't overpower the sun.

Formula for Figuring the Distance Your Fill-in Flash Should Be From the Subject

1. Use your light meter in the normal way to determine your exposure for the picture. Set your camera up for the shot. (1/250 second at $f/20$)

114

2. Consult your guide number in the flash factor table to find what flash factor is used with a speed of 1/250 second. (For films with an ASA of 160-250 it is 240)

3. To find how many feet the flash extension should be from the subject, divide flash factor 240 by $f/20$, the f/stop to be used. The fill-in flash should be 12 feet from the subject.

With a bit of intelligent experimenting, you can learn to use maximum fill-in, producing flat lighting, or just enough fill in for some tonal contrast to be apparent to the eye. In color work and in photographing babies, use a maximum fill-in. Color is best in flat light. Babies and brightness go together. In shooting a man's portrait, use only moderate fill-in to preserve character. In shooting a dramatic portrait or a pictorial, use only enough fill-in to hold a little of the detail in the shadow, so the shadow won't block up.

Synchronization—What Is It?

The original method of using flash lamps was the system known as "open flash." In this system, the photographer, having his camera mounted on a tripod, would first open the shutter, then fire the flash lamp, and finally close the shutter again. This system is still used with certain very large flash lamps which are not intended for synchronized shooting.

Obviously open flash would not do for shooting action pictures, and news photographers devised several mehods of firing a flash lamp at the same time the shutter was tripped; this was known as synchronization. In the earliest synchronization systems, the shutter was tripped by means of a small magnet which was operated by the same battery that fired the flash lamp. Since the flash lamp reaches full light output or "peak" rather slowly, the time taken by the magnet to release the shutter was adjusted to delay the shutter opening until the flashlight was fully ignited.

After World War II, shutter manufacturers installed contacts to fire flash lamps inside the shutter itself. The shutter mechanism also had a "delay train" consisting of several small gear wheels, which delayed the opening of the shutter blades after the flash contacts were closed, so that the shutter would not open until the flash lamp had reached its peak intensity. Almost all modern camera shutters have synchronization devices of this sort built in; some are adjustable to three positions. In the M position, the contact is made first and the shutter opens 20 milliseconds (20/1000 second) later; this is for all "press" type lamps. In the F position, the shutter delay is only 5 milliseconds, and is suitable for the gas filled lamps like the SM and AF types. And in the X position, the contact is made at the exact instant the shutter is wide open, and is used with strobe lights, which have no time delay.

115

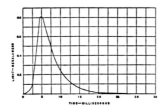

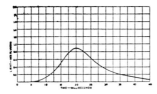

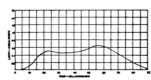

49. FLASH BULB GRAPHS. (Top) A high narrow peak indicates a bright flash of short duration. (Middle) A lower, broad peak indicates a flash lamp which is less bright at its peak, but burns for a longer period of time. (Bottom) A relatively flat "plateau peak" indicates a lamp which burns at an even level for relatively long period; it is used mainly with focal-plane shutters, to get even exposure over the entire picture area. The upper two types of lamp are used mainly with between-the-lens shutters.

Three Types of Peaks for Flash Bulbs

Photographic literature uses drawings to illustrate the light characteristics of flash lamps. The three kinds of peaks are high peaks, broad peaks, and flat peaks.

A high narrow peak indicates a bright light which burns for a short duration of time.

A lower, broad peak indicates a flash lamp which isn't so bright, but which burns for a long period of time.

A flat, plateau peak indicates a lamp which is not so bright but which burns for a longer period of time. Lamps with such a light characteristic are for focal plane shutters (back of the camera).

The first two lamps are for between-the-lens shutters.

Strobe Light And Its Development

A strobe is an electric source of light which has been adapted to photography. It is also known as high-speed light. Portable units may operate either on batteries or AC lines with an extension cord plugged into the wall socket. Studio units usually operate on AC lines.

Depending on the kind of batteries used in a portable unit, you can get from 80 to more than 150 flashes of light. Some batteries may be recharged for another series of light flashes.

Why consider strobe when you have chemical flash equipment? Each is a useful tool. In some photographic situations, either one will

116

do the work of the other. In other photographic situations, one will be superior to the other. Generally speaking, where you need only one source of light rather than multiflash for a volume of exposures, and if you hope to make a profit, strobe is excellent. Suppose you had to shoot 200 party pictures during a single evening. Your flash lamp bill would be high! You'd have the problem of what to do with the used flash lamps. Of course, the initial expense of a reliable strobe unit is over $60, although strobes are advertised from $19.95 to over $100. So before you invest in a strobe light, you need enough flash work to justify its purchase.

News photographers who need 3 or 4 synchronized flash lights for one exposure find it simpler to use flash lamps than strobe equipment. The latter is bulky to carry and requires more time to set up. There was a time when a strobe light and the pack (or power source) weighed 8 to 15 pounds. The intensity of the light produced was in proportion to the weight or size of the power pack. Generally speaking, this is still true. But thanks to some scientific improvements, smaller and less bulky capacitors are producing enough light so that weight of the power pack of a strobe is no longer a factor in deciding whether to use strobe or flash. Even a husky lad gets weary of lugging around 10 or 15 pounds! Practical, compact portable strobe units are available now which weigh no more than 24 ounces without batteries. Duration of strobe light varies among the different units. Range of the duration of the light is from 1/600 second to 1/1200 second.

In the late 1920's Harold E. Edgerton began his work at M.I.T. on refining and synchronizing an elementary stroboscope which had been used in industry for years. During the summers when Edgerton was in college, he worked for a power and light company. When the big generators gave trouble technical experts had to guess at what needed repairing. Parts in the generators moved faster than the eye could see. Apparently there was no way to synchronize the elementary stroboscope then in use so that it would emit a quick, powerful spark of light at a given moment, or when a specific mechanically moving part of a machine was in a certain position. Edgerton wanted to see how the parts of the big generators worked. He spent 30 years perfecting, improving and synchronizing the stroboscope, so that he could photograph the moving parts of the generator.

Basically, a stroboscope is a gas-filled tube for electrical control work. A capacitor acts as a reservoir for electricity. Either at a regular interval or as the result of a pressed button, this stored electricity is released in the form of a light in a flash as fast as 1/1,000,000 of a second. This swift, blinding light, which is brighter than the sun, is formed in the gas-filled tube.

117

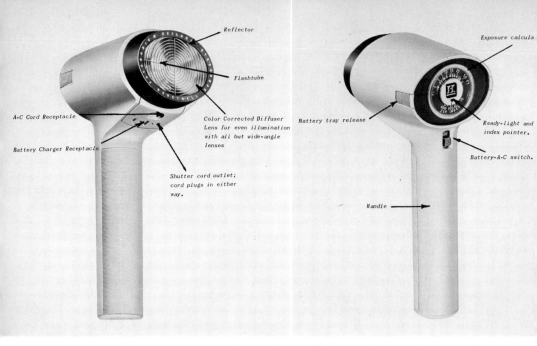

Reflector

Exposure calcula

Flashtube

A-C Cord Receptacle

Color Corrected Diffuser
Lens for even illumination
with all but wide-angle
lenses

Battery tray release

Ready-light and
index pointer.

Battery Charger Receptacle

Battery-A-C switch.

Shutter cord outlet;
cord plugs in either
way.

Handle

50. Front and rear views with parts labeled, of the Heiland Futuramic Strobonar electronic
flash unit, for battery and a-c operation. Photos courtesy Honeywell.

With the refined strobe which came from Edgerton's work, one was able to photograph and study many things the human eye had never seen. The wings of a flying humming bird were frozen in photographs. With strobe lights and photography, researchers were able to find how a cat which is held upside down always lands right side up. So swift is strobe light that it is possible to hit a milk bottle with a hammer and still freeze the motion of the moving hammer and the shattered pieces of the bottle before they fall into a mass of broken glass.

BATTERY OPERATION OF THE STROBE — CHART 19

1. Form the capacitor on AC.

   a. Switch the battery-AC switch to AC (See Figure 50).

   b. Insert the extension cord into the strobe and plug the extension into an AC circuit.

   (No batteries are in the strobe. Batteries are taken out when the strobe isn't in use.)

   c. Flash the unit nine or ten times with the camera release. This flashing forms the capacitor or gets the unit ready for action.

   d. Remove the extension cord from the strobe unit.

2. Insert batteries into strobe unit.

3. Mount strobe unit on camera.

4. Attach shutter cord to flash unit and camera.

5. Set film exposure index on exposure dial, and determine exposure, and set camera. (Figure 50).

118

Example:

Your ASA film rating is 250. Set on exposure dial. Lamp to subject distance is 10 feet. On the dial under 10 feet is your f/stop opening, f/16

(Always set your shutter on its fastest speed, since the swift burst of light coming on and off will perform the function of the shutter.)

NOTE: If your camera is a Polaroid which uses the EVS system instead of f/stops, use the special EVS scale sticker.

For films with speeds faster than ASA 400, divide the film speed by two or four, or eight, etc.) to obtain an index of 400 or less. Take readings from the scale as described in step 5, then stop down one f/stop if you divided by two, two f/stops if you divided by four, etc., to compensate for the faster film speed.

6. Push switch to BATT.

7. Wait for Ready-Light to glow (in the ASA indicator on the exposure dial).

8. Shoot the picture.

9. Wait for the Ready-Light to glow again before shooting the second picture. Cycling time between flashes with fresh photoflash batteries is 10-12 seconds. When a longer interval occurs between two pictures, turn off the strobe unit to save your batteries.

10. Turn switch to OFF-AC when through shooting as well as between shots of longer time lapses than 10-12 seconds.

AC OPERATION OF THE STROBE

1. Attach the AC cord to your strobe.

2. Plug AC cord into wall outlet.

3. Switch remains at OFF-AC.

4. Form capacitor on AC.

5. Mount unit on camera

6. Attach shutter cord.

7. Set film exposure index on exposure dial.

8. Determine exposure.

9. Set lens aperture and shutter speed.

10. Wait for ready light.

11. Shoot picture.

12. Wait for Ready-Light to glow before shooting each picture.

51. TWO ON ONE. Action shots like this one were seldom obtained before strobe light made it possible to "freeze" action. Photo from Wide World.

Development

Units which have a very short flash duration (1/2,000 second and higher) require up to 50 per cent longer film development for normal contrast. Use normal development for flash durations of 1/1000 second and slower.

Camera-Flash Synchronization

Most strobes are built for cameras with built-in flash contacts. If your camera has a between-the-lens shutter with X-contacts (zero delay), the strobe will synchronize with it at all shutter speeds. If your camera has a focal-plane shutter with zero delay synchronization, it will synchronize only at slower speeds — up to 1/25 or 1/60 second. Most cameras without the built-in X (zero delay) synchronization can be easily adapted for a strobe by a competent camera repairman.

Battery Power

Heiland Permacad rechargeable batteries	80 to 120 flashes per charge
Eveready E93 batteries	150 or more flashes from a set
Ordinary C cell photoflash batteries	40 to 60 flashes

Remove batteries when gun will be out of use one week or longer. Battery corrosion could ruin your unit if left in it over 30 days.

120

52. THE PAY-OFF PUNCH. The high speed of strobe lighting captured the spray of perspiration from the head of Jersey Joe Walcott from the punch of Rocky Marciano. Photo by Herb Scharfman, UPI.

A Permacad Charger is designed to charge the three Permacad cells without removing them from the strobe unit. Plug the charger into the special cord receptacle on the strobe, then use the AC cord furnished with the strobe to connect the charger to any household AC outlet. Be sure the strobe switch is in the OFF-AC position. The charger may be left plugged in overnight and the batteries will take a maximum charge in 12 to 16 hours. A yellow indicator light in the charger reminds you that it is operating. If the yellow indicator is not on, the cells are not charging.

Checking Synchronization

Set the diaphragm at its widest opening with your camera back open.
Point the strobe at a light-colored wall.
Fire the strobe.
If you see a full circle of light through the shutter, your synchronization is good.
Multiple Flash is possible with slave units built to accompany the strobe.

Bounce Light

Estimate distance from flash to the ceiling to the subject.
Find the f/stop for this distance on your strobe exposure dial.
Open up one full f/stop to compensate for light absorbed by the ceiling.

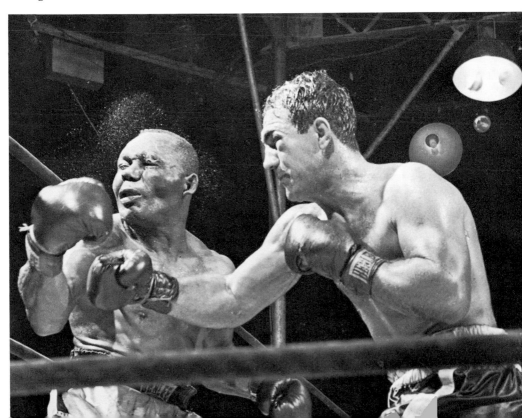

Close-Up Photography

Most strobes are designed for use at distances of three feet or more. If used closer to the subject than three feet, an adapter (an opal diffuser) should be used. When such an adapter is used, open up four stops.

Strobe as a Fill-Light Outdoors

Use an exposure meter to determine the *shutter speed* (Take usual range of brightness reading).

Since you will be working with two light sources (sun and strobe), let your sun light dominate and use strobe for filling in the shadow areas.

To determine your f/stop opening, set your film ASA rating on the strobe exposure dial.

Read the f/stop for your lamp-to-subject distance.

Now, stop down one additional f/stop for color film and two additional stops for black and white film.

Example: ASA of Tri-X Pan is 400. Set 400 on the strobe exposure dial. Subject distance is 12 feet, indicating an f/20 aperture. BUT for black and white film, you must stop down two additional stops. Stopping down to f/32 is only one stop. But this is your smallest aperture. So you must increase the distance between the light and the subject to avoid having the strobe too hot.

You know that any time you double or halve the distance between your subject and a light source, you may open up or close down two full f/stops.

We must compensate for only one f/stop. The original subject distance is 12 feet. Half of 12 is 6. So put your strobe on an extension 18 feet away from the subject.

Use your light meter to measure the shadow-highlight areas of your scene. Set the normal arrow on a number on your meter circular scale mid-way between the shadow-highlight readings.

Select a shutter speed which will go with an f/32 aperture.

Checking the Manufacturer's Guide Number for a Strobe

Some manufacturers state the power of their strobes. They supply a guide number which may result in underexposed film. It is a simple matter to check your guide number for a strobe.

Set up a photo situation in which the subject distance is 10 feet. Make an exposure at each f/stop on your camera (f/4.7, 5.6 on through f/32). Develop all negatives the same length of time. Select the best negative. Multiply the f/stop used on that negative by the subject distance (10 feet) and the result is your strobe guide number.

Recycle time depends on the capacity of a capacitor, the condition of your batteries, temperature, and humidity.

122

CHAPTER 9

Posing People
for the Record Shot

Newspaper Space Is Valuable and Demands Tight Posing

A majority of the photos which the news photographer shoots will be of groups of people. These *record* shots are made to show the reader what the subjects look like. These group shots of people won't be as interesting to the photographer or to a majority of the readers as the emotional shot — the picture which strikes the reader's emotions. The picture is funny, so the reader laughs. Or the picture plays on the reader's sympathy, so he sends in a $10 donation. The photo reminds the reader of the good old days, or of his youthful antics, and for a brief moment the reader indulges in nostalgic reminiscing.

Since record shots are more numerous and fill more space in any single edition than the emotional feature shots, a photographer has to understand the problem and techniques involved in making the record shot — a group of people printed to show what the people look like.

It is ironical that today readers want more pictures and bigger pictures at a time when the editorial side of a newspaper has less space than it had before World War 2. Before that most self-respecting newspapers devoted about 60 percent of their space to editorial matter and 40 percent to advertising. And few newspapers with a circulation of less than 100,000 did much about local photos before World War 2. The average publisher considered using photography as a reporting tool for the local scene a luxury which he couldn't afford. Secondhand photo engraving equipment would cost a minimum of $5,000. Photographic tools — camera, enlarger, darkroom equipment — could easily cost another $2,000. An employee to produce photo-engravings would draw a salary of $100 a week. The photographer would cost $50 to $65 a week. And the bill for paper, film, flash lamps, and chemicals hadn't even been considered.

53. VERTICAL DEAD SPACE. When two persons stand side by side before the camera, don't permit a vertical space between them. Don't be satisfied to have their shoulders touch. Move the people closer by overlapping their shoulders. Dick Cobb, Oklahoma City.

Most publishers with a circulation of less than 100,000 settled for mats bought from picture syndicates. Editors regarded the pictures produced from such mats as "art," something to put on a news page to give it change of pace from the usual tones of the gray body type, the black headlines, and the white of the newsprint. If a big fire burned half of the main street in the business section, the local portrait photographer was hired to get a photograph. The photo was then sent to the nearest big city to be engraved on a zinc plate by a commercial engraver. And the home folks were treated to a local picture!

World War 2 changed this way of newspaper life. Both *Life* and *Look* magazines had already shown before the war what a tremendous appetite readers had for picture stories which reported events of the day. World War 2, the biggest continuing news story since the First World War, had outstanding photo coverage. Folks got used to seeing their news in pictures. Immediately after the war, TV came to the masses. Magazines were first to realize how greatly the monster TV would cut into both reader and advertising markets. Magazines reacted quickly by using more and better photos. News editors also felt the pressure from readers for more news pictures.

Almost simultaneously with the arrival of TV for the masses, came the Fairchild Scanagraver for the small publisher. This simple, easy-to-operate machine produced a plastic "engraving" of a newsphoto. The Scanagraver wasn't for sale. The publisher leased it. Cost was tied to circulation. The bigger the circulation, the more the machine rent cost. Plastic was a lot cheaper than zinc. But best of all, anyone could operate the machine in a very short time. Acids were not involved. A receptionist, a bookkeeper, reporter, or photographer in his white-collar clothes could double in harness by starting the machine

124

on an "engraving," and then continuing with his regular job. Progressive publishers soon discovered that it was cheaper to print photos than it was to set the same amount of space in type. Further, papers which used photos aggressively to report the community generally whipped the opposition badly, circulation-wise. Pictures had high readability. Often a "bad" photo and its cutline had higher readership than the best read word story.

After World War 2 readers wanted pictures — more of them and bigger than ever. Publishers of the smaller papers responded by using the Fairchild Scanagraver at first and other similar machines later. But editors had a problem. Advertising had taken over some editorial space, so that the paper could maintain its profit and continue to operate. After the war the increased cost of newsprint and employee salaries shot up about 200 percent for many papers. The only way to increase revenue to help with these expenses seemed to cut back on editorial matter and give more space to advertisements.

With less editorial space, how were the editors to use more and bigger pictures? This space problem of editors is why the posing of the record shot of a group of people is important to the news photographer. News space today is at a premium. Any run-of-the-mill news photographer has to know the techniques of saving space in a news shot or he won't continue to get his pay check.

Before considering the specific problems of posing a group of people, consider three common-sense principles and four don'ts which apply to any photographic situation.

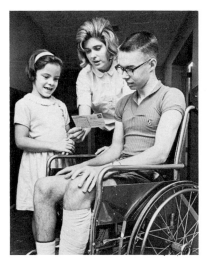

54. HORIZONTAL DEAD SPACE. Don't let one person stand while another sits. The face of the sitting person is some distance below the face of the standing person. Intervening space between the two faces (each is a separate center of interest) is dead space. Here a boy sits in a wheel chair on the right. The woman in the center has leaned forward to bring her face closer to his and that of the little girl on the left. Now, all three faces are a common center of interest. If the woman in the center stood upright, she would have towered over the boy in the wheel chair, creating two centers of interest and an intervening dead space. Tom Blevins, Norman Transcript.

125

Three Common-Sense Principles

The thinking photographer will find a way to *use a plain background*. A good photo should focus reader attention on the central object of interest — the reason for making the picture. No other details in the photo should compete with the central object of interest for attention. A cluttered background, a brick wall with its busy pattern, a big blob of a white tone in the background which will draw the reader's eye away from the central object of interest — all of these will be avoided if the photographer sets up his photo so that he can have a plain background.

Out-of-doors the sky makes an excellent background. Put your subject on a hill and shoot up. If there's no convenient hill at hand, have the subject sit on the back end of a car while you sit on the ground and shoot up, taking care that no distracting tree limbs show in the view finder. If the photographer is higher than the subject and shoots down, the ground will provide the plain background. The side of any building which has no pattern of brick and mortar or lumber siding will provide the plain background. A sheet thrown over a clothes line can provide an uncluttered backdrop. And if a plain background isn't possible under shooting conditions, the enlargement background can be airbrushed so that distracting objects won't show.

Getting the plain background also includes checking the view finder before snapping the photo to make certain a telephone pole, a vase of flowers, or some other distracting object isn't directly behind a model's head, and seeming to grow out of it.

A second common-sense rule is to *get the camera as close as you can to your subject*. By working close to your subject, you get a big image outline on your negative. This is especially important when working with small cameras. The negative with the big image outline is easy to enlarge. The enlarger head will not have to be up very high because with the big image outline, great magnification in enlargement is not needed. But a negative with a small image outline needs great magnification. As you magnify your small image outline many times, you will also enlarge the grains of silver bromide which form the image outline. The resulting enlargement will be grainy.

Third, by getting the camera up close to your subject, you *eliminate distracting objects on either side of the subject* which would have to be cropped out of the photo in enlarging the negative. The fewer the objects which are seen in a photo, the greater the emphasis which is given to your central object of interest. Learn to eliminate as many unneeded details as possible from a scene. Pictures do the best job when they have the minimum of detail needed to tell the story and

126

55. (Upper left) THE INVERTED TRIANGLE is a good pose for four people. Used with three,
    a dead space behind the center man is created. Dick Cobb, Oklahoma City. (Upper right)
STAGGERED COUPLES work well with four people. Note that the shoulders of the back couple
do overlap. The front couple is placed in front of one of the back couple. The little girl,
whose height is the least, was placed directly in front of one of the back couple. Her partner
is to the side of the man in back. The gesture adds action. What is the significant detail which
tells you where the picture was made? Such significant detail helps a photographer tell a
better story. Pictures using significant detail require fewer explanatory words in the cutline.
Dick Cobb, Oklahoma City. (Lower left) THE TRIANGLE POSE works well with either three
or five persons. Oklahoman & Times. (Lower right) This pose could be described as either
a triangle or a STAIRSTEP arrangement. The steps descend from the highest head to a lower
head. Some dead space appears on the left, and the tall boy on the left should have been
down one step to get his head lower than that of the man with the pipe. Steps are a great
help in a pose like this one. What are the significant details which tell you what kind of a
group this is? Dick Cobb, Oklahoma City.

get a message to the reader. Patience, practice, and constant vigilance are needed by a photographer to develop an eye which can quickly eliminate unneeded details from a scene.

Four Don'ts

1. Don't have dead space in a photo either vertically or horizontally. 2. Don't put too many people in one shot. 3. Don't permit one person in the picture to block out the view of another person. 4. Don't waste space by lining up people in a single line. Use geometric posing for more compact placement of subjects.

Too Many People in One Picture

A 2-column photo shouldn't contain more than four people. A 3-column photo should not have more than six people in it. A great deal of original detail in the glossy photo is missing in the reproduction which is printed on newspaper. Because so much detail is lost between the glossy and the reproduction, the head-size of a person in the photo must be big — ½ column (one inch) or bigger in size. Even with loss of detail, a big head-size will hold enough detail to be recognized by the reader. Small head-size plus loss of detail result in photos which cause readers to strain to recognize people in pictures. Such photos waste space. The average reader won't strain to try to recognize someone in a picture. Some limit must be placed on the number of people in a photo so that space will permit big

56. UNITY is helped by pointing lines and overlap. This excellent advertising photo achieves unity by overlap and pointing lines. The pointing lines, carrying the eye to the cigarettes, are the two coffee spoons, the rose, and the man's hand. If overlap were not used, and each object in the photo was isolated, then unity would be lost.

57. LINES OF TRANSGRESSION AID UNITY. In "Wild Ducks" the water is one tone. The sky is a second tone. Without the black, perpendicular reeds in the foreground crossing both the water and the sky, and tying these two separate tones together this photo would be a layer-cake photo. That is, the sky would lie on top of the water, like one tier of a cake upon another. Wild Ducks in Flight: Dave Corson from Shostal. (Right) In this desert scene by Andreas Feininger, the Cacti serve as "Lines of Transgression" to unify the landscape and keep it from appearing to be just a mass of small, scattered objects with nothing to connect them to each other.

head-size for those photographed. The only purpose of the record shot is to show what something looks like. If the photo doesn't perform this function, space given to the photo is wasted.

One Head Partially Obscures Another

Often this happens when one person shifts his position after the photographer has arranged the group. Solution: check in the view finder before shooting the picture.

In a large group (more than 12 persons), get the camera up higher than the group and shoot down. Stand in a chair or on a table. The high camera view will keep one person from blocking out another.

At least once a month, some business tycoons get together around the board of director's table and want their picture taken. Unless the photographer carefully staggers those in the scene, someone will surely block out someone else. The two persons at the head of the table, on either side of it and farthest from the photographer, should be pushed up right against the table. The next two on either side of the table should be out a bit from the table. The third pair

129

58. UNITY is broken here because the man looks out at the viewer instead of at the object. His look would cause the viewer to also look at the object, too. Because the framed certificate is the lightest area in the picture besides the shirt, the viewer's eye will quickly go to the certificate. Dick Cobb, Oklahoma City.

59. GOOD EYE DIRECTION helps unity. Usually when people work, they look at what they're doing instead of looking out at the reader and giving him a big, toothy grin. Some photographers encourage the model in a pose like this to look out and smile at the reader to get action into the model's face. However, this creates two centers of action, because the model is already doing something. Dick Cobb, Oklahoma City.

60. What could one of the subjects do to add more action to this photo? While the eye directions here are satisfactory, the picture is static. Perhaps the child could have been posed with arms outstretched to receive the doll from the hands of one of the persons in the background. Dick Cobb, Oklahoma City.

should be out still farther from the table. The last pair, nearest the camera, should be the farthest from the table.

When two persons stand side by side before the camera, don't permit a vertical space between them. Don't be satisfied to have their shoulders touch. Move the people closer by overlapping their shoulders.

One center of interest in a picture is best. Therefore, don't let one person stand while another sits if their faces are a great distance apart. Intervening space between the two faces (each is a separate center of interest) is dead space. Have both persons stand or both sit, to get the faces into a common center of interest.

In this example, a boy sits in a wheel chair on the right. The woman in the center has leaned forward to bring her face closer to his and that of the little girl on the left. Now, all three faces are a common center of interest. If the girl in the center stood upright, she would have towered over the boy in the wheel chair, creating two centers of interest and an intervening dead space.

If three people are placed before a camera, shoulder to shoulder, two dead spaces separate the three heads. Move the third person behind the other two. Now, no dead or open spaces are left. Moving the third person eliminated one. Putting the third person behind the other two killed the second dead space. Now, your picture is only two people wide instead of three people wide. This narrowing of your subject matter will probably permit you to make the resulting photograph at least one-half column bigger in size, so that all of the image outlines will benefit by being bigger.

The *inverted triangle* is a good pose for four people. Used with three, a dead space behind the center man is created.

Nine Points on Setting up the Record Shot of a Group of People

1. In a record shot, your objective is to show what something looks like. With a group of people, this means arranging them so no space will be wasted while head-sizes are blown up big enough for each person to be recognized after the loss of detail occurs in reproduction. You don't have enough space to be either too original or clever. If you avoid the "don'ts" and use several of the points now being listed, and show what your group looks like, these steps are sufficient for the record shot. Use originality, cleverness, and see a photo where many wouldn't for feature or emotional shots.

2. *Avoid dead space.*

3. *Get action into the photo.* The action may be either real or simulated. Action adds tons of interest to any photo. A photo of a person who is static and merely looks back at the reader is dull. Have

131

a girl powder her nose or take a swig from a soft-drink bottle. A man can gesture, talk on a telephone, or sign his name. These poses are over-done, but they do add action. If the occasion justifies it, animation in the faces of the group is better than listless expressions.

4. *Eye direction aids the unity of any photo.* Let's analyze photo unity and then see how eye direction helps it.

Unity in a photo means that all the parts of the photo seem to be a united whole, that all parts look like they belong together. Unity in a photo results from one of three methods: 1) *Overlap*, in which objects in the photo touch one another; 2) *lines of transgression* — usually a vertical line running up through several horizontal objects or tones, tying all into a united whole; 3) *one person looks at two people* in a group while the two look back at the one.

In *"Wild Ducks"* the water is one tone. The sky is a second tone. Without the black, perpendicular reeds in the foreground crossing both the water and the sky, and tying these two separate tones together, this photo would be a layer cake photo. That is, the sky would lie on top of the water, like one tier of a cake upon another.

If the foreground of a photograph is mostly a light, monotonous tone, the photographer should back up and cross the fence, as Josef Scaylea did. Now, with the dark lines of the fence in the foreground, the monotonous light tones are broken up by the strong, black silhouette of the fence. Also present in this picture is the third dimensional effect: fence in the foreground, buildings in the mid-area, and the mountain in the background.

Unity is broken because the man looks out at the viewer instead of at the object which he holds. If the man looked at the object, his look would cause the viewer to look at the object, too. However, because the framed certificate is the lightest tone in the picture besides the shirt, the viewer's eye will go quickly to the certificate.

Good eye direction helps unity. Usually when people work, they look at what they're doing instead of looking out at the reader and giving him a big, toothy grin. Some photographers encourage the model in a pose like this to look out and smile at the reader to get action into the model's face. However, this creates two centers of action, because the model is already doing something.

Figure 60 is a different matter. It does not violate any rule of unity, all eye directions are correct, yet it is static and dull. The need here is for some sort of action, either real or implied, to liven up a dull situation. Perhaps one of the persons in the background could have been shown handing the doll to the child?

132

61. DEPTH OF FIELD adds interest to photos of groups. Good cropping has been used on the young lady in the foreground, and she forms a partial frame about the person in the background. Jim Argo, Oklahoman & Times.

62. (Left) A variation of the first depth of field picture, this one lacks the action of the first, and consequently the interest, too. Dick Cobb, Oklahoma City. (Right) Depth of field and action are combined in a good picture for the woman's page. However, the left quarter of this picture is dead space. A smart editor will put a copy block or a headline in this area. Joe Miller, Oklahoman & Times.

63. (Left) Depth of field and emphasis on the man in the foreground are combined in this shot. The man in the foreground is in action while the other two aren't, and he's closest to the camera. Heads form a diagonal line, increasing a feeling of action. Tom Blevins, Norman Transcript. (Right) Cropping is used to assist depth of field and action. Dick Cobb, Okla. City.

64. (LEFT) Aside from the fact that the only two people are in this photo, why is this pose different from the tradiional triangle? Figure this out and you have the key to change of pace posing. Dick Cobb, Oklahoma City. (Right) Change of pace can be built around one sitting and a second standing directly behind the sitter. Dick Cobb, Oklahoma City.

5. *Depth of Field.* Once in the early days of flash photography it was sufficient if a newsphoto of a group was in focus and had the technical qualities to reproduce on newsprint. People in a line at right angles to the camera — that was enough. If the photographer didn't put them against a brick wall (busy pattern) and if he watched his dead space, he got by. But all this was before TV. Now, plain vanilla isn't good enough for newspaper group shots.

Instead of having the group line up shoulder to shoulder at right angles to the camera in the traditional triangle pose, the progressive photographer is striving to get depth of field into even his group shots. Depth of field is a scene with objects in the foreground, the mid-area, and the background, and all in focus. Using depth of field technique gives a photo the added illusion of third dimension — depth. Photographing an object and reproducing it on flat enlarging paper generally yields only two dimensions — height and breadth. Depth, the third dimension, is lost unless one purposely plans for it.

6. *Change of Pace Posing.* Compare the pose used in the traditional triangle, Fig. 55, with those used in Fig. 64, 65, 66. The cutline under the traditional triangle explains the variations in pose which bring about the change of pace which is desired in arranging people.

134

65. (Above, left) This is the same basic pose as that used in 62 yet it seems different. Dick Cobb, Oklahoma City. (Above, right) Change of pace works well on the woman's page, too. The photographer began with a sit-stand arrangement and asked a couple of more guests to move into the picture. The resulting picture has two profiles, a full face, and a three-quarter face.

66. (Below, left) Possibly this prize winning picture in the 1955 competition of the "News Pictures of the Year" had a lot to do with making other news photographers aware of the value of depth of field in group shots. Techniques include change of pace, big head size, animated expression, and depth of field—all in one shot! Earl Seubert, Chief Photographer, Minneapolis Tribune. (Below, right) An unposed photograph of a cabinet member and a senafor comes out with big head size, change of pace, depth of field, action, spontaneity of expression. Oklahoman & Times.

7. *Get the biggest possible image outline in your given space.* Remember how you lose a lot of detail between the glossy print and the reproduction in the paper? That's one reason for a big image outline. Another is that people see big image outlines quicker and easier. Readers like big pictures. A quick glance at the photographs in any mass circulation magazine will show you that one way to increase the size of your image outline without wasting space is to *crop a photo severely.* Look at your negative blow up on the easel critically. What parts of the photo tell the story? Crop away everything else. As you glance at the photographs in a mass circulation magazine, notice that the back of the head, shoulders, and many parts of the anatomy are cut off. The big image outline and cropping go hand in hand.

Readership studies show that if a 1-column photo is enlarged to a 2-column cut, readership doubles. This process continues until the 4-column cut is reached. People just naturally respond to the big picture.

A mug shot should more than fill a 1-column space, so that a part of the head will be cropped. Small important details of a person's face are his features — eyes, nose, mouth, expression. The bigger these small, important details are, the easier it is for readers to recognize the person in the picture, even with a loss of detail due to reproduction.

67. If this uncropped 8x10 photo were reduced to a 2-column cut in a newspaper, the arrows (important detail) would be so small that after the loss of some detail they would not be recognizable. But the right cropping will correct this situation. Dick Cobb.

68. Now, properly cropped and blown up to fill the same 8x10 area, this picture when reduced to a 2-column cut, will present a bigger arrow (small important detail) outline which the reader should be able to see clearly and recognize readily. Dick Cobb.

69. This advertising photograph uses cropping to permit the biggest image outline in the given space. The ad is selling suits that fit so well that male wearers are irresistible. The look of the girl in the background emphasizes, like a pointing finger directed at the central object of interest. The reader will look to see what is so interesting to the girl. Dick Cobb.

8. *Important small detail which must be seen and emphasized will determine the size and space which are given to a photo and also how severely the photo must be cropped.*

A reader must see all important detail quickly and easily. He should not look at a photo and wonder what some of the story-telling details are. To help readers get the message from photos instantly, blow up all small, important detail so that it can be seen easily and recognized. Of course, as the small detail is increased in size, so is the rest of the photo. Severe cropping will save some space required for the photo after small detail is blown up. But if the small detail is important, then whatever space is required to properly display the important small detail should be utilized.

A photo which doesn't display the important detail in this fashion wastes space because readers won't work to get the message. They just pass on to something else.

9. *When action is introduced into a group of people, limit the action to only one or two of the group,* with the others watching the action. The two who are in action are the center of interest. They are further emphasized by the watchers. If every one in a group is in action, many centers of interest compete with one another. All emphasis is no emphasis. The poor, confused reader quickly leaves such a photograph.

137

70. The drama cast is a problem. You can only use one picture in the school paper. Both the cast and the teacher want everyone in the cast in the picture. A photograph results which has two centers of interest because two separate actions are going on. Dick Cobb.

71. Now that only one action is presented to the reader, his interest won't be divided. Most editors would prefer this simpler photograph with bigger image outlines and one center of interest. But actors who were left out of this shot will like the first picure, even though it's a bad picure. Dick Cobb.

72. It's Christmas. So everybody gets into the act. And two separate actions result, two different pictures. How can you get one center of interest and a unified picture? Dick Cobb.

73. Pull the group together. Have one person in action (girl showing others the card holder) while the others look at her. Good eye direction and overlap bring unity. For even greater action, the girl could hang the card holder on the mantel while the others watch her. Dick Cobb.

Feature Section and Magazine Group Poses

The feature section of newspapers and magazines aren't quite so conscious of space limitation as is the general news area of most newspapers. Even if the feature section and magazines do feel the pressure of space limitation, they don't act as if they do. A more liberal use of white space and less tight group poses both indicate the feature section and magazine approach in using photographs.

138

CHAPTER 10

Making Photos with a Message

What Is an Emotional Photo?

Photo content which causes the reader to feel emotion has a strong message. The photo says something to the reader. The photo content causes the reader to laugh, to feel sad, or to experience revulsion. The photo content may cause the reader to remember the past nostalgicly. Or the photo content may depict universal events that most readers have experienced and understand and readily identify with. Such events include birth, childhood, teen-age life with its special set of problems, marriage, death, war.

Psychologists say that man has certain basic emotions. Photos with content related to these emotions will hit the reader in his emotions. Four basic emotions are survival, sex, ambition, and escape.

The *survival* appeal may be seen in photos of floods, tornadoes, a championship boxing match, two New Year's Day bowl football teams. or two candidates for president of the United States. *Sex* is interpreted in news photos as a pretty girl announcing her engagement, the wedded couple as they leave on a honeymoon, the kiss of two movie stars, and cheesecake and sweater-girl photos. The following photo situations would have the *ambition* appeal: a mug shot of an executive who began as an office boy and has just been promoted to corporation president; a photo of the current glamour girl in the movies, being escorted by the current male lead; a photo of a scientist who has just discovered the way to cure some dread disease. Pictures of those who have achieved success in any area — business, the movies, science, athletics, cultural — represent ambition. Many who see the photos think, "If he did it, I can do it." Or the reader may wistfully reflect, "Why can't I scale the heights?" *Escape* is the desire of all to get away from their immediate surroundings, the humdrum of daily living and the press of their responsibilities. Photos which show people in recreational ac-

74. SPOT NEWS: A boy loses his life on a bicycle. The boy, the dog and the woman running to see if it is her child, all have emotional impact. George F. Tapscott, Oklahoman & Times.

tivities, on vacation, or having fun, show man in his pursuit of pleasure, man attempting to escape from the cares of sameness which bore and depress him.

A spot news photo is represented by 74. The photographer shooting spot news doesn't have either the time or the right to tamper with details. The camera is reporting objectively. Any emotion present will be there without assistance from the photographer.

75. BUS STOP. Who hasn't fretted and fumed at a bus stop (or a taxi stand or an air terminal?). Nearly everyone has had a similar experience, so readers will identify with such a picture. Austin Traverse, Oklahoman & Times.

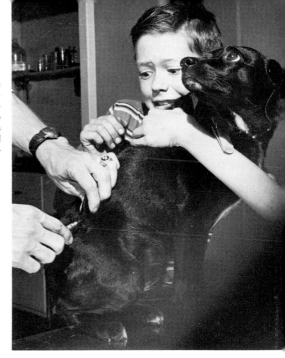

76. EASY, DOCTOR! Kids and animals rate high in reader preference; a picture like this generates reader sympathy for both. Important small detail is the vaccination needle itself; the vet had to be cropped out so the important matter could be as large as possible. The hands and needle are all the detail needed to tell the story. Julius Greenfield, Akron Beacon-Journal.

Most parents can identify with the picture of a crushed bicycle and be thankful their child wasn't killed or injured. Or this event will remind parents of some past bicycle mishap of one of their children.

Seeing Emotional Photos

Photos which sock readers in their emotions have three points of origin. (1) Some spot news pictures have content which moves the

77. NEW BUILDING. Photographers get tired of making pictures of houses and buildings to show the growth of a city. Such pictures look pretty much alike and there is little one can do to inject a fresh approach. But this photographer caught the reflection of a new building in the bystander's glasses. Joe Miller, Oklahoman & Times.

78. ANIMALS AND HUMAN INTEREST. It's hard not to be amused by these photographs, isn't it? In fact it's downright hard to suppress a good chuckle. (Above left) George Honeycutt, The Houston Chronicle. (Above right) Bruce Roberts, Charlotte, North Carolina. (Below, left) Clint Grant, Dallas Morning News. (Below, right) courtesy Kodak High School Photography Awards.

reader. (2) Imaginative and resourceful photographers on routine assignments often return with photos which provoke reader reaction. These photos are shot because the photographer has the ability to see and *make* emotional photos out of straw and mud. (3) An emotion photo often starts with an idea in a photographer's head which he plans and executes.

Formula for Seeing Photos

The art of seeing a photo possibility can be developed. Many fine emotional photos have been *made* from unpromising subject matter. What kind of hocus pocus does a photographer use to transpose barren scenes into pictures worth a byline?

Three simple rules — so simple that many will read and discount them or ignore them — have been used to develop the ability to see the photo potential of a scene.

1. Look at the scene which you plan to photograph. *Ask* yourself these questions:
   a. What feeling or message does the scene convey to *me*?
   b. How can I best convey the same feeling/message to the readers?
   c. What am I trying to tell the reader?
   d. How can I make the reader see/feel what I see/feel?
2. Emphasize the details which help tell the story. (See techniques on emphasis, Chapter 11)
3. Exclude or subordinate details in the scene which do not help tell the story.

Remember. The three rules about how you handle your raw material alone don't cause the reader to feel emotion. First, you must select subject matter with universal appeal or which is related to one of man's basic emotions. Then apply your three rules to record the potentially emotional subject matter on film in the most forceful way to make your point or tell your story.

More Questions to Ask Yourself Before Exposing Your Film

During the Easter vacation break each spring, student photographers at the University of Missouri may sign up for a workshop. Participants spend about three days photographing some Missouri town, trying to catch the spirit and the flavor of the town and its people. Professor Cliff Edom always has able professionals on hand to view and criticize the work of the students and to offer tips. One of the professionals who has assisted several times in this worthwhile workshop is John Morris.

Mr. Morris has been an assistant to Wilson Hicks, former *Life* picture editor; picture editor of the *Ladies Home Journal*; picture editor for Magnum; and assistant managing editor in charge of photography, the *Washington Post*. At present he is director of a government project in Washington which probably will result in a national archive for significant photos of the United States.

Mr. Morris posed a list of 21 questions for the student photographers to mull over as they looked at the town to be photographed and tried to select the most representative and revealing scenes. Any thinking photographer can adapt this list of questions to projects he is photographing, and his work should improve as he gets in the habit of thinking through what his objective is, instead of exposing a lot of film without thought and hoping that something will be good.

The Morris Question List

1. Is this picture a good one, or is it merely a good subject?
2. What might occur here which would make this situation worth a picture?
3. How's the weather in my pictures?
4. What is so special about this city (scene, subject matter)? Am I trying to capture it in my pictures, or do I prefer to show what this city has in common with other communities?
5. If I had to spend a week in this city just to take one picture, what would it be?
6. What matters are of great concern to the people of this city? Have I shown any of them?
7. Have I taken any pictures which could not have been taken last year? Do my pictures show some details which will say specifically what the date of the year is?
8. Whose name is most frequently seen in this city?
9. Am I ignoring things people are proud of?
10. Will my picture help the town to understand itself? Will my pictures hurt feelings? Is this good or bad?
11. Do I have any witty pictures? Do I have a single picture that will make someone laugh or smile?
12. How many of the basic human emotions — love, fear, anger — have I photographed?
13. Do I find this community pretty or ugly? Have I shown either or both?
14. Do people here show any visible reaction to the outside world? Have I caught it?
15. Have I taken pictures which might better have been made at another time of the day?
16. Have I caught expressions — or merely faces? Do my pictures look right into people's eyes?
17. Have I caught any pictures expressive of nature?

144

79. HANS WERFEL AND HIS NEW SHOES. (Left) Everyone who has been in need and has then received his desire can associate himself with the thrill of this little war victim when he was given a pair of new shoes by the American Red Cross. Such a picture has universal appeal and great emotional impact. Gerald Wallar, American Red Cross.

80. LIFE'S LABOR LOST (Right) War is not the only destroyer. Here we have the victim of a tornado, standing amid the ruins of her farm and all her possessions. Neils Lauritzen, Milwaukee Journal.

18. Have I found details which are significant? Have I taken a good still life?
19. Have I ever stood still 20 minutes before taking a picture?
20. What is the big news in my city today? What's the "talk of the town"?
21. Have I shown anyone having fun?

Emotional Photos vs. the Truth

Jenkin Lloyd Jones, a provocative speaker and newspaper publisher in Tulsa, Oklahoma, has commented that photojournalism can be one of the crookedest forms of journalism. In a speech before the National Press Photographers Association Convention, William P. Steven, a distinguished newspaper editor, quoted from a column which Jones wrote on photography.[1]

Jones cited an example of such crookedness as a photo taken for the Department of Agriculture in the middle 1930's. American farmers were pressed by both drought and debt. Henry Wallace's Agricultural Adjustment Administration was trying to prove that only by massive

---

[1] From a speech by William P. Steven, National Press Photographers Association Convention, Houston, Texas, 1965.

81. Integration has been a big story in many parts of the country. Oklahoma has been relatively free of bitterness; when integration came to formerly segregated restaurants, the Oklahoma City Daily Oklahoman told the story in this symbolic photograph. Staff Photo Oklahoman & Times.

government controls and spending could the farms be saved. The Department of Agriculture began collecting a series of documentary photographs, taken by eager-beaver photographers, anxious to please their bosses in the Department.

One series on North Dakota farms showed a number of dust-drifted fields, and in each picture was a whitened cow skull. Farmers needing money will turn dead animals over to a rendering plant. So some suspicious folks began examining those cow skulls through a magnifying glass. It was the same skull in each picture.

82. A fish-eye lens produced this "victim's eye" view of the aftermath of an accident, as the sheet was pulled over his body. Allen Litten, Harrisonburg, Virginia, Daily News Record.

146

83. (Left) Integration again; this picture shows Suzy Sterling, a Southern volunteer in the inter-racial war on poverty. Bruce Roberts, Charlotte, North Carolina.

84. (Right) When you see a photogaph with the quality of this one, you can't help exclaiming "Gosh, that's good!". It was undoubtedly this very feeling that prompted one of America's top photographers to shoot the picture in the first place. George Silk, LIFE.

A young government photographer found the skull in a Bad Lands arroyo. He hauled it around in his car trunk to "salt" his pictures. The photographer's defense: It dramatized a problem.

Mr. Steven, in his comments to news photographers, also quoted from Theodore H. Whit's *The Making of a President: 1964,*[2] which both applauds and condemns the use of TV reporting events. Of TV's coverage on the assassination of President Kennedy, White wrote: ". . . it achieved greatness in November, 1963, by reporting true drama with clarity, good taste, and responsibility, in a fashion which stabilized the nation in the emotional shock and on the verge of hysteria. By concealing nothing, by sharing all, by being visible when their private natures must have craved privacy, Jacqueline Kennedy first above all, then the grief-stricken Kennedy family, then the new President permitted television to give strength and participation to the citizens."

In condemning TV reporting of the Harlem riots, Mr. White wrote:

"It is important to stress for the record how splendid was the police work in New York City during this week of violence, for it was almost

---

[2]Atheneum Publishing Company, New York, 1964.

147

completely ignored; and the studied indifference of the great television media to the heroism of the city's police was as significant as any other factor in the spread of senseless rioting to other cities.

"For though one brick-thrower was shot to death and 92 civilians and 48 police were injured, never at any time did the police of New York lose control of the streets, even in the heart of the ghetto. But television, with its insatiable appetite for live drama, found in the riots gorgeous spectacle. Protected by the police from the mobs, cameramen could thus catch police at work in the ugly business of grappling with rioters, subduing them by clubs if necessary. For months TV had displayed a procession of brilliant, eloquent Negro intellectuals who . . . denounced . . . the city's power structure . . . providing the moral absolution of juveniles for any form of Negro violence against any form of law and order.

"During the week of violence, the police, pictured with their clubs and helmets over and over again, were denied the support of public opinion so essential to quiet civil disturbance.

"At no time, to this writer's knowledge, has TV ever shown the nation the spectacle of a Negro community of decency. All across the country . . . are Negro communities — working class and middle class — of dignity, tranquillity, quiet and decency far above the average of their white neighbors . . . TV, reaching for distorted dramatic effect has ignored the triumphant achievements of such Negro communities . . .

". . . The New York riots were capped by a national network's half-hour show of one of the foulest and worst blocks in Harlem, as if indicting the city and holding the city responsible for the riots. Completely ignoring the fact that New York has built more public housing in the ghetto of Harlem than most other cities of the nation have built for all their people, or that Harlem to an overwhelming degree is composed of decent people living in decency, TV gave its implied absolution to the rioters, further embittering the best of Harlem's leadership and terrifying the whites, already simmering and ready for a counter explosion of their own."

Mr. Steven made the following comment on White's example: "What happened in White's examples was that the camera men yielded to the inevitable temptation to take the stuff that makes the best pictures. By what terms were these the best pictures if the information they convey are not the truth? How are these best if they are distorted in favor of lawlessness and insurrection against peace and order?

"A camera journalist uses the camera as a device for reporting truth. He must be as concerned as the word reporter that the whole story is told. He must ask, when he takes violence, whether he also must show the strength of law and order."

148

CHAPTER 11

15 Techniques
for Improving Photos

Documentary or Record Shots vs. Mood or Emotional Shots

The viewpoint of your camera — the angle of it in relation to the subject, and how close or how far the camera is from the subject — depends on the kind of a photograph you want to make. If you want to produce a conventional picture which most people will understand to illustrate a point or to show what something looks like, your objective is a *documentary photo* (record shot). In such a photo, no distorting angles will be used. If you're striving for dramatization, which demands exaggeration, your objective is a creative *mood photo* (emotional). In such a photo you have greater latitude to choose your own way to tell the story. Abstraction and distortion are in order if they help your reader in feeling and seeing "harvest abundance" or the great power of two opposing football teams. Angle shots are excellent when you have a logical reason to use them, when the photo situation justifies them. Used indiscriminately, they lose their effectiveness and can be ludicrous.

Perspective, the way you're used to seeing objects in which vertical and horizontal lines are straight and at right angles to one another, can be controlled in two ways: 1) By changing the point of view; 2) by changing the position of the film with regard to the optical axis.

The trick in avoiding distortion is to keep the plane of the film parallel to lines of the object which you photograph. Photographing a tall building without distortion demands a special tool — a camera with a lens which can be raised and lowered, and tilted back and forth, and a swinging back — a view camera. Most cameras don't have these adjustments. Without such a camera, you have to tilt your camera upward to include both the top and bottom of the building. With the camera tilted, the film is no longer parallel to the lines of the building. So in the negative, the building is unbalanced and leans crazily. Tilting your easel restores verticals to parallelism, and stopping down the enlarger diaphragm to $f/32$ will correct focusing distortion. By tilting both the negative and the easel in opposite directions, you can produce a distortion-free image without having to stop down the enlarger diaphragm excessively.

Angle shots mixed indiscriminately will detract from smooth continuity by requiring the reader to re-orient himself constantly.

EFFECT OF ANGLE SHOTS — CHART 20

Low Angle Shots	High Angle Shots
Make a girl's legs appear longer	Produce a stopper effect
Make a victorious general seem taller	Yield the overview or the long shot
Add to the impressiveness of height	Are used when there's no other way to get shot
	Often distort
Eye Level Angle	May add a feeling of complete, intimate reality
Yields the most natural pictures	
Is excellent for children	

In choosing viewpoint for whichever kind of a photo (documentary or record, mood or emotion) you're making, ask:

Why am I taking this photo?

What are the characteristics of the subject?

What is typical of this subject?

What do I want to emphasize?

What quality should I concentrate on?

Which viewpoint will best depict the most important element of my subject?

A number of times, you have been advised to get as close as possible to your subject. As good as the advice is, it can be overdone. Getting too close to the subject will produce distorted perspective.

Composition—Arrangement of Line, Tone and Mass to Tell Your Message or Convey a Mood*

A. *Some useful don'ts*

1. Don't put your center of interest in the exact, "dead" center of your picture.
2. Don't let a line cut your picture exactly in half, either horizontally or vertically.
3. Don't allow any long uninterrupted line to parallel either the top and bottom or the sides of your picture.
4. Don't have a lot of useless, stand-'em-off foreground.
5. Don't have more than one center of interest, and you won't if you know what you are taking a picture of.
6. Don't let your picture "weigh" too much on *one side*, or give the feeling of being off balance.

---

*From *The Fun o fPhotography* by Mario and Mabel Scacheri, copyright, 1936 by Harcourt, Brace & World, Inc.; Copyright, 1966, by Mabel Scacheri. Reprinted by permission.

85. WHEN THE CAMERA IS TOO CLOSE TO THE SUBJECT, DISTORTIONS RESULT
   A. Distortions are a massive chin and a low forehead.
   B. Dostortions are a top-heavy forehead and the chin is weak. Andreas Feininger.

B. *Some generalizations*

1. The slowest, least active line is the perfect horizontal.

2. The speediest straight line is the perfect diagonal. Other diagonals are speedy in proportion as they depart from the horizontal and approach the true diagonal.

3. The most active of all lines is the zig-zag. Artists have used it for years to portray lightning, although no one has even seen zig-zag lightning.

4. The most graceful of all lines is the curve, rather like an S. The sharper the curves, the more they approach the zig-zag, and the more movement the lines suggest.

5. The most dignified, solid, solemn line is the vertical. It suggests pillars holding up cathedral roofs, or "a tower of strength," strong to the imagination because of its vertical lines.

6. Two lines moving in opposite directions and crossing each other suggest resistance, sometimes action.

7. Lines which move in toward the center of interest will draw attention to it. Other lines may have an undesirable way of leading the eye out of the picture.

151

8. Objects in a picture may be grouped in a circle, a square, a cross, a triangle, or some other geometric pattern. Also masses of light and dark tones will form a pattern, pleasing or otherwise. A few dedicated, skilled professional photographers have learned to control this pattern, and shade from dark to light diagonally, vertically, or horizontally across their pictures, to increase interest in it.

9. If a picture confines itself chiefly to light tones, chiefly to dark tones, or chiefly to middle tones, it will probably be more effective than if the range of tones is complete and of even proportion.

10. The eye follows lines of light, goes from shadows to light spots, and will be more strongly attracted by a white spot on a black background, or a black spot on a white ground, than it will by either spot on a medium gray ground. The greater the contrast the greater the attraction.

    Also the nearer the edge of the picture an object is, the greater its attraction for the eye. The nearer the "dead" center, the less attraction it will have.

11. Light coming from above gives a serious or sad air to the subject, from below a dramatic, wild, or lively air. A light at an extremely acute angle brings out texture. A front light reduces the modeling of objects. A light from the side, at about 45 degrees, gives the greatest realism, as it is the one in which we usually see things about us illuminated.

12. The blind use of rules will not produce good pictures. Rules just help you get started. They make you aware of what you should do, goals to work toward, and give you standards by which to judge your work.

You will have to develop an awareness of when to use which rules. You do this by experience, trial and error, and intelligent evaluation of your work. There is a limit to the number of balls a juggler attempts to handle at one time. When you apply your rules to a photo situation, know what your photographic goal is, then use only the rules which will help you achieve your goal. Keep asking, in relation to every picture: What am I trying to do? What am I trying to say in this picture? What feeling do I want to stimulate in viewers?

With your aim clearly defined, then decide how to achieve it. Which rules will help you? If in doubt about whether to attempt to apply a rule, make a couple of shots. In one shot, try to apply the rule. In the other, omit the "questionable" rule. Don't hesitate to shoot 4 to 5 times as much film as you expect to use.

86. POINT OF VIEW OF CAMERA.

Above left: Normal angle taken from waist or eye level.
Courtesy R. J. Reynolds Tobacco Co.

Above center: High angle, looking down on subject.
A. Y. Owen, LIFE Magazine, © 1961 Time Inc.

Above right: Low angle, shooting up at subject.
Elliot Erwin, from Magnum Photos.

87. PROXIMITY OF CAMERA TO SUBJECT. Pictures are also classified by camera-to-subject distance, is still pictures as in the movie.

Below left: A long shot; usually more than 25 feet from the camera.
Ted Rozumalski, The Houston Chronicle.

Below center: A medium shot; from 6 feet to 25 feet from the camera, depending on the size of the subject.
Bob Taylor, Cordell, Okla.

Below right: A close-up. Less than 6 feet from the camera, again depending on the the size of the subject. Courtesy Nikon, Inc.

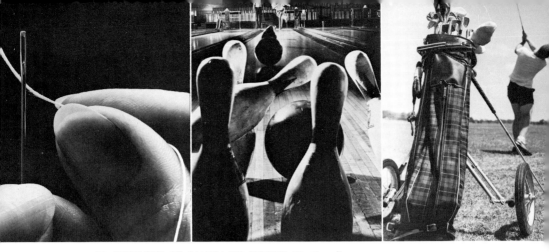

88. PROXIMITY OF CAMERA TO SUBJECT (Continued)

Left: Extreme Close-up—closer than normal viewing distance.
Courtesy Better Vision Institute.

Center: 2 in 1—a combination of close-up and long shot in one picture.
Joe Clark, Friends Magazine.

Right: Another 2 in 1 combination close-up and long shot.
Jim Bruce, University of Oklahoma student.

89. SIGNIFICANT DETAIL. Something to tell you why this woman is so frightened—is missing. Her husband may have just dropped dead. A threatening intruder may have walked in. Or she may be enjoying TV. The detail which would give you some clue—tell you who, what, when, where, why, or how—isn't in the picture. Ewing Galloway, New York.

90. SIGNIFICANT DETAIL IS THE STEERING WHEEL. Now, you know more about why the driver may be frightened. When significant detail is used, the photograph tells a more complete story, and fewer words will be required in the cutline to explain the picture. Ewing Galloway, New York.

91. SILHOUETTE. Because details—how the woman is dressed and her facial features—are not shown, the reader's interest is focused on the action. Silhouette is good in symbolic photographs. It also blots out details which help to date a photograph—cut and style of clothes. Yseult Mounsey, courtesy, Newspaper National Snapshot Awards.

92. INDIVIDUAL. By the costume, props and surroundings, you can tell that this individual is a butcher. Photo, courtesy Armour & Co.

93. INDIVIDUAL. With this photograph, you could recognize the man reading his mail. You could pick him out of a line-up of several people. When a photograph shows enough detail for the individual to be recognized, you have a contrasting situation from the silhouette. Bob Taylor, Cordell, Okla.

94. SYMBOL OF ACTION: FREEZE. There is always a question of whether or not to freeze action completely. In some cases the result would end up as a picture of a thing standing still. In this picture, even though the dogs are all "frozen", they are obviously in motion, simply because they could not be in the positions shown if they were stationary; several of the dogs are actually in mid-air. Don Sturky, Charlotte Observer.

95. SYMBOL OF ACTION: BLUR. This is the classic way artists and painters have represented action for hundreds of years. For some reason, photographers avoided it until quite recently. Here it is used most effectively to give a feeling of even greater speed than the action really was. Leo J. Pesh, Jr., Peshtigo Times.

155

96. IMPLIED ACTION. Sometimes action is indicated by the composition of the picture where no action really exists. (Left) in this magazine cover, action is implied by the diagonal lines in the background. (Courtesy Woman's Day). (Center) The diagonal line of the surf likewise implies action, though the boy in the picture may have actually been standing still. Charles Fretzin, courtesy Kodak High School Awards. (Right) Action is implied by the off-center balance of the picture elements. Richard Bauer, Milwaukee Journal.

97. FRAMING PHOTOGRAPHS. There are many ways of framing the subject matter of a photograph to put greater emphasis on it. These three photographs show only a few—the ingenious photographer can think of many more. (Left) a foreground object forms a partial frame for the background—in this case, one horse partly frames its colt. John Gould, Kodak High School Photo Awards. (Center) A somewhat artificial framing device, yet legitimate, is this use of the coil of rope in the foreground to frame the cowboy in the rear. Bob Taylor, Cordell, Okla. (Right) Totally artificial—you couldn't possibly climb down into the cup on a golf course to take a picture like this "worm's eye view". Pictures like this are real "stoppers" when it comes to catching the reader's eye. Austin Traverse, Oklahoman & Times.

98. EMPHASIS AND SUBORDINATION. When two or more objects are in one photo you must decide which one to emphasize and which to subordinate. There are various ways in which this can be done and these pictures show six of them. (Left) Two persons in the picture, only one in action, draws attention to the latter. Jim Pond, Dallas. (Center) Emphasis is on the object nearest the camera, aided in this case by an out of focus background. Either may be used alone. Thomas Smith, Vandergrift, Pa. (Right) Emphasis is on the teacher; the unique object. One teacher vs. many students, with their backs to the camera. Lewis Sprunger, Kodak High School Photo Awards.

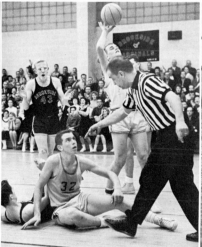

98. (Continued) EMPHASIS AND SUBORDINATION. (Left) Sometimes the object nearest the camera is subdued, by being darker in tone allowing the emphasis to be placed on those farther from the camera. Ike Verne, New York. (Center) With several objects in motion, the pointing hand provides the emphasis. Harry Snavely, Chronicle-Telegram. (Right) Emphasis by converging lines which lead the eye to the main subject. Perspective is often an aid to emphasis. David Stark, courtesy Kodak High School Photo Awards.

99. ILLUSION OF SPACE AND SIZE. (Left) Without the tractor in the foreground, the viewer would not know how large this expanse of cornfield actually is. The man on the tractor provides an object of known size to scale against. Photo, courtesy International Harvester World. (Right) This bottle might be a pint, a quart or a 5 gallon jug. But comparing it with the hand, an object of known size, it is seen to be a regular "stubby" beer bottle. Photo, courtesy Glass Container Manufacturer's Institute.

Emphasis Versus Subordination

One central object of interest against a plain background poses no problem in emphasis. All the reader can look at is the one object of interest.

When two or more objects are in the same photo, you must decide what to emphasize and what to subordinate. Otherwise, if both objects get the same amount of emphasis, the reader is confused. The poor reader doesn't know what to look at, so he quickly leaves the picture.

Six ways to achieve emphasis and subordination:
   a. Allow only one person to be in action. Others watch the action.
   b. Put the object to be emphasized nearest the camera so it will be the biggest in size.
   c. Place a unique object among several of the same kinds of objects.
   d. Use lighting or tone to gain emphasis: the eye goes to white or light tones.
   e. Converging lines force the eye to look at an object.
   f. A model who points at an object, or several people all looking at an object cause the reader to look at the object.

Four Ways To Achieve Illusion Of Space

   a. Illusion of scale or size of photo content is made understandable to readers by a contrast of the size of a known object (hand, human figure, car, animal) with other objects such as the Grand Canyon, the sea or a mountain. A reader, seeing a photo of just the Grand Canyon or a mountain, has no way of gauging the size of either. But put a man on the rim of the canyon, or a man riding a horse up the mountain, and you give the reader a known object to compare with the canyon or the mountain. If the man at the canyon is very small, the reader realizes a great expanse is being shown. If the man and the horse on

158

the mountain are normal in size, the reader realizes only a small portion of the mountain is being shown.

b. Illusion of *distance and space* can be achieved by background objects which are indistinct. You know from experience that objects which are close to you are sharp, and you can see many details — a person's features, whether he wears glasses, the color and style of his clothes. But as objects get farther from you, details are lost, and the objects become indistinct.

One way to increase the feeling of depth of field is to *use a large diaphragm opening* (compensating with the speed of your shutter to keep from overexposing) to purposely fuzz the background details.

If there is haze in the atmosphere, and *no red filter is used,* this haze will make distant objects indistinct, increasing the feeling of distance or depth.

c. *Third dimension*—placing objects in the foreground, midground, and background to enhance a feeling of distance—was discussed in Chapter 9, Posing People for the Record Shot.

Suppose three 6-foot men were in a scene, one in the foreground, another in the midground, and the third in the background. From experience, you know that as object gets farther away from you, this object seems to your eye to be getting smaller.

Also as parallel lines recede into the distance, they seem to converge.

Since both you and your readers associate diminishing size and parallel lines which converge with distance, you can use both of these illusions to create an impression of distance. You can make the distance in your scene great or small, depending on how close the converging lines come to one another and the difference in size of people in the foreground and the background.

Poster Effect

Poster Effect is achieved by four principles:

a. Photo content is a simple, clear message, quickly and easily grasped without study.

b. One dominant object is placed against a plain background.

100. EMPHASIS BY SELECTIVE FOCUSING. In these four pictures we see the same group of objects—a foreground grille, a statue in the middleground, and a poster in the background. In the first picture, a small lens stop was used to get everything in focus and the result is a confused jungle. With the lens open, in the second shot, we have the grille sharp, everything else blurred. Still keeping the lens wide open, we shift focus to the statue in the third picture and the poster in the fourth. Photos by Andreas Feininger.

c. If more than one object is used, make only one object dominant.

d. Have no important small detail which is not big enough to be seen quickly, easily.

Expository Load

Expository load is present in any photograph which has a great many details, each one helping to tell the story. The more details a photo has, the more involved a story it tells. And the longer it takes the reader to comprehend the full story.

Many magazines favor the poster effect approach for their covers. However the *Saturday Evening Post* has been very successful in many of its covers by using expository load.

Obviously, one approach is that of sparseness and the other is that of abundance. Both can't be used in one photo. You must decide in advance which approach you're trying to employ. Generally, the simpler you keep your shots and the less detail you have to employ, the less risk you run of botching a picture.

News magazines have devised a cover approach which differs from these discussed. The central object of interest is placed in the foreground. In the background will be *significant details* to tell a fuller story about the central object of interest.

Physical Appeal

Physical appeal in a photo refers to either 1) repeated pattern which gives a rhythm and feeling of motion to the picture or to 2) a bizarre photograph—a big enlargement of an insect—which holds the reader's attention because it is unusual. The appeal is called *physical* because the characteristics of the photo content—repeated pattern of the insect blow up—are seen with the eye.

101. POSTER EFFECT CONTRASTED WITH EXPOSITORY LOAD. (Upper left) Poster effect includes a simple message told with one or two models, closely unified against a plain background. No important detail should be so small that it is difficult to recognize quickly. Bob Taylor, Cordell, Oklahoma. (Upper right) Expository load—lots of detail—in Steven Dohanos' Saturday Evening Post cover will hold the eye of the reader for a long time. Reprinted by special permission of Steven Dohanos and The Saturday Evening Post, © 1953, The Curtis Publishing Company.

102. PHYSICAL APPEAL (Center left) Repetition of pattern of similar objects adds rhythm and action to a photograph. Bob Taylor, Cordell, Oklahoma.
(Center right) Physical appeal is also obtained through subject matter which is bizarre. You tend to think of a grasshopper as an insignificant insect. If a photograph of a grasshopper is greatly enlarged, readers will be confronted by a fierce and awesome spectacle. Because they haven't seen this kind of a photo before, most readers will continue to look, even though what they see repells them.
This montage which presents two moods of Red Skelton is different enough that it will attract and hold the attention of most readers. Philippe Halsman.
(Lower left) Possibly this subject matter is a combination of both kinds of physical appeal—and the bizarre. James L. Shaffer, Dubuque Telegraph Herald.
(Lower right) Another combination of repetition and the bizarre. Bruce Roberts, Charlotte, North Carolina.

103. EFFECT OF FOCAL LENGTH ON PICTURE AREA. (Upper left) This picture was taken with a wide angle lens, from the opposite corner. (Upper right) The same scene taken with the standard lens; note the narrower angle of view, but perspective has not changed. (Left) the same scene taken with a telephoto lens gives a closeup effect but again without change of perspective. Tom Blevins, Norman Transcript.

104. COMPOSITION. (Left) the horizon is too close to the center of the picture, which divides it into two nearly equal parts. This tends to weaken interest in it, since the eye has to choose from between two things which are almost alike. Toby Massey, Miami News. (Center) Readers will look at the big black object in the foreground because it is emphasized three ways—size, action, and the look of one of the boys on the hill, but most of all, because it is in the lower one third of the picture. Vincent S. D'Addario, Holyoke, Mass. (Right) Now the space division has been reversed; the foreground gets about two-thirds of the space while the background gets about one third. Yet the action is in the background. The reader's attention will be drawn to the baby because of the implied action—reaching for the dangerous objects. Courtesy, Bell System, American Telephone and Telegraph and Associated Companies.

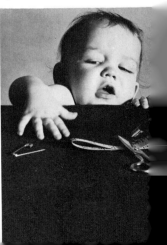

A print's vertical area should not be divided equally between the foreground and the sky. A more pleasing division is to use one-third of the vertical area for the foreground and two-thirds for the sky. Or this same formula of one-third versus two-thirds can be reversed. The foreground can be given two-thirds of the vertical area while only one-third is used for the sky.

Night Photos by Time Exposure

Procedure for time exposures:

1. Select a film about as sensitive to light as Tri-X.
   Suggested developers: D-76 or Promicrol. Tri-X can be rated at the equivalent of ASA 650 if developed in Promicrol at 68 degrees for 14 minutes.

2. Place your camera on a tripod.

3. Focus and stop down to $f/11$ or smaller.

4. Make at least three shots of the same subject.
   a. Some trial and error on your part will provide you with the basis for an estimated exposure for the first shot.
   b. Cut your estimated exposure in half for the second shot.
   c. Double your estimated exposure for the third shot.
   d. Develop all films for the same length of time. One of the three negatives will be a usable one.

105. NIGHT TIME EXPOSURES. (Left) Main Street at night. During the time the shutter was open, the headlights of moving automobiles registered on the film as the long streaks down the middle; here and there a streak gets out of line as a car swerved to pass another or to change lanes. (Center) The Railroad Station. Night pictures are especially effective when taken during or just after a light rain, producing interesting reflections on the otherwise dull pavement. (Right) Checking with Headquarters. Snow on the ground also helps in the making of night time exposures, because it reflects a good deal of light from the overhead street lamp.

5. Use a cable release in opening and closing your lens for the time exposures to avoid jiggling your camera.
   Exposures can vary from 15 seconds to 5 minutes or longer, depending on your scene light conditions and how small an f/stop you are using.

6. A pedestrian who walks in front of your lens probably will not be recorded on the film if the exposure is 30 seconds or longer. But bright car lights will be recorded. If you don't want the light pattern on your negative, merely cover your lens with a lens cap or your hand as car lights approach. Then uncover the lens when the lights are out of range. Take care to note the length of time the lens is covered (or count off the time: 1 and 2 and 3) and add this time to your exposure.

CHAPTER 12

Selecting Good News Photos

Three Characteristics the Editor Seeks

The record/documentary photo has been discussed. So has the emotional/mood picture. So you realize that all photos fall into one of these two classifications. Newspapers and other publications use both kinds of photos, and would be incomplete without both kinds of pictures. A paper which published only record shots or only emotional shots would be like a car trying to run on two wheels.

The record shot helps a newspaper give information to readers, and giving information is the paper's chief function. Emotional shots either amuse or make the reader feel. They're the icing on the cake. An editor glows when his paper can publish an emotional shot or feature type picture, and reader response justifies the editor's expectations. Though you may put more effort into the planning of emotional pictures, and have more fun shooting them because they challenge your creativity, emotional pictures are neither more nor less important than record shots which supply information. In communicating with readers, newspapers need both of these tools.

A photo editor sees hundreds of pictures every week. Only a small percent of the pictures which cross his desk are published. The rest are put in a file if they seem to have some use, or they're thrown away. What yard stick does the photo editor use to separate the wheat from the chaff?

A photo editor is concerned with three characteristics of any photo: 1. Its physical qualities; 2. The photo's relation to paper editorial policy; 3. Photo content.

Most of the time the first two characteristics require only a glance to determine whether a photo measures up to publication standards. The third problem, photo content, is the thorniest decision the editor faces. You know what the editor seeks in a photo with good physical characteristics. He wants a picture which is in focus, which is not blurry (unless purposely to indicate action) because of camera movement. The editor needs a positive print which has good separation of tone and good contrast. He doesn't want a man in a dark suit against a dark background. True, retouching will help the photo but retouching is time consuming and expensive. And the editor expects a photographer to be able to match the contrast in the negative with the right grade of paper, so that the picture will have some pure black tones, some pure white tones, and a great many in-between-gray tones.

So the photo passes the physical qualities test. Now the editor mentally checks to find if the story/message in the photo will violate the policy of his publication. A photo suitable for a medical book could shock the readers of the *New York Daily News*. A cheesecake picture of a model, clad mostly in pulchritude, would be good enough for a cover shot in the *New York Daily News,* but in extremely poor taste in the *Christian Science Monitor.* Many papers will not publish a picture of a corpse if the individual lived in the paper's circulation area. Why shock and distress friends and relatives of the dead person?

Life magazine has published some gruesome photos of death. Examples include an individual lying in a pool of his blood on the street minus an arm and a leg which were blown off. Both the arm and the leg lay near the dying person. Another *Life* shocker was a nude man jumping from a chimney to hang himself. Still another death picture was the outline of a human face and body in a mass of Italian mud in which the person suffocated during a flood.

Because of the mounting death rate of auto wreck victims, some newspapers are printing pictures of mangled bodies and crumpled, twisted cars. These papers didn't print such pictures before the present alarming death rate came about. The editorial aim is to shock readers into driving sanely, to impress upon readers that it could happen to them.

Some papers have policy about photographing women or teenagers smoking or consuming alcoholic beverages. A few well-known papers with large circulations do not accept either tobacco or alcoholic beverage advertisements. No reputable paper wishes to print subject matter which is in bad taste, which will offend readers or degrade morals. With a glance, most editors know whether a photo will violate an editorial "thou shalt not."

Now comes the third problem, that of deciding whether the photo content justifies publication.

Any posed record shot of a group of people which observes the eight points set forth in Chapter 9 probably will be published. Such photos were made to enable papers to give information to readers. Briefly, the nine check points for such pictures include:

1. Objective in making the photo: To show what something looks like.

2. Avoid dead space by posing the people in geometric arrangements.

3. Get action into the photo.

4. Have unity. Use eye direction to aid your unity.

5. Depth of field increases interest.

6. Use change of pace placement of people in geometric arrangements.

7. Get the biggest possible image outline in the given space.

8. Important small detail which must be seen quickly and easily will determine
   a. the size (space) the photo must be if it is effective;
   b. how severely the photo must be cropped to display the photo properly without wasting space.

9. Only one main center of interest with other action subordinate to it.

Ellard Formula

What if you have a *record shot of a news event*[1] which isn't a posed shot of a group of people. How will you decide whether to publish the picture? The Ellard formula[2] is a most useful aid in the absence of experience.

This guide assigns 33-1/3 points to each of three points on which you must score the photo content, and a photo must achieve 60 points to be published.

1. Action: How much is in the photo? 33-1/3 points

2. News value: Does the photo depict an event of much or little news interest? 33-1/3 points

3. Personality: Is the person in the photo someone whom most readers readily recognize and know something about (political leaders, Hollywood stars, sports performers)? 33-1/3 points

Look at the four photos on the next page and score them by this formula. After you do this exercise, you probably will conclude that

---

[1]News has been defined as a record or photo of an event which will interest a lot of people. The more people which the account/photo interests, the more important the news is. Elements of news, which help the inexperienced know news when they meet it, include immediacy, timeliness, personality, oddity, drama, proximity, survival, conflict, progress or change, human interest (emotion), sex, ambition, and escape. People read only three kinds of items: 1. That which touches their lives directly (a better job, higher taxes, their family or friends). 2. That which entertains and amuses them (often emotion). 3. That which is significant because it affects many lives (war, flood, tornado).

[2]Vitray, Mills, and Ellard, *Pictorial Journalism*, McGraw Hill Book Company, Inc., New York and London, 1939, Chapter 3.

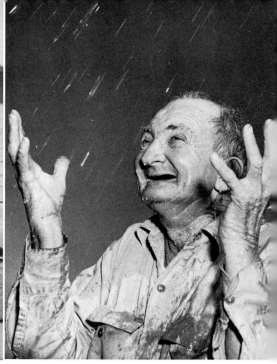

106. USING THE ELLARD FORMULA. Compare these four pictures with the criteria in the text and try to rate them according to the Ellard scale.

(Above left) Wet Rooster in a Flood, Keith Barlow, Ryde, N.S.W., Australia.

(Above right) Thou Waterest The Earth. Harvey Belgin, San Antonio Light, Texas.

(Below left) Angry Mother, Jerry McNeill, UPI.

(Below right) Conversation. William C. Beall, Washington, D.C. Daily News.

the Ellard guide, while useful for judging news-type photos, has its limitations. If relied upon for all photos, some interesting photos which readers enjoy would not be published.

Any emotional shot which also includes either news or a personality or both is of more interest to the reader because of these added values. But the emotional picture merits publication even if these other two values are missing. Many wordminded news editors have a tough time accepting this idea. But progressive, thinking editors do believe and use this idea.

Kalish and Edom[3] also mention two other important factors that merit consideration by editors in judging photos. These two factors are (1) the physical appeal in photo content and (2) reader preference for subject matter in photo content.

Appeal, according to Kalish and Edom, deals with photos which repeat the pattern of similar objects or which have bizarre subject matter. Repetition of pattern in a photo gives the content rhythm and a feeling of action, even when the objects are inanimate. An example of bizarre subject matter would be any kind of subject which is unusual enough to cause the reader to take a quick second look. An ant in a 3-column blowup is a terrible creature to behold. So photos with either repetition of pattern or odd or repulsive subject matter are said to have *physical appeal* — physical because you see the outlines of the subject matter with your eyes.

Another kind of appeal is *universal appeal*. The theme of a novel or short story or the content of a photo has universal appeal when a lot of people understand the situation, have a strong interest in it, and readily identify with the situation. People usually understand situations best which they have experienced. Examples of universal appeal would include birth, love, marriage, death, war, and disaster. For years covers on the *Saturday Evening Post* have helped sell the magazine because artists have captured in paint moments out of the lives of many people: A teen-age girl after her first dance puts her orchid in the family refrigerator; an over-weight woman at a soda counter drinking a No-calorie drink as she looks longingly at a hot fudge sundae with whipped cream which another customer is enjoying.

Studies of reader preference for subject matter[4] seem to indicate that readers enjoy the following topics in the order in which they are listed: 1. Babies and children; 2. a. travel and scenery; b. people and places in

[3]*Ibid.*, Kalish and Edom, *Picture Editing*, Holt, Rinehart and Winston, Inc., New York, 1951.
[4]*Ibid.*, pp. 89-90. Based on two readership studies, *Graphic Graflex* Photography; Copyright, 1948, by Morgan & Lester, and the second by Bert W. Woodburn, "Reader Interest in News-paper Pictures," *Journalism Quarterly*, September, 1947.

169

the news; 3. human interest: a. human, b. animal, c. nature, d. science; and 4. special interests. Some of the special interests would include sports, society, fashion, and finance.

Summary

1. Physical characteristics. Will the photo reproduce on newsprint?

2. Paper policy: Will the photo offend or startle the paper's readers?

3. Photo content: Does it a) have a message, b) tell a story, c) or evoke emotion?

    a. The *record* shot gives information. It may be either a

        1) Posed photo of a group of people (Observe nine points in shooting it);

        2) A news event or a personality. Action added to either kind of a photo results in a picture worth publishing, says the Ellard formula.

    b. The *emotional* shot makes the reader feel or it amuses him.

        A photo which causes reader feeling/amusement merits publication, even though it has no news value or a news personality. A picture with emotion + either news or personality or both is a better picture than one with emotion alone.

        1) Physical appeal enhances a photo by giving it rhythm and motion (by repetition of pattern) or by giving it shock value (bizarre subject matter such as enlargements of insects which readers aren't accustomed to seeing).

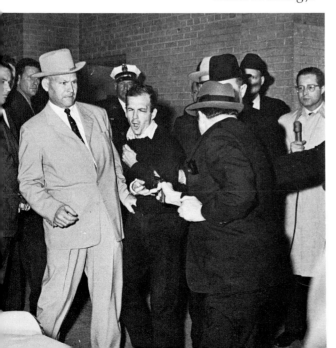

107. A top spot news photo is this widely used photograph of the death of Lee Harvey Oswald, the man accused of killing President Kennedy. Bob Jackson, Dallas Times Herald.

108. SOTP! An alert photographer out on another assignment noted this error in spelling and brought back a page 1 feature shot which gave readers a chuckle. Tom Blevins, Norman Transcript.

2) Universal appeal: Is the story so well understood and so widely experienced that readers readily identify with it?

3) How does the subject matter rate with readers?

4) The following principles discussed in relation to the posed group record shot apply to emotional photos: Dead space, action, depth of field, unity, one center of interest, biggest image outline in a given space, and having small important detail big enough to be seen easily.

SUMMARIZED CHECK LIST — CHART 21

I. RECORD OR DOCUMENTARY SHOT: To show what something looks like (See Chapter 9).

In Exposing Your Negative

1. Use *geometric arrangement* of people to save space: Triangle, stair-step, stagger.

   a. Eliminate *dead space* horizontally and vertically.

   b. Use *change-of-pace placement* of people in geometric arrangements.

2. Get *action* into the scene: A gesture, lively facial expression; have *one* do something while others watch.

171

109. Man's technical genius has put satellites into orbit, but he still is failing miserably on the solution of social problems. One of the straws in the wind of human frailty and lost hope is the rising tide of suicides. This one was posed for a story on suicides. Bob Albright, Oklahoman & Times.

3. Achieve *unity*. Use eye-direction to help with unity and emphasis.

   Aids to unity:

   a. Overlap

   b. Lines of transgression

   c. Diagonal lines, converging lines

   d. Subjects look at point of interest, point to it.

4. Achieve *depth of field* by placing subject matter in foreground, midground, background.

5. Have *one* main *center of interest* with other action subordinate to it.

In Making Your Enlarged Positive

1. Get the *biggest image outline in the given space.* Increases reader impact.

2. *Important small detail* must be big in outline and easily recognized.

   Important small detail determines

   a. The *space* which will have to be *given to a photo* to make it effective. Photos with important small detail require more space than those without such detail.

   b. How drastic the *cropping* must be to conserve space and still tell the story and have the small detail easily recognized.

II. EMOTION OR MOOD SHOT: To affect the reader's emotion, causing joy, sadness, laughter. (See Chapter 10).

    1. *How do you feel about the subject* matter which you are about to photograph?

       What does this subject matter say to you?

       How can you convey your idea/feelings to the reader?

          Ask yourself: What am I trying to tell the reader or to make him feel?

              How can I make the reader feel/see what I feel/see?

    2. *Emphasize* details in the scene which convey your feeling/theme/emotion.

    3. *Exclude* or subordinate details in the scene which detract or add nothing to the feeling/theme/emotion.

III. OTHER USEFUL TECHNIQUES for getting better photos (See Chapter 11).

    1. Camera angle
        a. Normal: Eye level, waist level
        b. Higher than normal: Shooting down on subject
        c. Lower than normal: Shooting up on subject

    2. Proximity of camera to subject
        a. Long shot for overview   d. Extreme close-up
        b. Medium shot   e. 2-in-1 shot: Combine a
        c. Close-up   close-up + long shot

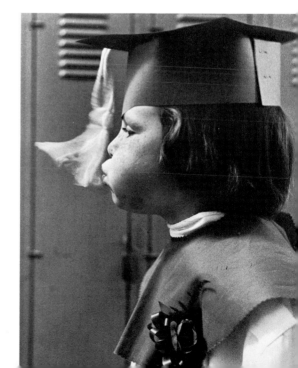

110. An ingenious yet simple approach to telling a story that rolls around every year—graduation. Photographers who consistently bring back bell-ringing photographs like this from routine assignments win a warm spot in the editor's heart. Such a quality photo will get a 3-to-4-column spread on page-1 with a by-line. A clip book of such photos is your passport to a higher paying job. Edward R. Noble, Pontiac Press.

111. (Left) How would you have shown your readers the winners in a target-shooting contest in just one photograph? How about placing the winners behind a torn-out hole in the target? Add drama by showing bullet punctures in the target. Don't forget to get action into the faces. Edward R. Noble, Pontiac Press.

112. (Right) Human interest involving animals and humor is a sure-fire formula. This photograph was good enough to make *Life* Magazine. Elaine Wilsey, Virginia, Minnesota.

3. Significant detail: A detail or details in photo content which clarify, tell story to reader, or answer such questions as who, what, when, where, why, how.

EX. Man in work clothes could be any kind of a laborer. Add a pitchfork (significant detail). Now the picture says "farmer."

4. Silhouette emphasizes *action* because details of person's expression and dress are eliminated. Its strong contrasting tones (black of the silhouette) is excellent in a picture series for *eye contrast*. Use it when you need a *symbolic* photo: Burden Bearer — he represents hard work to the reader.

5. The individual is the photo of anyone which would assist you to identify the person in a police line up. Features and expression of the person are shown. The individual and the silhouette represent opposites. Each has its particular place in photography and should be used properly.

6. Symbols of action
   a. Freeze action
   b. Blur it
   c. Diagonal lines
   d. Content off balance
   e. Series of photos
   f. Pattern of lights at night.

7. Frame your photo to hold the reader's eye in the photo longer. Dark tones of frame provide contrast.

8. Emphasis v. subordination must be used when you have more than one object against the plain background.
   a. One person in action, others watch.
   b. Make one object bigger; put in foreground.
   c. Eye goes to white, light tones. Control light, background tones.
   d. The unique: one girl, many boys.
   e. Converging lines: railroad tracks.
   f. Arrow, hand, "look" all point to object to be emphasized.

9. Four ways to achieve illusion of space
   a. Scale or size: Show a known object (hand, human figure, car) in a scene to tell reader whether photo content covers a big, normal, or small area.

113. One of the fringe benefits of being a hard-bitten city editor is that you get first claim on photographs like this one which newspapers refuse to publish, even though such photographs turn up nearly every week from a variety of sources. But the editor's "art collection" must be kept under lock, or lesser staff members will filch their favorite prints. Ewing Galloway, New York.

114. (Right) Other poses suggestive of unbridled love or sex are not published by family newspapers, even in the amusement section. Film publicity agents keep a fairly steady stream of such photos in the mail. The photos are thrown away or find their way into the editor's private collection. But they don't get published.

      b. Depth of field is achieved by

          1) Indistinctness, fuzziness. Lack of sharp outlines in background objects suggest distance between the foreground and the background. Achieve by

              a) Using a big f/stop

              b) Exposing a scene where haze in the air causes distant buildings to be indistinct.

          2) Backlighting which produces long shadows which enhance the illusion of space and size.

      c. Third dimension increases illusion of depth: Place objects foreground, midground, and background.

      d. Perspective

         You associate distance with diminishing size. Foreground people are large and sharp while background people are smaller and not so sharp.

         You associate distance with converging of lines of a street or a railroad.

10. Poster effect

      a. Simple clear-cut message that's quickly/easily grasped without study.

      b. One dominant object against a plain background. If scene requires more people than one object, subordinate the others.

      c. No important small detail should be too small to be quickly, easily seen.

11. Expository load is a photo with a great deal of detail. Details in the photo content should tell the story. The more detail a photo has, the bigger the story it should tell. A photo can't have both expository load and poster effect. Decide which is your goal.

12. Composition rules. See page 150.

13. Physical appeal results when you repeat a pattern of similar objects in the scene (marching soldiers, picket fence, sand dunes) or when the subject matter is so bizarre that the reader will do a double take on seeing it (blow up an insect which looks like a fierce, pre-historic monster).

14. Night time exposures.

15. Changing from the standard lens to either a wide angle or telephoto lens.

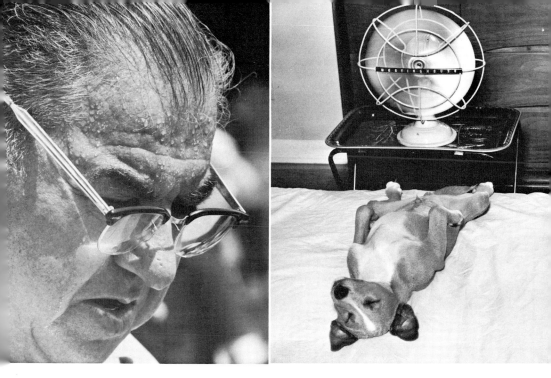

115. WEATHER PICTURES. Weather is a big continuing story for the news photographer. It isn't easy to make a top weather shot that will make page 1. The story has to be told in the picture so the reader will feel it; if it generates a chuckle, so much the better. (Top left) This perspiring gentleman typifies summer. But will the droplets reproduce in a newspaper cut? Earl Seubert, Minneapolis Tribune. (Top right) No question of this summer shot catching the reader's eye! Jack Tinney, Plymouth Meeting, Pa. (Bottom left) Thunderstorm breaks the heat—a good change of pace from the usual rain picture. (Bottom right) Winter, and this poor duck froze to the ice. Jim Argo, Oklahoman & Times.

IV. THE GOOD NEWS PICTURE (See Chapter 12).

1. Ellard formula, 1939. Score a photo on following three items:
   a. Action — 33-1/3
   b. News value — 33-1/3.
   c. Personality — 33-1/3
   > To be published, a photo must score 60 points. The formula works well on newstype situations, but it eliminates a lot of photos which are bell ringers with readers.

2. Kalish-Edom idea: Any photo which will cause reader EMOTION is worthy of publication. If the photo also depicts a news event, so much the better. BUT news value is NOT essential in a photo which does have emotion.

   Newspapers need and use both the record and the emotion shots. Record shots do not have emotion. They show what somebody looks like and provide information. They have greater reader interest if the person is a personality. Emotional shots provide either amusement or emotion. They sometimes also provide information, but this is not their main function. Emotion plus appeal is better than appeal alone.

3. Consider reader preference for subject matter (listed in order of decreasing preference):
   a. Babies and children
   b. 1) Travel and scenery
      2) People, places in news
   c. Human interest
      1) human   3) nature
      2) animal 4) science
   d. Special interests
      1) sports
      2) society
      3) fashion
      4) finance

4. Readers like big photos.

   A glossy print loses about 1/4 of its original detail in reproduction on news print. When big photos are used, this loss of original detail is partially compensated for. But with a small image outline plus this loss of detail, the reader won't quite figure out what the picture content is trying to say. The space used for a small photo with indistinct details is wasted.

   Get the head size of a 1-column mug shot bigger than the space it must fill, so that part of the top of the head and the back have to be cropped off.

   Each time a photo is doubled in size (up to 4 columns) the number of readers who will spend time looking at the photo will increase.

CHAPTER 13

Getting Photo Ideas

Seek Ideas Editors Will Buy

This discussion on finding photo ideas will be from the view of what kinds of photos will sell in specific markets. Half of the battle is knowing what your client wants and then supplying his need. Probably the section in this chapter on photo stories ideas for Sunday news feature and roto sections and for general-interest house publications will have the information which you expected.

A free lance can point his camera at any one of four kinds of photo situations and probably find a market for his prints. Newspapers and press services want pictures of people and events in the news which will interest readers. Newspapers, magazines, and advertising agencies need pictures for advertisements. Many manufacturing companies have house magazines in which they publish pictures and stories of how their products are used. Sunday news feature sections, and general interest house publications, and magazines need good photo stories. Since each of these four situations is a different market, ideas for photos must be considered in relation to each market.

Newspapers as a Market for the Single Photo

Newspapers use both record shots and emotional shots. As indicated in Chapter 9 the record shot shows what something looks like which is in the news: State University's new coach, a clash between strikers and police, or the fire department putting out a blaze at the Mayor's home. Emotional shots make the reader chuckle, frown, or slam his fist down on a desk. Either type of photo situation is a proper news picture. The record shot of a news event is the pack horse, carrying most of the picture load. However, the emotional shot — even though it has no news value — gets the big play on page one and is the spice for the paper.

116. SEASONAL AND HOLIDAY PICTURES ARE ALWAYS IN DEMAND. (Left) Early morning on the river during a vacation. Bob Taylor, Cordell, Okla. (Right) Summer heat drives kids to the "ole swimmin' hole" for a cooling off dip. Bob Taylor, Cordell, Okla.

From the standpoint of time and space, news events fall into one of three categories: 1. Past events which are being written or photographed in the present: newly elected officers of a club are photographed; 2. future events which are being written or photographed in the present; a governor is photographed as he declares he will be a candidate for a third term; 3. and spot news which is described (Radio and TV) or photographed as it happens: Sports events and disasters like fires and floods.

No newspaper or press association is omnipresent. In spite of the fact that a sound metropolitan paper has staff photographers, correspondents scattered throughout its circulation area, and the services of AP and UPI, big news events break without a professional's camera being on hand to film the story. Who often films this spot news? Amateurs who were nearby with their cameras.

Arnold Hardy was a student at Georgia Tech when the famous Winecoff Hotel fire broke out in Atlanta around 4 a.m. in December, 1946. For his photos, Hardy was paid $1,290 by Associated Press.

TEST YOUR IDEAS BEFORE TAKING THEM TO AN EDITOR — CHART 22

1. Will it have reader interest?
   a. Will the photo content touch an interest of readers or show the familiar?
   b. Does the content contain
      1) human interest
      2) the odd or unusual
      3) conflict or combat
      4) universal interest situations
      5) Four basic instincts
         a) survival
         b) sex
         c) ambition
         d) escape
   c. Will the content entertain or create an emotional spark?
2. Is the idea photogenic?
   Some ideas do not lend themselves to being photographed.
3. Will the finished picture say something, have a message?
   EX. Suppose the President of the United States makes a tough speech warning Russia to take care.
   NOT GOOD: A mug shot of the President with a friendly smile.
   GOOD: The President gesturing vigorously with a hard fist. His expression should be either earnest or grim.
4. Couples must be married 50 years or more before editors show much interest. An action shot of the couple working on their ceramics hobby will be preferred to a bust shot. And a lively or tart quote for the cutline will help.
5. People have to die in wrecks before editors want wreck photos. Try for more than twisted steel and torn bodies.
   How about a speedometer stuck at 110 miles?
   Or a broken whiskey bottle in the foreground with the car behind?
6. If the following are accepted by an editor, the picture and cutline must have a twist, a news angle, or an oddity:
   a. Dance school recital — a personality like Fred Astaire doing the routine with the kids
   b. School play
   c. Children's birthday parties
   d. Miniature villages, electric train layouts, etc.
   e. Gardens, flower beds
   f. Payment of election bets
   g. Someone who has "earned" recognition for a good deed
7. Queens of any kind — band, Maypole, tomato — are usually welcome.
   A story-telling photo with action is better than a pretty girl with a big grin.
   Shoot as she's crowned, as she throws her flowers to her attendants, checks her "war" paint before she makes her appearance, kicks off her high heels after the event.
8. Many papers insist that a scholarship be at least $200 or more before using a photo of the recipient.
9. Editors want pictures that
   a. Show how people live and what they do;
   b. Reflect the current scene.
10. Contrived pictures are frowned on.
11. Editors consider good taste and good will in pictures they buy.
12. Most group shots, unless by assignment, are a gamble. A definite news angle helps the sale if you don't have an assignment.

181

117. MORE SEASONAL PICTURES. When school
starts you know summer is officially ended.
Myron Harding, Boulder Daily Camera.

The S. S. Vestris, en route to South America in 1928, was wrecked and
110 lives were lost. A crewman, Fred Hanson, photographed the story
of destruction and death. The New York Daily News paid him $500
for his undeveloped film and a $500 bonus when his pictures were
good. Max Peter Haas, a professional photographer, made pictures of
the mad dog killers, Anthony and William Esposito, during a 20
minute gun battle in downtown New York in which two were killed
and two others were wounded. Haas realized more than $4,000 for
the sale of these photographs.

Spot news is exciting and when one hits the big story, it is profitable
to photograph. But anticipating spot news is like trying to predict
where lightning will strike. If you should find the big story in front
of your lens, get the *undeveloped* film to some newspaper office or
press association quickly. If you have to mail the film, use a light-tight
container and clearly label "undeveloped film." Be sure to get names
and addresses of people in the pictures. Check the spelling of the
names. Other vital information which will help you sell your spot news
photos includes the information you'd want to know about the event
if you read about it, the who, when, where, why, what, and how of
the situation.

More than likely, most of your sales possibilities for newspaper
photos will have to come from either past events or future events
filmed in the present, rather than from spot news. Remember, news
is the account/photo of an event which will interest many readers.
An important point about reader interest is that it is sparked by most

182

any topic which touches his life, which will benefit him, or which depicts the familiar to him. Teen-agers are interested in clothes styles, cars, vacation jobs, how to attract and interest the opposite sex. College students share some of these interests. Too, they're concerned with selecting the right preparation for their life work, getting a job after graduation, and marriage. Picture stories will be read which show readers how to do something they're interested in a better way: how to play a better game of golf or bridge or poker, how to plan an inexpensive but stimulating vacation, get ahead faster, build a patio, or care for the lawn. If a photograph doesn't present information which touches the reader's life (his interests or the familiar places and people he knows about) or if the photo content doesn't entertain or strike an emotional response, it won't get reader attention. When the following elements are present in photo content, the chances of achieving reader or entertainment or emotion are increased: Human interest, the odd and unusual, conflict and combat, universal interest situations, and four basic instincts which psychologists say all people exhibit in varying degrees — survival, sex, ambition, and escape.

Survival is in flood pictures as well as the battle of two football teams in a New Year's bowl game. Someone has to win and lose. Sex in photos can be the kiss of two movie stars, the picture of a girl announcing her engagement, or a shapely lass with very little on. The picture of any form of achievement in any field — science, sports, society, religion — can be achievement. Some people are spurred to greater effort by pictures of those who do succeed; some wonder why

118. MORE SEASONAL PICTURES. And for the grown ups, with summer over, it's harvest time. Bob Taylor, Cordell, Oklahoma.

119. MORE SEASONAL PICTURES. (Above, Left) School brings football, band practice, pep squad, meetings, working on the school paper, new clothes, new teachers, new friends, and the opportunity to learn and mature. (Above right) Before you quite realize it, Thanksgiving has come. (Below, left) Hard on the heels of Thanksgiving is Christmas. (Below, right) New Year's Eve party? It was the greatest! Anyway, I think it was. Wow, my head! (All photos on this page by Bob Taylor, Cordell, Okla.)

they don't accomplish more when they see others forging ahead. The desire to escape one's immediate responsibilities and problems is represented by photos of man pursuing recreation, on vacation, engaged in a hobby, or participating in a sport.

Chart 22 offers some points against which to test your picture ideas.

An important quality of the straight news photo is immediacy. The event must have just happened. It's possible for one of your news shots of human interest to be rejected through no fault of your photo skill or the picture's content.

Every story and every picture has to compete for the right to be published. On a good news day when space is tight, many good stories and photos get left out. On a bad news day when the paper is loose, some poor stories and photos can land on page one.

As capable as an editor with intelligence and experience can be, he often finds himself publishing a photo which he has told you he wouldn't be interested in. Or he may reject a photo which he has said he probably would be interested in. This situation results because often editors honestly don't know whether they will or will not use a photo until it reaches their desk. On the day before, or the day after, the photo might be rejected. Today, however, it seems to fill a need. So it gets the green light.

In this daily battle of events and pictures for a place in the paper, the editor's basis for acceptance or rejection is his nose for news, his experience with what has clicked or failed in the past, and his ever present desire to print what will fit a need or have appeal for his readers. Subconsciously, the editor asks himself: Will my readers like it? Or, will it tell my readers something they need to know?

Summary on Ideas for Single Newsphoto

1. Look for and shoot photos of people and events in the news.

2. Seek the feature type, human interest (emotion) photo which can be built around universal situations of how people live and react. Good text books for ideas are covers of the *Saturday Evening Post* and cartoons in most slick publications which poke fun at people. Either of these may be found in any library. Look at 100 *Post* covers and make a few notes you will want to study on the kind of content used, the details of the picture, and the appeal and emotion factors in the cover. Do the same for 100 cartoons. If these experiments don't turn the light on for you, so that you can know what to look for in the people around you, concentrate on being a documentary photographer.

185

120. (Left) Girls are supposed to be romantic but this one was more interested in the Valentine candy than in the kissing. (Right) At Easter, you've almost got it made. Soon the grass will be green, flowers will bloom, and school will be out again. Photos by Bob Taylor, Cordell, Oka.

Advertising Photos

Some free lancers have done pretty well with shooting single photos which they marketed through a New York agent. The agent then sold the photos to publications for either article or advertising illustrations. These photographers looked for simple or symbolic ideas. Examples of symbols for photos which might sell include:[1]

Wipe the slate clean	Hit the nail on the head
Don't cry over spilt milk	Hit the bull's eye
A new broom sweeps clean	Against the grain
A worn strap holding a child's school books	Cat licking a kitten
Rooster crowing	Holly wreath
Boy shouting, hands on either side of mouth	Frost on a window
	Easter lilies
	American flag
Hands pulling a wishbone	Human bucking wind, rain
Quick as a wink	Mistletoe bough
Like a cat at a mouse hole	Turtle walking alone
Strong tree roots in the ground	

The advice of two agents who have handled thousands of such photographs is pertinent. Ewing Galloway, New York City, has a file of 750,000 negatives. This firm pays from $5 to $50 for a black and white negative. Color brings higher fees and is in great demand.

Mr. Galloway died in 1953. Three associates who operate Ewing

---

[1]Scacheri, op. cit. p. 340.

Galloway now are Thomas McGeough, John C. Kane, and Joseph Hisler. McGeough says an amateur who wants to sell should spend a minimum of one afternoon a month in the library looking at the magazines. He must know what is being done, what competition he has to meet. He should study pictures, seek what caused the editors to buy them, then try to get the same quality into his work.

A tie-in exists between story content and advertisements, says Mr. McGeough. Why is a nationally circulated magazine interested in a story about girls who clerk in a department store? Two reasons. Most people know something about this setting. And department stores are filled with items which are advertised in the magazine — rayon, cotton, ready-to-wear items. A farm scene of grazing cattle which shows fences and a barn has a tie-in to advertised products: stock feed, fence, and roofing materials.

"You don't have to travel to Europe to take saleable pictures," says Mr. McGeough. "Start at home with a kitty on the back doorstep, a rosebush, a snow-covered street. Learn to use light properly, to emphasize people and life and action rather than things, and don't hurry. In our studio, we once spent a whole day photographing a cup of coffee before we got it to suit us."

Although Ewing Galloway has a staff of photographers, it is a ready market for free lance photographers. Changes in styles of clothes, hair, automobiles, and architecture force a constant discarding of outdated negatives and create a void that must be filled. Ewing Galloway and other picture agencies are always hoping the morning mail will bring them the work of a new free lance who can become the source of saleable material.

The biggest obstacle a free lance faces is not the technical end of photography, says Mr. McGeough. The ability to find proper subject matter or see pictures that will interest others and to use good composition — that's the problem! Yet this proper subject matter is everywhere: flowers blooming in a garden, a child at play, a pet which your neighbor owns. Advertising model releases are a must, even from your neighbor whose pet you have photographed.

A simple, well composed photograph of a newly painted, well-landscaped home is easier to sell than some arty, "way out" shot of a broken down barn, says Mr. McGeough. Possible clients for the freshly painted house would include paint companies, siding companies, roofing companies, nurseries and seed and landscape companies, and banks and insurance companies which lend money for mortgages.

Robert I. Nesmith[2], who owned a New York City picture agency for years, said: "*Subject matter does not really matter. How you think and*

121. ACCIDENTS IN THE HOME take a large
toll in lives and injuries. Pictures like this
sell for many purposes. Tom O'Reilly, Chief
Photographer, Toledo Blade.

photograph the subject matters. Just recording the object in front of the camera on film is not enough. *Make pictures which say something:* silent, noisy, strong, soft, smooth, reliable, comfortable, speedy, warm, cold, fresh, pure, mild, lazy, busy, energetic, powerful, safe, quiet, dangerous, happy, worried, cool, refreshing, peaceful, dark, bright, hard, mysterious, graceful, careless, lucky.

"Make pictures which convey a feeling.

"We sold a picture of a cat's paw. The buyer wasn't selling cats. He was selling typewriters. The picture in the advertisement said the typewriter was quiet and cushioned."

Other photo ideas showing feeling which Mr. Nesmith has sold include the small hand of a baby in the large hand of a man (life insurance advertisement); a chain descending tautly into water which says, "Are you dragging anchor?" or "What's holding your business back?"

Landscapes don't sell well. Pictures which say spring, winter or vacation do sell. Cute baby pictures don't sell. But a picture of a baby which says "comfort" would sell to a talcum powder company. The picture has to say something, have a message. Placing a can of talcum powder in the picture of the comfortable baby limits the sale of the picture to that particular talcum powder company. Many other baby products want pictures which say "comfortable," but not with the can of talcum powder in the background.

188

Again, study and analysis of advertising photographs in current magazines show you how selling photographers build a photo around an idea and produce a saleable picture.

The House Magazine Field

This field is a rewarding market for those who understand it, and a frustrating one for those who do not. The product-application story demands a certain editorial type of thinking which many experienced, successful writers in other fields don't seem to grasp.

For the moment, forget about general interest material, which will be discussed in the next section of this chapter. Now, you are concentrating on the product-application story and photo, which has every chance of success. As a matter of fact, 15 or 20 or more product-application stories are possible in nearly every event worthy of coverage.

For example, a soup company decides to build a factory in your town. Offhand, this seems to be a good story to sell to the soup company. Discard such an idea. The company's editor knows all about what his company is doing. He will get all the material he needs from his own organization. Your market will be 15 to 20 other house magazines whose companies had, or will have, some part in the new building.

Ground is broken for the foundation. Whose earth moving equipment is on the job? Shoot several pictures of the different types of equipment in action, write short factual captions, and send them in to the house magazines involved.

The editor of X-Construction Company will welcome the shots because they show his product in use, or they may show a different use for his products, or because the editor couldn't afford to send a staff photographer to get these pictures.

While at the soup company construction, check with the general contractor or the purchasing agent in charge and line up a whole series of pictures and caption stories. Is cast iron pipe used for sewage lines? Photos of the pipe will sell to a cast iron magazine. Whose concrete is being poured? How many firms are involved in the wiring? What kind of electrical equipment is being installed? Who supplies the steel framework? The roofing material? The paint?

What special construction material is being used: glass blocks, decorative brick, insulation material, special paneling, window frames? Whose office equipment will be used: typewriters, office desks, filing cabinets, tabulating machines, check writers, postage machines? Whose business forms and bookkeeping systems?

What delivery trucks are used? Who has the fuel contract? What kind of heating equipment is being installed? How about refrigeration and airconditioning? Who supplies the raw materials for the

122. WHAT DID I DO? People are always holler-
ing at little kids. Tom O'Reilly, Chief Photographer, Toledo Blade.

soup? Who supplies the can and the boxes in which the finished product is shipped to customers?

The possibilities of such stories are limited only by your imagination
and industry. It is at this point that many free lances fail. They cannot
visualize all the products and services which go into even the simplest
of ventures. They do not realize that somewhere, some place, a hard-
working editor would welcome fresh picture and caption material of
his products in use.

The pay? Few magazines pay less than $10 for an ordinary picture
and caption story; the majority pay between $20 and $30; a few at the
top pay $75 and $100.

There is no cut and dried formula, but in a few months the average
free lance finds by trial and error those magazines he likes to work
with. Not all product-application stories sell. Some ideas have been
worked to death. Much depends upon the quality of the free lance's
photos — how well he shows the use of the product. A good craftsman
with imagination and tenacity will make a lot of editors happy. The
craftsman's bank account will grow, too.

Markets for these photos are listed in the Gebbie Press House Magazine Directory, Box 1111, Sioux City, Iowa, 51102.

Photo Stories for Sunday Magazines and General Interest House Publications

Getting ideas for the photo story consists of two processes: 1. Finding out what a specific editor wants; 2. finding topics which are photo-

190

genic in the area in which you live and putting your story together for a particular reading audience.

Two sources can tell you what an editor wants. One source is the editor's own publication. You have to analyze it, take it apart, and study the techniques and the emphasis which the editor will buy. And the second source will be market information published in the following: *Author and Journalist, Writer's Digest, Writer's Market, Gebbie Press House Magazine Directory,*[3] *The Literary Market Place,*[4] *Universal Photo Almanac,*[5] *Editor and Publisher Year Book,*[6] *Printers' Ink Magazine House Organ List,*[7] and *Ayer's Directory of Newspapers and Periodicals.*[8]

REASONS FOR ANALYZING POTENTIAL MARKETS — CHART 23

1. To see what kind of subject matter the editor uses (See Chart 25).

2. To see how the subject matter is handled so you will know how to slant for a particular publication. What is emphasized? What is omitted? Why?

3. To discover the kind of a reader the magazine is aimed at.

4. To note what the editor has published recently so you won't duplicate an idea he has just used. Photographers who query on an idea recently used are confessing that they don't do their homework. Editors are busy, busy, busy. They don't have time for a lazybones. One blooper like this gets you on the editor's dumbbell list. Your next query may be a world beater, but the editor will look at it with a jaundiced eye.

5. To see how the cutlines and the copyblock are written: how many words; any particular style?

6. To learn from those who are publishing how they take a simple idea and make it seem important and interesting enough to earn a check from an editor and attention from readers who have more to do each day than they can possibly get to.

7. To clip and file, or to make a file card of the ideas behind stories which could have happened in your area, and which you could have shot. You can't quit school or college or your job and dash off to the West Coast for a story, then to the East Coast, then abroad. A few photographers for magazines like *Life* lead such lives. But most photographers must consider their investment of time and money when they seek saleable picture ideas. You will make the most money by sticking to your area, which has more stories than you can possibly shoot, if you can only see them.

---

[3]*Gebbie House Magazine Directory,* Box 1111, Sioux City, Iowa 51102, 1954.
[4]R. R. Bowker Company, 1180 Sixth Ave., New York, N.Y. 10036
[5]Tlak Publishing Company, 10 West 33 Street, New York.
[6]1475 Broadway, New York.
[7]205 East 32 Street, New York.
[8]N. W. Ayer and Sons, Philadelphia, Pa.

You may not be enthusiastic about analyzing a lot of picture stories in a publication to which you hope to sell. However, it is essential to do so if you don't want to doom your efforts to failure. Chart 23 outlines the reasons for analyzing picture stories. Chart 24 is a suggested guide for your analysis and Chart 25 shows the possible subject matter classifications for photo ideas.

Too often, a person with creative ability thinks all he has to do to become a selling author is to know how to write. And one who wants to be a free lance photographer often thinks if he has mastered his photographic techniques, his career is launched. Of course both the writer and the photographer are wrong.

Agent Paul R. Reynolds,[9] who handles writers, says five steps are involved in getting an idea and selling it. The Reynolds steps, adapted to photography, include: 1. Getting the idea; 2. researching the idea and writing the shooting script; 3. picking models and setting, readying equipment; 4. shooting the story; 5. selecting the best negatives, enlarging and cropping photos properly, and writing informative, complete cutlines and a copyblock.

In this 5-point program, the photography is step number 4. A lot of other things take place ahead of step 4, or your photo ability and efforts will be wasted. Each step in the 5-point program is essential to turn out a saleable picture story. Analyzing potential markets to which you hope to sell is just as important as shooting the pictures.

Slanting is mentioned, Chart 23, point 2. Because an editor aims at a particular audience which thinks a certain way, and has preferences in subject matter and biases, the editor wants to publish what his customers will buy. The editor has found from experience and reader reaction that a topic handled one way will reach readers, but if other approaches are used, readers do not respond. So the editor wants a picture story tailored to his specification, to fit his readers and what they expect to find in this publication.

ANALYSIS GUIDE FOR A PHOTO STORY — CHART 24

1. Name of magazine being analyzed? Date? Page number where story begins? Editor? Address? Photographer?
2. At what kind of an audience is the magazine aimed?

Age group	Group's special interests	f. travel
Income group	a. home	g. hobby
Vocational group	b. family	h. cultural
(white, blue collar)	c. security	music
Level of education	d. sports	books
Religion	e. clubs, fraternal	art
	groups	drama

---

[9]Paul R. Reynolds Inc., Literary Agents, 599 Fifth Avenue, New York.

3. What subject matter category/categories and elements of interest are in the story? (Chart 25)

4. Write a brief summary of the story idea.

5. Why will the story appeal to, attract, and hold readers?
Subject familiar to many readers?
Universal interest subject?
Strong emotional impact (which emotions)?
Vicarious thrill (entertainment, escape)?
Other?

6. How is human interest (emotion-conflict) introduced/used?

7. Has the focus of the story been limited sufficiently? (Simple theme instead of a complex one?) Think in terms of what this story is a part of and try to evaluate how much the focus has been narrowed.

8. How does each photo advance the action (help tell the story simply, clearly, forcefully)? Begin with the first picture and list the function of each shot in relation to the whole story.

9. Examine the first and the last photos and justify the arrangement.
Does the lead photo cue the reader, prepare him for the subject matter to follow, have top action?

10. Make a note of anything you observe in either photo technique or subject matter which might be of use to you later. Where possible, clip the photo or the story and attach your note and place in right file folder.

11. Note the following on each photo in the story:
    a. Proximity of camera to subject: Long, medium, closeup, combination of close + long?
    b. Angle of camera to subject: Normal, high, low.
    c. Unity present?
    d. Significant detail: Man in work clothes + pitchfork = Farmer
    e. Action: How is it attained?
    f. Emphasis v. subordination. What is emphasized? How? Why? What is subordinated? How? Why?
    g. Use of space illusion
       Scale or size: Include a known object (man, car, hand) in scene to cue reader on whether photo includes a large or a small area
       Depth of field: Background is fuzzy to indicate distance
       Third dimension: Place objects in foreground, midground, and background
    h. Poster effect v. expository load
    i. Physical appeal: Rhythm by repeated pattern; startle reader with bizarre subject matter
    j. Special effects
       1) Lighting, tone used to create mood
       2) Silhouette used

12. How many photos are in longest story? Shortest? Average number in most stories?

13. Are all photos black and white, all colored, or some of each?

14. Was a photo from the story used on the cover? Color?

15. How many words in the longest, shortest, average cutline? Copyblock?

193

Topic Classification of Photographic Subject Matter— Chart 25

1. Children and babies
2. a. Travel and scenic pictures
   b. Persons and places in the news
3. Human interest subjects
   a. Human   c. Nature
   b. Animal   d. Science
4. Topics appealing to a particular group
   a. Business and finance
   b. Cultural pursuits
      1) art   3) ballet   5) theater
      2) books   4) music
   c. Education
   d. Fashion
   e. Food, home furnishings
   f. Outdoor stories
   g. Politics
   h. Religion
   i. Science, medicine
   j. Sports
5. Accidents, disasters
6. Ambition: any form of accomplishment in any field.
7. Conflict, combat
8. Contrast and comparison of past with present
   Present: A big fire in your town
   Photo idea from past: Layout on local big fires for past 20 years
9. Crime
10. Current life of people
    Everyday activites of everyday people.
       EX. How a city rescue squadron operates
11. Escape: Desire to forget the humdrum present for a little while
12. Familiar and unfamiliar: Every community has its special characteristics. What is the most unusual, typical, biggest, smallest, or newest in your community?
    New York has skyscrapers.
    New Orleans has a French quarter.
13. History, historical dates
14. Hobby
15. How to —
16. Interesting people: If not known by name to mass public, they're not celebrities.
    Have overcome handicaps (physical or personality); unusual hobbies; interesting jobs.
    Adventurous: Oil company employees live all over world.
       Missionaries live with strange, little-known people.
       Career diplomats and army personnel.
17. Lawful theft: Keep a file of good picture ideas which you can adapt.
    Another's Picture   *Suggests to You*
    A child's photo   Series of children from many nations
    A toothy horse   Laughing animals
18. Mood
19. Oddity, unusual objects, events, customs
20. Personality, celebrity: Individuals known by name, photograph to mass public
21. Problems
    Revive old stories: Famous unsolved murders
       CBS took President Eisenhower to Normandy Beaches on 20th anniversary of the end of World War 2 and interviewed him on many of the decisions he made 20 years earlier.

22. Sex
23. Seasons, holidays, special events
24. Sidebar to news developments
   EX. Queen Elizabeth's coronation was the news.
   A photo story on the troops which guard her is the sidebar feature.
   People read it because of their interest in Elizabeth, a personality often in the news.
25. Significance: how an event affects the reader's life, affairs.
26. Survival
27. Trends of the times.
   Developments in local, state, national levels
   Cold war between US & Russia: Picture story on the effect of the cold war on the taxpayer.
   Today's inflation: Picture story on things a nickel used to buy.

Slanting is simply shaping a topic to the taste of the audience at which it is directed. In life you talk to different people in different ways, and you discuss different topics with different people. You don't talk to your grandmother, the person to whom you're engaged, your best friend, your boss, or your little brother in the same manner. Nor do you impartially discuss the same topics with each. Topics you hash over with your best friend might offend your grandmother. Some of your grandmother's interest might bore your friend. Well, this same principle holds in either photography or writing, and that's all slanting is: selecting topics and presenting them in a manner calculated to interest a particular audience. There's nothing dishonest or underhanded about it. It's just common sense.

So you have analyzed publications to which you hope to sell. You know the subject matter and the point of view a specific publication desires. Now you know what this publication prefers to consider for purchase.

123. No one wants to be dull, so most play as well as work. An excellent advertising photograph emphasizes the product by putting it in the foreground, by the look of a prop (the boy) and by the zig-zag line action formed by the two bottles and the boy's head. Note how a big image outline is obtained and how extreme cropping has been used. How is unity obtained? Is a frame present? The message: Pepsi and youthful joy and companionship go together. Courtesy, The Pepsi Cola Company, New York.

195

What about those ideas for photos? The receptive mind finds ideas for photos by disciplined observation and by seeking ideas.

You seek tips for ideas *externally:* 1. By reading newspapers and magazines, technical and trade magazines, and books; 2. in your experiences; 3. in the study of your community, state, and region; and 4. by the use of the library. *Internally,* your mind must be active. It must digest and evaluate your findings and suggest ideas to you. Some say you "live pictures" when you ask constantly of all the grist which runs through your mill, "Will it make a picture?"

Reading Newspapers

Stories on the following activities provide tips for individual photos or picture stories: chamber of commerce, extension division of the state university, short courses and hobby interests sponsored by the YMCA, and all organizations which sponsor the appearance of speakers, Hollywood personalities who do readings, singers, Broadway plays and opera, trade and professional associations — steel, oil, beer, American Medical Association, and American Bar Association — are sources for saleable ideas.

MARKETS FOR YOUR PICTURES — CHART 26

Your Situation	*Possible Markets*	
You are in high school or college	School newspaper School yearbook Local newspaper Scholastic Roto	Nearest metropolitan newspaper Roto section or feature section of either metropolitan or regional paper
You are employed but you're a weekend, vacation hobby photographer	Local paper Nearest metropolitan newspaper Roto or feature section of either metropolitan or regional paper Following roto sections are strongly regional in interest: Chicago Sunday Tribune Magazine Courier Journal Sunday Magazine, Louisville, Ky. Detroit News Sunday Pictorial Dixie Roto, Times-Picayune Magazine, New Orleans, La. Empire Magazine, Denver Post Picture, Minneapolis Sunday Tribune Providence Sunday Journal, Rhode Island Following Sunday newspaper sections are broader in interest and more difficult to sell:	

American Weekly	Parade
Family Week	Star Weekly,
New York Times Magazine	Toronto, Ontario
	This Week Magazine

 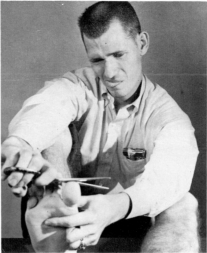

124. A TOUCH OF HUMOR SELLS PICTURES, TOO. (Left) Window shopping, as seen by a University of Oklahoma student. (Right) Right of Privacy? Can't a fella trim his toe nails without some photographer sneaking a shot? Paul Burns, University of Oklahoma student.

Industrial publications of general interest for customers

Standards are very high, but the pay is good

Friends, Chevrolet Division, General Motors
Buick Magazine, General Motors
Chrysler Events Magazine, Chrysler Corporation
People & Places, De Soto Division,
    Chrysler Corporation
Lincoln Mercury Times, Ford Motor Company
Ford Times, Ford Motor Company
Pontiac Warrior, Pontiac Division,
    General Motors
Monsanto Magazine, Chemicals
The Four-Leaf Clover, Clover Farm Stores Corp.
Farm & Home News, Farm, grain, feed
Lever Standard, soap
Hometown — The Rexall Magazine, drugs
Prudential Family, insurance
Savings & Loan Publications, Columbus 12, Ohio
Ford Farming, Ford Motor Company
Farming Today, Ferguson tractors

Fraternal Magazines

American Legion Magazine	The Lion
Elks Magazine	Optimist
Kiwanis Magazine	Rotarian
	VFW Magazine

Top Slicks: Life, Look

197

Newspapers and magazines contain stories on interesting people: men performing a job done by a woman or vice versa (Cabby is a Lady: Macon, Missouri),[10] those who have overcome handicaps, either physically or in personality; those who have achieved success in jobs; those who are adventurous and spend their lives in foreign countries with oil companies, the armed forces, in the diplomatic service, or as missionaries.

Newspapers and magazines use copy on problems which suggest ideas for "how-to" picture stories: gain weight, lose weight, be popular, get a job, hold a job, avoid slums, get more people out to church, improve human relations in the labor-management area.

The following news clippings provided tips which could have made good picture stories.

Henryetta, Oklahoma — Jim Shoulders was notified he had been chosen World Champion All-Around Cowboy, making him the official rodeo champion of all time. A lot to work with: personality, action, animals, achievement, conflict (man v. brute strength), escape for the reader who can vicariously ride to victory with Shoulders, and survival (can he outlast the bucking horse; will he win again next year?).

Midland, Texas — Two painters bet $1,000 that one can stay awake longer than the other. They were groggy by the 87th hour. Their activities, facial expressions during the test would be the story.

Presbyterian Louis H. Evans, 55, one of the most successful clergymen in the U.S., was relieved of duties in relation to only one church and made minister-at-large for the Board of National Missions, because Presbyterians felt that his preaching should reach people from coast to coast.

A 15-year-old girl had her own dance studio where she taught pupils from age 3 through 50. She had more pupils than she could handle and maintained a waiting list.

What about the couple with 14 children? The angle used for a picture story was that everyone in the family shared the work required to keep the house clean, clothes ready, and meals prepared.

A champion of anything (golf, bridge, football, basketball, baton twirling, tap dancing, ballet, hair styling, crime detection, rose growing, ceramics, judo) conducts a clinic. These are naturals for the "how-to" story. Champions have other angles. For example: A German Shepherd which won 150 shows made a picture story.

The annual announcement of the college yearbook queens is accompanied by formal portraits. The metropolitan/regional roto or

---

[10]*Friends, Chevrolet Dealers,* 3-135 General Motors Building, Detroit 2, Michigan, Jan. 1959.

magazine section probably would use the formal portraits plus a picture of each girl as a baby, or formal portrait plus an informal action pose of each girl engaged in her hobby.

LIFE MAGAZINE ANALYSIS FOR A 6-MONTH PERIOD[11] — CHART 27

Subject Matter Published	Number Stories about Same Subject	Reader Interest Elements
1. Animals, nature	9	Unusual, odd, HI (emotion) Trend of times, current life of people
2. Personality, celebrity	9	Sex, oddity, successful in work
3. Trends of the times	9	Youth, oddity, problem, significance, HI (emotion) children
4. Science, medicine	3	Oddity, children
5. Education	4	Unusual, children
6. Religion	3	Odd, celebrity
7. Seasons: Spring in Arkansas Winter in a Summer Resort	2	Children, sex, scenic
8. Problem: Economic Labor v. Management	1	Oddity: One company which succeeds in human relations
9. Hobby	1	Oddity: Man collects confederate money

EXAMPLES

Animal
Oddity: How geese are fattened by stuffing them mechanically.
 A Minnesota man keeps otters for pets. He's had 150 in 25 years.
HI (emotion): Greedy $9,000 Hippo eats a straw hat and has the stomach ache.
Trend of times: A Rage for Parakeets.*
Current life of people: A child's dog has a spring litter of pups.*

Personality/Interesting People
Sex: Prize Blackboard Beauty: Prettiest US School Teacher.*
Unusual: Nation's biggest landlord is Secretary of Interior.

Trends of the Times
Youth, oddity: Topping Time in Idaho: Goofy Haircuts of High School Boys.*
Problem, significance: Working Wives: Have 4 million and Number Is Rising.*
 Consider the Lowly Penny: How It Touches Many Lives.

Education
Unusual, sex: High school students help their teacher with her wedding.*

The local paper has a good feature story on a group of 10 business men who get together frequently to indulge in barbershop harmony. One photo shows the group singing. A photographer who spends an evening with the group certainly ought to be able to get an interesting, action-filled series of pictures. How about expressions and gestures as they sing different kinds of music: love, humor, spiritual, folklore, railroad, military?

---

[11] From January 1 through June, 1953.
* These are stories which you could have planned, shot, and sold in *your* own area.

125. THE GAG PICTURE. Dad and Junior ham it up for Mother's camera. Clarence Earl Norris, University of Oklahoma student.

The opening of a new lake swimming area is announced. This is a natural for kids and ham humor. Try a series of 4-7 photos all on the diving board: a formal diving position; arching the back in air; weak knees tumbling off sideways; the kid who slips and sits down suddenly on the board; a poor diver as he is about to hit the water in a belly buster.

A story about the state penitentiary rodeo where convicts will do the riding, roping, and bulldogging holds interest.

The closing of school brings problems. How will the kids spend their time? What will this change mean to mothers? What kinds of jobs will some kids gets? How do they get these jobs?

The opening of school brings another set of problems. One is traffic safety, getting kids to school and back safely. A picture series on common sense rules for kids to observe has been good for a long time. Another series on bicycle traffic safety precautions might be done.

A 3-paragraph story serves as a photo story tip. The story says a nursery will begin practice on its annual spring operetta which will be "Goldie Locks" and involves 38 children. The rehearsals, getting costumes, and then the big afternoon plus spontaneous improvising by members of the cast should make a good picture series. Children rate highest in reader interest.

A group of 40 former professional showmen and amateur performers including clowns, gymnasts, comedians, and magicians have been staging shows at orphanages, hospitals, and before underprivileged audiences around Oklahoma City for 10 years. Mmm, excellent raw material for a picture story. Kids again. Lots of emotion. Action.

Your Experiences

Your present, the past, and future hold endless ideas for picture stories. The alarm rings in the morning. How do you respond? Do you leap up cheerfully or do you stumble groggily out of bed? Or do you go through a series of morning antics calculated to postpone the inevitable? A couple of story ideas here, maybe. In shaving, you become aware of how silly your expressions are in the mirror. This idea has been done. Maybe you saw it. But it will be done again somewhere. Or you might do a slap-stick story of a man trying to decide whether he needs a shave.

Looking forward to vacation, your wife has found a good article on ways to keep the kids quiet and busy during the long drive. Make pictures of this.

Your little daughter is having trouble with dandruff.

A physician provides the solution. Your wife tells you how she will apply his advice to your daughter. Dandruff — a common problem of people plus an authoritative solution. A natural for a how-to story with pictures.

Don't count the past as lost. It isn't. It's fallow ground for picture story ideas. Spend time making lists on the following questions:

What are the places for which you have a lasting interest? Why? Are there a lot of other people who feel the same way you do about these places?

Recall experiences which caused you intense emotion. What were the emotions? Probably many of these emotional moments are universal experiences which many others have had. A cartoonist had one panel a week for years on "Life's Darkest Moment." Could you put together in one series of pictures "Life's Most Embarrassing Moment?" Were you a small town kid? Did you take in the wonders of a big city on an all-day trip or during a visit to relatives? Such background as this provided the idea for a "A Big Time in the Big City."[12] You can think of a lot of pictures that would be possibilities for such a series: the kid at the governor's office, in a museum, at the state fair, watching a new skyscraper go up, at the zoo, the airport.

Remember how you used to hate dancing school, and the manners you had to use, the giggling little girls in starchy white dresses? Kids still go to dancing schools. Some of these schools emphasize etiquette. The story could be documentary: what happens and when. Or how manners are emphasized. Or from a little boy's point of view, showing

---

[12]Friends, *op. cit.*, June, 1960.

all the things about the dancing school that he hates. A published picture story on a dancing school was titled "Charm School for Cool Cats."[13]

Conjure up the "character type" people you have known. What traits made these people characters? How did others react to your characters? This ought to be good for a series of ideas. An obvious one: irritating habits of bosses, secretaries, teachers, speakers. Others: the party bore and his habits; the biggest gossip you know and how he or she operates. On these and similar human foibles at which we can laugh, magazines have printed many single panel cartoon situations which can be clipped over a period and translated and adapted to a picture story. The spending wife and her agonizing husband is a favorite theme.

What about the problems in your personal life which affected you deeply or shaped your attitude toward life? Are you up to adapting a *Reader's Digest* article on the art of living into a photo story? Left-handed people have trouble in a right-handed world. This idea made a good picture story.[14]

Your observations will provide good photo story tips. What about those gargoyles on the court house which intrigue you? Most people ignore them because the gargoyles can't be seen without looking up. How about a series of pictures of the hideous stone figures and title it, "Anyone Here You Know?"

Seeing the neighborhood kids play at being grown up people by dressing in cast-offs of their parents inspired a picture story titled, "It Takes Practice to Be a Lady."[15] You go by the feed store to buy some fertilizer for your lawn. The biggest truck you've ever seen is pulling away from the curb. It has a sign on the door indicating that it belongs to a chicken hatchery. A few questions asked in the feed store reveal this hatchery is one of the biggest in your part of the country. It ought to be good for several stories. One might be titled, "His Chickens Cross Many Roads."[16]

Study Your Community, State, Region

How do people in your area make their living? What are the economic resources of the area? What is the community noted for?

---

13 *Ibid.*, April, 1959.
14 *Ibid.*, March, 1959.
15 *Ibid.*, April, 1961.   16 *Ibid.*, May, 1959.

126. Happy people often have a hobby which provides a creative outlet and rewards them with objects which their hands have produced. Al McLaughlin, Chief Photographer, Oklahoman & Times.

How does the state spend the taxpayer's money? What activities cost the most? Where did the people come from who settled the area? What was the cultural heritage? Their present customs? Any interesting foreign communities? What are the most interesting, unusual, different, least known, best known features of the community, the region, and the state? What about the folklore? What is happening in business, politics and government, education, agriculture, religion, civic activities, clubs, recreation, law enforcement, human relations, social conditions, science, and culture? Who are the leaders in these areas? Who are the nationally recognized authorities? What is the source of pride or shame in the community, the region, the state?

The yellow pages in a telephone directory are an excellent place to begin a survey of your community. A fertile mind can get many ideas to check out for picture stories by flipping through the yellow pages.

As you travel about your area, don't overlook a common theme around which you can build picture stories. For example the theme, "Patterns in Stone and Steel,"[17] would permit pictures to come from scenes which are miles apart. In this story, the content of the photos would have the physical appeal of repeated pattern.

[17]*Ibid,* October, 1959.

127. PITCHER. This very unusual photograph was made by utilizing the huge depth of field of an extreme wide angle lens, to show us how the pitcher's hand looks to the batter whom he has just thrown. Joe Clark, Detroit.

Other themes which have been published by *Friends Magazine* include:

Theme	Scenes Used
Adventures in a Child's World[18]	
A Moment of Quiet[19]	Child studies a checker move; old man and woman hold hands; mountain is reflected in a lake; sail boats riding at anchor
Most Pictured Time of the Day: Sunset[20]	Different sunsets
Winter on the Farm[21]	Scenes show what happens on the farm in winter

A family in Louisiana which enjoys outings on a river on a home-made raft made a story.[22]

Who owns the biggest business, the most land, the most unusual economic enterprise, or the biggest fortune, the most beautiful home, the best landscaped grounds? How did these things come about? A top zoo in any region will be one of the most interesting places to visit. Any attraction which has such magnetic drawing power holds a lot of picture ideas. Spend some time at the zoo and ideas will come to you.

[18]*Ibid*, March 1959
[19]*Ibid*, July, 1958
[20]*Ibid*, April, 1961
[21]*Ibid*, February, 1960
[22]*Ibid*, August, 1959, p. 2.

Are some rivers and lakes nearby? Fishing and boating and week-end excursions are photogenic. Fishermen of our town, the different kinds of boats on the lake, teaching your wife to fish (slap-stick, ham humor), safety considerations, the kind of guy you don't want on a fishing or camping excursion — are a few of the possible themes.

How people relax and their recreations have been good for many a picture layout: picnic candids, beach scenes, water sports, golf, and billiards.

How about the different kind of clubs in your community, state, region: fencing, Mayflower descendants, Daughters of the American Revolution, coin collectors, cat fanciers, fat people at the reducing gym?

It's remarkable how a dog will take on the characteristic of his owner — confidence, timidity, insecurity, belligerence. And you've seen a layout somewhere of dogs dressed as humans. Candids of dog owners walking their pets could be funny.

Take a street or a state highway and show how it changes from one end to the other, or its contrasting or unusual aspects. What is the effect of seasons and holidays on your community? Summer and how people keep cool: kids play in water, park swims, old ladies rock and fan on the front porch or do they all sit in an air-conditioned room and watch TV. Harvest, Thanksgiving, Halloween, Easter, Spring Comes to Your Town.

128. (Left) Buildings, landmarks, and monuments which change little through the years are excellent bread and butter shots for a beginning free lance. This particular photograph has been selling for the past 20 years for Ewing Galloway Photographic Agency, New York City. (Right) This appealing picture of mother-love has been selling steadily since 1950, and it will probably sell just as steadily for the next 15 years. Bob Taylor, Cordell, Okla.

Using the Library

The library has a dual purpose for the photographer. It's the place you get tips for picture story ideas and research your article — learn as much information as you can about your topic, see what has appeared in popular publications, check to find if picture stories on it have been done, and if so, from what point of view.

Libraries hold reports from government bureaus, trade associations, and surveys and polls. Paul De Kruif, a writer of medical and scientific articles, has a knack of taking technical information and transforming it into everyday language and making it interesting because he related medical and scientific advances to the individual lives of his readers. Now a photographer can do the same things with tips he gets from dry government reports or from trade association journals. A technical subject with photographic potential must be simplified into every day language, and the application of the topic to a reader's interests of his life must be obvious.

Useful reference books on people in professional fields include:

American Labor Who's Who
American Medical Biographies
American Statesmen
Appleton's Cyclopaedia of American Biography
Authors of Today and Yesterday
Bryan's Dictionary of Painters and Engravers
Cyclopedia of Painters and Paintings
Dictionary of American Biography
Dictionary of Canadian Biography
Dictionary of Christian Biography
Dictionary of National Biography (English)
Green Book (oil, paint, drug industries) Who's Who
Grove's Dictionary of Music and Musicians
Lippincott's Pronouncing Biographical Dictionary
Living Authors
Musical Bluebook of America
Notable Americans
National Cyclopedia of American Biography
Oriental Biographical Dictionary
Pratt: New Encyclopedia of Music and Musicians
Who Was Who
Who's Who
Who's Who Among North American Authors
Who's Who in Advertising
Who's Who in America

129. A man at work in the rain who is suffering from the common cold — something most everyone has at least once a year. So people are interested in a remedy for their colds. A simple photograph with a strong message like this pays for the space it takes in the advertisement many times because it catches the interest of the reader long enough for him to read the ad copy about Bufferin. Courtesy, Bristol-Myers Product Division, Bristol Myers Company.

Who's Who in American Education
Who's Who in American Jewry
Who's Who in Colored America
Who's Who in Government
Who's Who in Journalism
Who's Who in Literature
Who's Who in New York
Who's Who in Science
Who's Who in the Theater
Women's Who's Who of America
    Background information may be found in:
Reader's Guide to Periodical Literature
International Index to Periodicals
Public Affairs Information Index
Industrial Arts Index
Agricultural Index
New York Times Index
Annual Magazine-Subject Index, combined with Dramatic Index
Education Index
Bibliographic Index

Idea File

It should be a thing which really pays you back for the time it takes, or it isn't worthwhile. Take care that the file doesn't become busy work.

People are different. The thing that helps one person is a burden to another. Some rely on memory. Others like notes. Others play each scene by ear. Probably you will have to evolve the idea file which will be most helpful to you by trial and error.

207

130. THANKSGIVING DINNER. This photograph is like some of the classic Saturday Evening Post covers of former years. Neither yields its full message to a quick glance; you have to look for some time to get the whole story. Cliff Yeich, Reading Times.

131. (Below, left.) The raw material for the picture above. The table layout is photographed, with three empty picture frames on the wall. (Below, center) The staff artist made this drawing of "Mother's shadow". (Below, right) And here are a variety of poses of Dad and the two girls, from which to choose pictures on the wall. Now, to assemble the whole—the photogapher made his exposure of the main negative, on a sheet of bromide paper, but did not develop it. Next, a high contrast negative of the shadow was put into the enlarger, and thrown out of focus for the soft effect desired. This, in turn was exposed on the same sheet of paper, to get mother's shadow into the print. Now this sheet of paper was developed, fixed, washed and dried. Finally, smaller prints of Dad and the two girls were pasted into the picture frames. The candles? They were drawn on the final print by a staff artist.

Chart 25 offers some subject matter headings under which you might want to file some clips. If you prepare a letter folder headed "Children," don't waste time clipping and filing cute kids. But the baby photo that says "comfort" could go in the folder.

A photo problem of editors is getting some variation on holiday themes. A folder titled "Seasons" compiled over a period of years might grow into several folders headed Harvest, Halloween, Christmas, New Year, and the rest of them. Photos which are unusually well done or which involve enough variation to seem fresh and original are worth filing. You may want two folders for the same topic. One folder might be "Seasons — Ideas" and the second might be "Seasons — Techniques." The labels explain the purpose of each folder.

A good daily paper will yield several clips a week for an idea file — tips on topics which probably will make good photo stories. At least two folders should be used: one for immediate action tips because you know they'll sell, and a second one to hold the rest of your clip ideas until you can get to them. You may prefer to break the second folder into many by topic headings, so clips of a similar nature will automatically be grouped together.

Your reading and analysis of published photo stories, and your observation will yield you saleable ideas for photo stories. Each idea should be put on a 5x8 card with the proper subject matter heading, so you can readily locate cards. In the beginning, one folder may hold these cards. In time, you may have to work out a more elaborate arrangement.

Quite a few of your letter folders will be given such headings as "Winter on the Farm," "Historical Monuments," "A Moment of Repose," "Churches With a Different Look," and "Goofy, Unusual Houses." Each heading represents a story you have working. As you pick up individual photos at scenes miles apart which fit a folder, the print and the information are dropped into the correct folder. When you have between 6 and 10 photos, your story is ripe. Look over the series of photos critically. Is the series rounded out pretty well or does it seem to lack a photo which would complete the story? If a lack is apparent, what kind of a photo is needed? On a series like "Patterns in Steel and Glass," make certain that you have variety in the patterns. If the series seems complete, and if you have a great enough variety between each scene, write your copyblock and your cutlines, and send the story to the right editor.

Several letter folder files, each with different headings, will be needed for clipped cartoons and other photos. Folders might be headed "Life's Most Embarrassing Moment," "No, I'm Not Henpecked," "I Love My Husband, But —" "Home Sweet Home," and "Life at the

Office." Into these folders you're putting clips which will be the basis for a photo story when you have enough situations.

A good idea file is a catalyst. When one story is mailed to an editor, you don't have to wonder what to do next. You have a lot of choices about what you do next. Pick out what you consider to be the next most saleable idea and begin thinking about your script.

When you look at a set of contact prints to pick out the best of the lot, occasionally you may decide even your selected prints are plain vanilla. How to get more oomph into the set? Review your set of prints against the list of techniques which should make photos more interesting. If you don't immediately think of a way to re-pose a shot to improve it, look at your example clips on this particular technique. Maybe your clips will suggest a better use of a technique which will liven up your shot.

Watch Your Calendar

A free lance has to live and work in the present, but his sales will be keyed to the future. In the summer, you shoot summer pictures: people in short sleeve shirts with open collars, some one cutting the lawn, a group splashing in a swimming pool. You'll have no immediate market for these pictures because most publications work from three to six months in advance of publication. You'll have to hold these summer pictures and hope for a sale between next January and the end of March.

Model Release

Photos which are used in advertisements — for purposes of trade — cannot be published without the consent of the models. So you must get a release from your models. Several of the house publications of general interest will not buy your picture story unless model releases are available.

RELEASE FORM

Date. . . . .

In consideration of . . . . taking photographs of me (my daughter — son) . . . . I hereby irrevocably authorize him, in his discretion, for his own account and without control of any kind by me (and whether such photographs are taken now or at any time in the future), to use, display, sell, publish, modify, alter and combine with others, and otherwise treat or deal with any and all such photographs and any and all such plates, films, prints, copies, enlargements, etchings, modifications, alterations, combinations, and other treatments thereof, hereby conveying to him all property rights and privileges in connection therewith as well as in connec-

210

tion with any photographs heretofore taken by him, together with the right to confer any and all such rights and privileges upon others, without obligation of any kind by him or anyone else.

Except that . . . . shall receive $ . . . . per hour for . . . . services as a model.

Signed. . . . .

. . . .

Rubber stamp form for stamping message on the back of each print:

License to reproduce this photograph will be granted upon acceptance of terms quoted. If purchased it is for your one-time publication only and must not be syndicated, rented, loaned, televised, copied, or used for advertising purposes without written permission. Use of credit line is a condition of sale.

Your name   Street address   Town, zone, state

132. FORWARD PASS. This change of pace effect was made from a straight print of the picture, simply by telling the engraver to omit the halftone screen when exposing the sensitized zinc plate. A similar effect can be obtained by shooting on high contrast film or making a copy of the original print, on "litho" film. Toby Massey, The Miami News.

Photo Copyright

Form *J* applications for this registration are secured from the Register of Copyrights, Library of Congress, Washington, D. C. This form should be filled out and filed with a copy of your photo and accompanied by a fee of $4 for each photo. The © must be put on the face of all prints.

Preparing Prints For The Mail — Chart 28

1. Straighten or flatten prints
   a. Pull each print, emulsion side up, gently over the edge of a desk.
   b. Put two prints face to face. Then put the whole set under a heavy book.

2. Stamp your terms of the sale with your name and address on the back of each print.

3. Cutlines and copyblock
   Two systems for cutlines. Probably the first system has the widest use.
   a. Paste each cutline on the photo to which it applies
   b. Key each photo on the back with a soft-lead pencil: a, b, c, d or 1, 2, 3
      Then when the cutline copy is written, the cutline to apply to photo **a or 1** will be so identified.

4. Place prints between two stout pieces of cardboard, larger than the prints. Use rubber bands to fasten the package.

5. Slip the packaged prints and your copyblock into a stamped, addressed manila envelope.
   Make sure your return address is in the upper left hand corner.
   Be certain you have enough first-class postage on the envelope.
   Print on envelope in big letters: Photos — Please Do Not Bend.

6. Also slip into your envelope a self-addressed, stamped envelope for the return of your picture story, should you not make a sale.

CHAPTER 14

The Photo Sequence

The photo sequence is a picture series of several photos dealing with the same subject. It may tell a story, record an event, describe a scene, reveal a person.

The two kinds of photo sequences

1. A series of photos on a subject which does not tell a story with a beginning, a middle, and an end.
   Examples: The Most Photographed Time of the Day: Sunset. A Moment of Quiet: Shots of an old man and a woman holding hands; boats at anchor; a boy studying a checker move.
2. The photo story in which emphasis is on the *same* subject rather than a common subject, and the story has a beginning, middle, and end.
   A narrative form presents a complete, detailed account of
   A significant event   An aspect of contemporary life.
   A personality

Both forms of the photo sequence combine photos with short captions and a copyblock of 100 to 500 words; emphasize photos and subordinate words. Occasionally, a sequence depends on pictures alone to carry the story load; only head type or an overline will be used in the layout with the photos.

A SEQUENCE MAY BE SHOT 1 OF 4 WAYS — CHART 29

1. Camera and subject may be fixed.
   Woman talks on a telephone. You record her expressions.
   Two men at a table argue. You record their expressions and gestures.
2. Camera in a fixed position; subject changes position.
   A series of photos of a galloping horse.
   Photos of a World Series baseball game.
   Photos showing a football scoring play as it unfolds.
3. Camera moves, subject is fixed.
   The situation may reveal different aspects of a subject: a statue, building, person.
   Place a comedian in front of a medicine chest in the bathroom and photograph all that can go wrong:

213

    a. The vitamin pill jar is empty;
    b. A comb has no teeth;
    c. The toothpaste is used up;
    d. He cuts his finger with scissors.

4. The camera moves and the subject moves. This is the most dramatic of the four shooting situations. It is also the most difficult to shoot.
The photographer has to
    a. Follow the physical action;
    b. At the same time, he must produce a continuous series of exposures.

Example: You film the following scene as it develops — A thug killed a store owner, a policeman, and wounded a taxi driver before being captured.

Photos:

1. Wounded taxi driver lying in foreground. Background, a crowd around the dead policeman.

2. Wounded driver, dead policeman, and fleeing gunman in background.

3. The cornered thug, cringing against a wall.

4. Angry people, shaking fists at thug as he is put in patrol wagon.

A sequence may be either planned or unplanned. Above, the photographer happened on a dramatic event and he started shooting his picture story.

A photographer who knows in advance that he must cover a football game can make some preparations. He wants the plays that result in scores and the plays that prevent scores.

CHOOSING SUBJECT MATTER — CHART 30

1. Is the subject matter PHOTOGENIC?
2. Is the subject matter FAMILIAR to many readers?
3. Is your presentation a NEW ANGLE on an OLD SUBJECT? The INSIDE STORY? What then?
4. Can the subject be adapted to the narrative device of TELLING A STORY?
5. CONFLICT can be suggested in many ways: contrast, suspense, victory.
6. Is UNIVERSAL INTEREST present? Immediacy is important, but many excellent picture stories depend upon a type of interest which transcends spot news.
Such stories reflect the lives and feelings of great masses of people.
ASK: What does this subject mean to the reader?
      Will it affect HIS job, home, security, freedom?
        Readers are most interested in subjects which directly affect their lives or which touch their emotions and entertain them.
Topics of universal interest:

Cost of living	Increasing the regard which others have for me.
Happiness of children	
Increasing my income	Threat of war, disaster
Medical advance: cancer cure, longer life	Improvement for the golden years.

7. Will the story give readers a VICARIOUS THRILL? People want escape, momentary relief from the humdrum of life. They like change. They accept "make believe" which will give them vicarious thrills. They want to be entertained and amused.

   Examples: How A Champ Won" (Pictures show effective blows).
   "The Day Liz Taylor Married" (What she and the groom did before ceremony).

8. Can the scope of the subject be limited: SHARP FOCUS?
   A photo story on a whole town is difficult.
   Reducing the scope to one block would be less difficult.
   Further reduction to only one family in the block would be better still.
   And a story on one member of the family would be the best of all.

9. Focus on PEOPLE as opposed to things. Readers are much more interested in other people.

10. Will cutlines complete the story or will more copy be needed?

11. Is the idea significant enough to justify the effort?

12. What publications might be interested in buying the series?

Writing Story Script

The script is an outline of what you plan to do. It is your road map. It is your check list to make certain that you don't forget some vital shots, that you don't get on location, and find you've forgotten a needed piece of equipment.

The script does not have to be followed slavishly. But before it is written, you should have done your research and interviewing. Then you sit down and make notes on how each shot should be set up, and where the camera will be. The more clearly you see your shots in advance, the better your story should be.

SCRIPT OUTLINE — CHART 31

Category of subject matter? (how-to-do-it, animal, children?)
Subject: You Don't Have to Have Dandruff
Suggested by: Your name, address
Date:
Place: (Where will story be shot?)
   Can the story be done in one trip?
   How much time will be required for shooting?
   If retakes are necessary, how far is the story setting from your home?
Props: (List them)
Sources of information: (List them)
   How much research is necessary?
   Is information readily available for documenting the script? Where?
   Is other authority available for checking the script? Who, what?

Write a brief summary, overview of the idea in one to two paragraphs. Answers the 5 w's and h's so that you will include all needed information in your summary of the story idea. Use one or two sentences to show why your idea will fit the magazine at which you're aiming.

Outline each photo which will appear in the series.

Who will be in it?

Will models cooperate? Will they give releases?

Will they expect pay? What restrictions may be imposed?

Position, poses for each model in photo?

How lighted? Angle from which shot made? Long, medium, closeup, or combination?

Information conveyed by photo? How will photo advance the story?

Any other needed information.

Gathering Information[1]

Go to the proper source.[2]

Each subject will have different sources of information.

Topic 1: Cal Rogers has made his living inventing since college, a friend tells you. Go directly to Cal for his story. Talking to him on his porch for a couple of hours isn't enough. You need specific information on his inventions. You need to see them, his work shop, and his models. Cal will think of forgotten incidents as he tells you about his work in the shop. Take notes, listen, ask questions: His biggest flop? His first invention? His most important invention? Hardships of living on inventor's income?

Topic 2: A news clipping gives you the following facts — Dr. Oscar Title, professor of education, has just returned from Germany. He made a survey of education to find a way to clean out Nazi propaganda. He will speak on "Education in Germany Under Armed Occupation Forces."

Don't go to Dr. Title first. Get background information from the library: Encyc'opedia Americana and Britannica: See German Education. Cyclopedia of Education: See Information on German Education. Reader's Guide to Periodical Literature: Any articles on European education?

Go to Dr. Title's speech and take notes. He'll probably answer many questions you planned to ask him. He'll also give you ideas for questions to ask when you interview him.

NOW, you have enough background information to interview him. Write out your questions before you go to see him.

Topic 3: Recently you drove through what was once the Dust Bowl. You saw many earthen dams and tanks of water. Will these prevent wholesale cattle deaths in the next drought?

Possible sources of information: County Agricultural Agent will have figures on his county only. State Agricultural Bureau will have the

---

[1]Adapted from pp. 91-93, *Modern Feature Writing* by DeWitt C. Reddick. Copyright 1949 by Harpera nd Row, Publishers, Incorporated. Used by permission of the author and publisher.
[2]See list of library references, Chapter 13.

216

overall picture. The Federal Department of Agriculture probably will have a lot of printed information and pamphlets on this topic. Write them. In your request for information, be sure to get a pamphlet on how tanks are constructed.

Human interest is lacking, and it's essential. Look through the student directory at the State University for boys from the cattle country. Interview them about their tank building experiences.

Interviewing

Most of what you read in newspapers and magazines resulted from interviews. Your appearance and manner will influence your reception. Be thoughtful of the interviewee. Be pleasant, business-like and avoid a faltering, hesitant manner. Begin by explaining again (you did it when you got the appointment) the purpose of the interview. Begin with simple, direct questions (Why did you go to South America?) Avoid broad questions in the early part of the interview (What do you think of the people of South America?) The interviewee should get to read your copy.

Shooting the Photo Sequence

To avoid running out of film, estimate how many exposures you'll make. The number of photos which you shoot depends on the complexity of your theme and the amount of space the magazine will use for one story.

"Mountain Doctor" — a Typical Picture Story

Photographer Bruce Roberts has taken the book, *Mountain Doctor*, by LeGette Blythe (William Morrow Co.) and built a picture story around it.

Dr. Gaine Cannon came home to Balsom Grove, North Carolina, to retire. His father had been the local doctor as Gaine grew up. About 1,600 people live in the area. Its economy consists mainly of raising hogs and greens and making corn likker. When folks heard that Dr. Gaine had come home, they brought him their sick ones. Soon Dr. Gaine was working a 12-hour day, spending most of his time in the mountains, going to those who were too ill to be moved.

Albert Schweitzer has long been a source of inspiration to Dr. Cannon. He visited Dr. Schweitzer in Lambarene in 1961. His experience with Dr. Schweitzer crystallized Dr. Cannon's faith.

Because of the need for a hospital in Balsom Grove, and through the example of Dr. Schweitzer, Dr. Cannon began building a 30-bed hospital, mostly with faith and small material resources. Patients who can't pay something work off bills—about 40,000 hours of contributed work on the hospital so far. Most of the Mountain Doctor's waking

217

133. In 1961 Dr. Cannon had an experience which has greatly influenced his life. He went to Lambarene to meet Dr. Schweitzer. Le Grand Docteur "pulled my chair close and held my hand as he spoke. At one point he talked of Jesus and the Good Samaritan. It crystallized my faith." A bust of Dr. Schweitzer rests on his desk.

134. Dr. Canon tries to get as close as he can to his patients in his jeep. Many of the mountain "roads" are little more than trails, up the side of the mountain.

135. When the road ends, Dr. Cannon has to leave his jeep and
walk sometimes a hundred yards, sometimes miles, to reach
his patient.

136. Children nearly always watch Dr. Cannon from the open door as he arrives and as he leaves.

137. (Left) Having reached a patient in her home, Dr. Cannon begins to seek the cause of the "misery" which makes her feel so bad.

138. (Below) Sore throat? Dr. Cannon gently probes with flashlight and depressor.

hours are spent with his people who draw from him their strength, and hope and health. The story in pictures appears on the previous pages.

To fill six pages in a magazine, shoot about 40 different picture situations. Use two exposures for each of the 40 situations; total exposures = 80. Try varying light and pose in the second shot. Of the 40 photo situations, about 30 should be good. Select 6 to 15 of the best which will tell the story. At least four of the pictures should be prospects for blowups.

Film is the cheapest ingredient you use. Long run economy demands that you shoot a lot of it. Following this advice cuts down on remakes later, allows a wider choice in the final selection, and with many high quality photos to choose from, the editor may decide at the last minute to expand your story when another doesn't come in.

Every story should have one lead picture. It should contain the essence of the whole series in one shot. Put the lead picture first to introduce the theme; pictorially, this photo should have stopping power and impact.

The beginning, middle, and end of a picture story should be clearly and logically defined. *Example:* In a manufacturing story, the first and the last pictures should show the raw material and the finished product.

Story on steel: First picture shows ingot coming out of soaking pit.

Last picture shows a finished coil of sheet metal.

To hold the interest aroused by the lead picture, the following are important in the other photos: Variety in size and shape, change in content, lighting, photo angle.

Overall shots give the general setting of the story and orient the reader. They assist the reader in understanding the pictures which follow. Margaret Bourke-White used the long shot to inform editors even if they didn't use the shot in their stories. The long shot is good in mob and strike situations. Long shots are often made from roofs, telephone poles, the top of your car.

Medium shots are used for the majority of a series. They show people groups of 3-8, interiors, action.

Explanatory closeups show faces, hands doing things, the working parts of machinery, small objects of importance. Pictorially, closeups can be the most interesting of all photos. They allow a greater range for imaginative use of light, perspective, and viewpoint. Don't forget to combine closeups and long shots occasionally.

139. A MODERN TOM SAWYER. A small boy, a small town, a summer day make a timeless
adventure story. Here is an excellent example of how to tell a story in pictures, using
words from the original Tom Sawyer for captions. As originally published, the story started
with the picture above and the following text block. ¶ For an imaginative youngster, there is
nothing quite like a small town. It blends the spaciousness of the country with the compactness
of the city, provides a perfect setting for the high adventures of boyhood. ¶ Nine-year old
Mike Snead, a resident of tiny Maxton, North Carolina, recalls Mark Twain's word painting
of the world's best-known small-town boy, Tom Sawyer. He has Tom's spirit of adventure, his
sometimes mischievous spontaneity, his unlimited energy. The essentials of the Twain character-
ization are unchanged after more than 100 years. And just as the Sawyer image is durable,
so, too, are the words that created it (see captions) ¶ In Maxton, as Tom did in Hannibal,
Mike finds vent for his exuberance. For him, it's a boundless world, seldom quiet, always
exciting. It's a world of new sights, new sounds, new experiences. On these and the following
pages, the scriptless drama of a boy in his ninth summer — *Richard L. Wilson.*

This story is reproduced as it appeared in International Harvester; the photographs are by
Bruce Roberts.

"He was not the Model Boy of the village. He knew the model boy very well though—and loathed him."

"... a boy ... on all sorts of delicious expeditions ..."

"... he was always the first boy that went barefoot in the Spring and the last to resume leather in the fall ..."

223

TOM SAWYER A CENTURY LATER,
THE SAME BREATHLESS ROUGH AND TUMBLE.

"... everything that goes to make life precious, that boy had."

"In an instant both boys were rolling and tumbling in the dirt, covering themselves with dust and glory."

"He was always willing to take a hand in any enterprise that offered entertainment and required no capital, for he had a troublesome superabundance of that sort of time which is NOT money."

"All the different ways of getting hot and tired were gone through with . . ."

225

TOM SAWYER

A BOYHOOD BASIC:

THE HAUNTED HOUSE

"The 'ha'nted' house, utterly isolated, its fences gone long ago, rank weeds smothering the very doorsteps . . ."

". . . out of the stillness, little, scarely perceptible noises began to emphasize themselves . . . old beams began to creak mysteriously . . . the stairs creaked faintly . . . evidently spirits were abroad."

" 'Run!' said he, 'run for your life!' He needn't have repeated it; once was enough; Huck was making thirty or forty miles an hour before the repetition was uttered."

On location, watch for the cover shot. Poster effect is desirable. Content must be simple and clear. It must be seen and understood from a distance. Requirements for poster effect:

a. Subject: Single and clear cut in outline
A minimum of fine/small detail
Image outline should be large enough to fill most of the frame.

b. Background: Quiet and neutral in design and tone.
No distracting object to compete for attention with main object.

c. Space where the magazine name can be inserted.

d. One large, space-filling motif instead of a group of smaller ones is best.
A closeup of a head is better than a full figure.
A sitting figure is better than a standing figure.

e. The subject of a cover design depends upon a magazine and it is related to the magazine's content.

Keep your story in mind as you work. Every photo has to have a purpose, a place in the story. Every picture must contribute to the final goal — telling a story clearly, simply, forcefully.

To get story continuity, the photos must be connected by either a common subject person or thing which would be in every photo, or a common idea. The story must move forward, develop. Each photo should supply additional information or should show the subject/ event from another angle. If the subject permits, try to build up interest with each picture as you work toward a climax. Change camera positions, vary close-ups with distance shots when possible. This technique keeps your layout from being monotonous, as it will if every shot is taken from the same angle.

Aim for photographic quality, but do not miss a shot essential for the story because the photo "wouldn't make a good picture." Take it anyway. Take several shots for each picture in a story if you have time, but don't miss a shot by fooling around too long with the previous one. Slowness can spoil your opportunity on the next picture to be shot. Learn to work fast.

Basic shots which have to be taken for any picture story:

a. Establish locale where it is important to the story.

b. Show the subject or occurrence with several shots, varying the angle and distance;

c. Inject human interest whenever possible;

d. Show the climax, the result, if there is one.

In industrial plants be sure safety devices are in evidence if they belong in the picture: helmets, goggles, gloves. Otherwise, the plant public relations officer will not let you release the pictures.

If a model freezes, be patient. Talk casually, ask questions. As the model talks, the freeze will melt.

Remember to
a. Be on the lookout for unexpected shots;
b. Seek better angles and lighting than you put in the script;
c. Be ready to expand the shooting script if interviews and research justify it;
d. Look for odd angles, unique lighting, bizarre contrast;
e. Planning plus chance result in great photos;
f. During the interviews and the photo shooting
    1) Get names and quotations;
    2) Catch the sparkle and flavor of special slang and customs.

THE MAGAZINE COVER — CHART 32

It is a wrapper on a commodity that is offered for sale.[3] Anytime you shoot a story and use some color shots, try to get a picture that's so good the editor can't resist it for a cover. If you get the cover spot, your check will jump at least $75 to $100.

1. It should have EYE APPEAL to catch the potential reader's eye.
2. IDEA to entice reader to stop and look
    a. original (seeing with fresh eyes)
    b. timely
    c. appealing.
3. HUMAN INTEREST to make the potential reader pick up the magazine. If the scene depicted is so universal that it has been experienced by many readers, this helps.
    Human interest is based on emotion:
    What people like to do;   How they live;
    What they would like to be;   What they love.
4. LITERARY QUALITY to make the potential reader realize that "much that is unseen is also here," and so he buys the magazine.
    The story is told through
    a. selective visualization,   d. arrangement (composition),
    b. dramatization,   basic compositional shapes,
    c. characterization,   e. embellishment (lighting, props)
5. Other tips
    The general appearance of a cover is dependent upon the type of the magazine. Women's service magazines differ from men's sports publications. Specific appeal is usually
    a. sentimental,
    b. nostalgic,
    c. human interest.

---

[3]Godsey, Townsend, Materials used in teaching Photo Journalism at the University of Oklahoma.

6. TO SELL MAGAZINE COVERS
   a. Study magazine covers.
   b. Study specific magazine's covers for at least last 12 issues.
   c. Get an idea.
   d. Plan composition to fit.
      Leave space for magazine title, other matter.
   e. Keep background simple.
   f. Select suitable model — one that fits magazine; obtain model releases.
   g. Use clear, well balanced lighting to give poster quality.
   h. Submit only finest quality transparencies.
   i. Use cut out mounts for best presentation.
   j. Submit only a few transparencies at a time so you won't compete with yourself.
   k. Work six months to a year ahead of seasonal material.

SUMMARY: SHOOTING A PHOTO STORY — CHART 33

1. Select an idea which has photographic possibilities (see Choosing Subject Matter).
2. Make a preliminary outline of your idea (See Outline for Writing Story Script).
3. Do your research and conduct your interviews. These activities will yield a mass of notes.
   Before you grab your camera
   a. Get your facts.
   b. Check them.
   c. The more significant your story, the more you will have to dig for information. Superficial stories result from poor research.
   d. Eliminate unimportant material.
   e. Arrange what's left in an effective sequence.
   f. The theme or continuity device is established. Your editor will have a lot to say about what angle the focus will be. Your analysis should prepare you so that you can anticipate some of the editor's suggestions.
4. Write the final story script. (See Outline for Writing Story Script).
   Make your script definite.
      Example
      Too indefinite (description of a picture situation): Candidates' wives at convention
      Better: Mrs. Doodle and Mrs. Strodle in front row balcony. Mrs. D. has bored expression. Mrs. S. is intent upon the stage action. Back row faces should be in focus but only dimly lighted so they won't distract from Mrs. D. and Mrs. S.
5. Select your equipment, estimate film and flash lamps needed.
6. On location
   a. Explain to your models what they are to do and why. Tell them the idea behind the story. They'll respond better to your directions if they know goals.
   b. Make notes of other points to keep in mind on location (see Shooting Photo Sequence).
7. Select the contact prints which you believe will make the story.
   Enlarge negatives of these prints, taking care to crop each photo properly.
   Write and edit cutlines and copyblock.
   Spot prints carefully.
   Prepare prints properly to be mailed to editor.

PLANNING AND PHOTOGRAPHING A HOW-TO-DO-IT STORY

People like these stories for three reasons:[4]

1. They like to make things with their hands, and they like to have good directions.
2. They're interested in ways to improve themselves: how to give a talk or a party.
3. They're interested in how-to stories for utility: how to study, to make a pie.

How-to photo stories are found in many kinds of magazines[5]

1. Business journal: Ways of Improving a Business.
2. Religious magazines: Planning a Program; How to Give a Church Party.
3. Women's magazines: How to Cook Good Meals; How to Make Window Draperies, etc.
4. Family magazines: How to Rear an Only Child; How to Take Your Son Camping.

Restrictions in finding subjects[6]

1. Styles and food articles are usually done by staff writers and photographers.
2. No magazine is interested in a mere theory on how to do something. The idea must be tested, successful, and not too involved.
3. It must be something many will like to do and can do.
4. It shouldn't involve a great outlay of money. It's better if it can be done with a hammer and a saw instead of a lathe.
5. The procedure should involve relatively simple steps.

Examples of how-to stories which have sold

1. "How to Build a Lawn," *People and Places,* March, 1954.
2. "Expert Advice on Choosing the Right Pet," *People and Places,* December, 1954.
3. "Nurses Caps — How to Recognize," *People and Places,* November, 1952
4. "Play Safe in Your Workshop," *Friends,* July, 1954.
5. "How to Make Ornamental Tiles," *Friends,* December, 1954.
6. "Sam Snead Shows How to Use Golf Clubs," *Technique of the Picture Story,*[7] pp. 96-97.

Research[8]

1. Watch the procedure from beginning to end.
2. Make notes on essential points in the process.
3. Check with authority to find if all points necessary to understanding the process are included in your story.

---

[4]Adapted from pp. 236-241, *Modern Feature Writing* by DeWitt C. Reddick. Copyright 1949 by Harper and Row, Publishers, Incorporated. Used by permission of the author and publisher.
[5]Ibid.
[6]Ibid.
[7]Mitch & Eberman.
[8]Godsey, Townsend, *op. cit.*

Taking your eyes off the road, if only for an instant, to see what the children are doing could result in an accident. You can avoid this risk by teaching the youngsters that there is a proper way to ride, and by gesting car games that will stir their imagination, but not their ene

WHEN DRIVING, KEEP YOUR CHILDREN'S SAFETY IN MIND—

Don't Put Up With "Cut-Ups"

One of the hazards of the road that can threaten the safety of you and your family may be inside your own automobile. Too-playful children, riding beside you or behind you on a trip, often create dangerous driving conditions. Their antics (some of which are pictured on these pages) not only may distract the driver from the safe operation of the car—they also may endanger the youngsters themselves. To keep children in their seats and out of the driver's way on a trip, it's wise to plan, in advance, a number of car games they can play. It's a good idea, too, to arrange your packing—luggage, first-aid kit, vacuum bottle, toys—so that the trip will be made more comfortable for them.

THE HOW TO DO IT STORY. Here is a complete two page "how to do it" story, reproduced direct from the pages of the magazine in which it appeared to show how a story would be laid out. Note the sizes of the various pictures, in proportion to their importance, and the text in the copy blocks; these supplement the photos, they do not merely label them. Philip Foskett, from FRIENDS magazine.

Key dangling in the ignition invites trouble in an unattended car. For a six-year-old boy, it's an invitation to get behind the steering wheel, start the engine and "drive the way Daddy does."

Unlocked doors that can be opened by a child in the rear seat when the car is in motion can lead to tragedy. Keep all the doors locked; remove the inside rear door handles, if necessary.

Humpty-dumpties are riding for a fall, and perhaps serious injury, when they stand on a seat. At a sudden stop they could be thrown against the dashboard or sent tumbling to the floor.

Treats with hidden hazards—lollypops with wooden sticks, for example—are dangerous in a car. If the child were pitched forward by a quick stop, the stick could be pushed deep into the mouth.

...ndow "pilot" runs the risk of a serious mid-...ion if another automobile should pass. The ...rs should be taught the importance of al-...eping the head and arms inside the car.

Party-goer keeps party going while father drives, but if the noise has a disturbing effect on his driving, it's time to teach her an important rule of automobile manners—never bother the man at the wheel.

Misguided missiles should never be placed on package shelf of car. If driver makes a sudden stop, a flashlight or a metal toy can be a dangerous flying object.

Outline for shooting[9]
1. List essential steps in their proper sequence.
2. Make detailed list of all props and models needed.
3. Make rough layout sketches.

Shooting Preparations[10]
1. Assemble all props and models.
2. Assemble all lights, cameras, background.

The Shooting[11]
1. Plan session so that all photos in the sequence can be made in one session.
2. Determine the most desirable camera angle and set camera on a tripod.
3. Make simple, straight lighting setup.
4. Camera should be considered as a person (your reader who is being taught the how-to-do-it). A good idea is to consider the camera as seated across the table or work bench from the how-to-do demonstrator. Don't use confusing lighting or camera angles. Maintain proper scale from picture to picture in the sequence.

Developing and Printing[12]
1. Develop all films at one time (roll film is good) for matching contrast.
2. Print all pictures at the same time and match tonal quality. Remember, the pictures are to be seen on a page together and must match in quality.

Editing[13]
1. Write adequate cutlines.
2. Attach cutlines to print, or if sequence lines are on separate sheet, make certain that lines are numbered to match prints.

---

[9] Ibid.
[10] *Ibid.*　　　　[11] *Ibid.*
[12] *Ibid.*　　　　[13] *Ibid.*

234

CHAPTER 15

Editing the Photograph and Writing the Cutline

Will the Print Reproduce?

Prints with action and impact often have strong highlights and shadows. Readers respond to these contrasting qualities. Engravers curse the photographer for the strong highlights and shadows. They're difficult to handle. However, prints are chosen to please readers, not engravers.

PHOTO CHARACTERISTICS RELATED TO ENGRAVING — CHART 39

Photo Characteristics Which Are Easy to Engrave	Photo Characteristics Which Engravers Can Change
Flat light	Contrast can be added to a flat print just by re-photographing it during engraving
Short range of gray halftones	Highlights can be toned down by the Art department
No strong highlights or deep shadows	A print which is blurry (out of focus or camera movement) can be improved by the Art department

Photographs of big news events, such as the smuggled picture of a criminal in the electric chair or D-Day in World War 2, often are widely used, even though the pictures are technically poor. If prints with the same poor technical characteristics had little news value, they would be thrown in the wastebasket. The rule of thumb is that photos of little news value must be technically good to be considered for publication. But if the only available photos of big news events are weak technically, the Art department will doctor them some, and the pictures will be used.

WHEN ARE TECHNICALLY POOR PICTURES PUBLISHED?

140. D-Day, 1944 Storming the Beaches of Normandy. The technically poor photo above, of a big news event was used by *Life* Magazine. Taken from a rocking boat, the blur and flatness better depicts the feeling of this grim, dangerous mission, and the cold fear which gripped many who followed orders, knowing they would die before the day ended. Photograph by Robert Capa, Courtesy, *Life*.

The technically good photo on the right will end up in the waste basket. It has neither news value nor emotion. Photo by Joseph Scaylea, The Seattle Times.

WHAT DETERMINES THE SIZE OF A PUBLICATION PHOTO? — CHART 35

1. Space available in the publication?
2. News value and/or emotion in the photo?
3. Does the photo have a message that is apparent to readers?
4. Physical characteristics:
   a. Good tone contrast
   b. Sharp focus and no camera movement so the photo won't become fuzzy when enlarged.
5. Small, important detail must be easily seen and readily identified.
6. How does the subject matter rate with readers?
7. How much action and spontaneity are in the photo?

Suggestions

It's better to display one big, attention-getting photo properly than to have three smaller pictures, which are cramped for space and hard to see quickly.

Good pictures, properly displayed, have a large readership. A study indicates that an inferior photo can have a higher readership than the Number 1 word story.[1]

Size of Halftones

Probably the 2-column cut is used oftenest.

As the 2-column cut is increased to 3-columns, and then to 4-columns, readership will increase because big pictures have more impact.

If a mug shot is changed to a full-length photograph, readership will increase by about 1/3.

If a 1-column mug shot is reduced to a ½ column cut, about one-half the readership will be lost.

ENGRAVER INSTRUCTIONS SHOULD BE COMPLETE — CHART 36

Newspaper

1. Front of picture: Crop Marks indicate the size of the halftone.
2. Back of the picture: (Write with a soft lead pencil and don't press down)
   a. Size of the halftone
   b. Page and column where halftone will be displayed.
   c. If the photo is a mug shot of one individual, write the name and initials
   d. If the photo is a general interest picture, write the first two or three words of the cut line.

---

[1] Continuing Study of Newspaper Reading by the Advertising Research Foundation.

141. HALFTONES MUST BE LARGE ENOUGH TO BE EFFECTIVE. Sometimes an unusually shaped photograph may permit odd cropping. The subject matter demanded this cropping; in a more nearly square format, the picture would not have the same impact. Joe Clark, Detroit.

142. HALFTONES MUST BE LARGE ENOUGH TO BE EFFECTIVE. Even when tightly cropped as the small picture in the upper left is, its impact is less than the "looser" but larger picture. Hal Berg, courtesy Equitable Life Assurance Society.

Yearbook

Stickers with the following information should be attached to the back of each photo:

Name	Finish:	Square Oval Circle C.O.B.
		Check the style desired
Cut Number	Bleed	Right Left Top Bottom
Size cut	Plates	Check above edge of page
(width or height)		where plate extends off paper.
Remarks		Plate size must include ⅛″ in
		addition to regular size where
		bleed occurs.

Cropping the Photo

A crop mark is a line drawn on a photograph with a red grease pencil, boxing the area which you want the engraver to use. Grease pencil marks are easy to rub off with a Kleenex if the mark needs changing. Cropping enables you to pick out the only part of a photograph which tells the story, and to eliminate unnecessary detail. When the story-telling part of the picture is enlarged to the proper size, the central object of interest will have impact for two reasons. One, it will be dominant, without a lot of unimportant details dividing attention. Two, the big enlargement — just size — enhances picture interest.

In cropping a picture, an editor puts crop marks on the top and two sides of a picture, but none on the bottom. An editor knows how wide and how deep his photo will be in the finished publication, and he marks the exact size of the cut on his dummy.[1] An experienced editor can visualize and estimate about where the engraver's cut-off on the bottom of the photo will be. The editor makes certain that this cut-off will not eliminate any needed detail. The editor leaves the problem of cut-off on the bottom of the picture to the engraver for two reasons. It saves the editor time. And during the engraving, when the cut-off is made, it is exact rather than an estimation.

Proportion in Determining Size of the Printed Picture

Probably you wonder how an editor will know the exact size of his cut if he doesn't bother to make his fourth cropping mark on the bottom of photograph. Proportion is a useful picture-editing tool which supplies the answer.

Experience and common sense tell the editor that photos which are nearly square will have about the same relative proportions when either reduced or blown up in size. If he knows the width he can estimate fairly closely the height, and vice versa. Horizontals and

---

[1] Layout sheets are marked off in columns. The editor indicates on the dummy where each story and each picture will be placed, and how much space each will take.

verticals are like the square in that they keep this same relative dimensions as they are enlarged or reduced.

CUT AREAS INCREASE IN GEOMETRIC PROGRESSION — CHART 37

Increase 1 column to 2 columns — area is quadrupled, not doubled
Increase 1 column to 3 columns — area is 9 times greater rather than tripled
Increase 1 column to 4 columns — area is 16 times greater rather than quadrupled

Scaling to Determine Size of the Printed Picture

When an editor wants to know whether a picture will make a cut of a specific size and whether cropping will destroy the purpose of the picture, he often resorts to scaling instead of proportion. Either will work, but the former permits the editor to see exactly what will and will not be included in the cut.

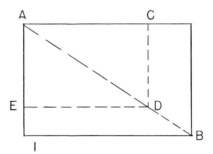

The Known Dimension Is Column WIDTH of the Cut

1. You know your cut will be smaller than the original photograph
   You also know the cut will be 2-columns wide
      Problem: Find the cut's depth.
   Place ruler on top of picture, and measure 4 inches horizontally, line AC
      At C draw a vertical line, CD
   Place ruler across the picture in a diagonal, from top left corner A through bottom right corner, B
   Where the diagonal ruler intersects your line CD put a light grease mark.
   Line CD = The depth of the 2-column cut
   ACED = The Cut

240

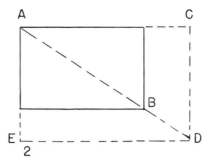

2. You know your cut will be larger than the original photograph.
   You also know the cut will be 6 columns or 12 inches wide.
      Problem: Find the cut's depth.
   Place the picture on top of a square sheet of white paper larger than the picture. Top left corner of the picture (A) and that of the white paper coincide.
   Place ruler on top of picture/paper and measure 12 inches horizontally, line AC
   At C draw vertical line, CD
   Place ruler as a diagonal from points AB.
   Where diagonal ruler intersects line CD, put a light grease mark.
   Line CD = depth of the cut
   ACED = The Cut

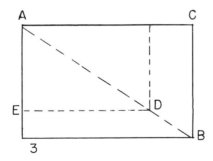

The Known Dimension Is Column DEPTH of the Cut

1. You know your cut will be *smaller* than the original photograph.
   You know the cut depth will be 3½ inches.
      Problem: Find the column width of cut.
   Lightly mark a diagonal, line AB
   Measure down from top of picture 3½ inches and lightly mark line CD where it intersects diagonal.
   Line ED = Column width
   ACED = The Cut

241

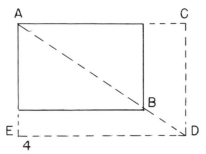

4

2. You know your cut will be *larger* than the original photograph.
   You know the cut depth will be 5 inches.
      Problem: Find the column width of cut.
   Place picture on top of square sheet of paper larger than the picture.
   Top left corner of the picture (A) and that of the white paper
   coincide.
   Lightly mark a diagonal, line AB
   Measure down from top of picture 5 inches and mark line CD which
   coincided with diagonal at D
   Line ED = Width of cut
   ACED = Cut

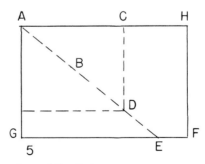

5

You Know Both Dimensions of the Cut

1. The cut will be smaller than your photograph.
      Problem: To find the necessary cropping needed to make the cut
      a specific size.
   Measure across the top of picture, line AC, the *width* of the cut.
   Make a light grease mark. Drop horizontal line CD, the *depth* of the
   cut. Place ruler in a diagonal line, AB, from top left corner A
   through the intersection of the *end* of line CD at D.
   Area EF = Space which must be cropped away from the picture
   sides vertically.
   EF may be all on one side or the other, or half on one side and half
   on the other, depending on which benefits the picture the most.

242

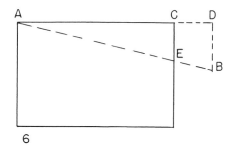

2. The cut will be larger than your photo.

   Problem: To find how much additional space must be added to the original photo in making a larger printing plate.

   Place picture on top of square sheet of paper larger than picture.

   Measure across top of picture and paper, line AD, the width of the cut.

   Drop horizontal line DB, the depth of the cut.

   Place ruler in diagonal AB from top left corner through point B, end of vertical line CB.

   Distance EF = amount of cropping to be taken off either the bottom, or the top, or ½ of EF off both the bottom and the top, depending on which enhances the photo the most.

Using a Scale of Proportions

The scale is made of two pieces of circular cardboard. The smaller circle is placed in the center of the larger circle and the two are riveted together, so that the smaller circle can be rotated in either direction. On this inner and smaller circle are the numbers which designate the

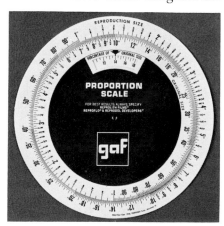

143. PROPORTION SCALE. Actually, a circular slide rule which makes it easy to calculate proportions of any picture and the engraving from it. Courtesy General Aniline & Film Corp., Manufacturers of Ansco Products.

243

original size of the photo which you are editing. On the outer circle are the numbers to indicate the size of *desired reproduction*.

1. Problems in Reducing the Size of the Photo to a Smaller Cut
   A. Photo dimensions: 8¾ inches (width) x 15 inches (depth)
      You want to reduce the depth to 9 inches
      Problem: Find what the width would be.

   STEPS:
      1. Rotate the inner circle so that the original size of the photo depth, 15 inches, is opposite the desired reproduction depth, 9 inches.
      2. Find the original width of the photo (inner circle), 8¾ inches. Opposite this original width on the outer circle is the reproduction width, 5¼ inches.
      Original width was placed opposite desired reproduction width. Original depth was then opposite the answer, desired reproduction depth.
      Your answer: The cut will be 5¼ inches.

   B. Photo dimensions: 8 inches (width) x 10 inches (depth)
      You want to reduce the *width* to two columns or 4 inches
      Problem: Find what depth would be.

   STEPS:
      1. Rotate the inner circle so that 8 inches is opposite 4 inches on the outer scale (width)
      2. Find 10 inches on the *inner scale*
         The number on the outer scale opposite 10 inches = 5 inches
         Your answer: The cut will be 5 inches deep.

2. *Problems in Increasing the Size of the Photo to a Larger Cut*
   A. Photo dimensions: 8¾ inches (width) x 15 inches (depth)
      You want to increase the depth to 20 inches
      Problem: Find what the width would be.

   STEPS:
      1. Rotate the inner circle so that 15 inches (depth) is opposite 20 inches
      2. Find 8¾ inches on the inner scale
         The number on the outer scale opposite 8¾ inches = 11¾ inches
         Your answer: The cut will be 11¾ inches wide.

244

B. Photo dimensions: 8 inches (width) x 10 inches (depth)
You want to increase width to 12 inches
Problem: Find what the depth would be

STEPS:

1. Rotate the inner circle so that 8 inches is opposite 12 inches on the outer circle.

2. Find 10 inches on the inner circle
   The number on the inner scale opposite 10 inches = 15 inches
   Your answer: The cut will be 15 inches deep.

144. (Above) Uncropped photo; a good picture but with a good deal of waste space on the sides of image. (Right) cropped to a long narrow shape, the actual image is not much bigger but elimination of the waste area puts greater emphasis on the important detail. Oklahoman & Times.

145. OTHER WAYS OF HANDLING PICTURES. (Left) Collage or pasteup method of making a picture out of pieces of two photographs. Tom Blevins, Norman Transcript. (Right) Montage; multiple exposures on one negative or multiple printing from several negatives on one sheet of printing paper. A. Y. Owens, Oklahoma City.

Summary of Procedure

Always place the original size on the inner circle opposite the reproduced size on the outer circle.

   a. If *depth* (inner circle) is to be either reduced or increased to a known number of inches, find this known figure on the outer circle. Opposite the known figure (inner circle) on the outer circle will be the unknown width, the answer you seek.

   b. If *width* (inner circle) is to be either reduced or increased to a known number of inches, find this known figure on the *outer* circle. Opposite this known figure (inner circle) on the outer circle will be the unknown depth, the answer you seek.

Other Ways of Handling Pictures

A *mortise* is cutting away a portion of a halftone which is waste space. Into the cutout, type lines are placed. Used occasionally, the mortise is effective. Type should be given space in which to breathe and not butted too close to the edge of the mortise.

A *montage* can be result from one of two methods. *One,* a photographer has two or more exposures on one sheet of film. *Two,* several negatives are exposed on the same piece of enlarging paper.

A *collage* is made by pasting together several photographs or parts of photographs. Newspapers favor this method rather than the montage. The latter takes much time, skill, and patience. A pasteup can be done in minutes. Then the joints are airbrushed, and the collage is sent along to engraving or photographed again and enlarged. This print is then sent to the printer.

In the fall when football is king, the sports page will carry a *diagram* — a blow-up of an important play with each player identified. Name labels in the diagram are set in type and pasted onto the photo or the labels may be typed onto paper, cut out and pasted onto the enlargement. But arrows, crosses, and other symbols are drawn directly on the photo.

To emphasize the key photo in a page layout, the background is eliminated, leaving the person in action against the white of the page. Such emphasis is called an outline, drop-out, block-out, or *silhouette*. The halftone is made as usual. Then the engraver cuts away the background.

Books on typography will describe how to achieve other effective uses of pictures such as the combination of halftones and line drawings, and the Ben Day patterns in the place of backgrounds which have been dropped out.

Writing Captions

Too many newspapers are using labels instead of captions. They're merely identifying the people involved in the pictures. Captions should sell pictures to the public — help the reader understand and appreciate the photo.

Any sort of picture can be improved with a good caption. A good picture can be made even better with a first-rate caption.

First job of the caption writer is to get the mood of the picture. (1) The content of a picture, (2) the circumstances which made the photo news, (3) and the information from which the caption will be written will indicate the mood of the photo. Some photos will need light, humorous cutlines; others will be only informative; others will be pathetic, or involve some other emotion.

Key words used in a kicker (the first three to seven words set in either bold face or caps) do one of two things or both: (1) Summarize the action in the picture, causing the reader to look back at the photo to check on the accuracy of the writer OR make a specific reference to some part of the content of the photo; (2) Set the mood of the photo

247

by use of a twist or angle: figures of speech, puns, twisted cliches, current slang, titles of books, songs, movies.

SAYS PRINTER WASN'T HER TYPE — (Gal reporter was kidnapped by composing-room employee for short while and returned to safety.)

SCALE OFF THE OLD FISH — (His dad was one of the original college boys who swallowed live goldfish. Now son has swallowed one at college.)

It's more difficult to write kickers which catch the mood and use a twist or angle than it is to summarize the action in a photo or make a specific reference to some part of the content in the photo. Everyone can learn to do the latter. Some won't have the touch to do the former. Many believe it can't be taught.

Second job of the caption writer is to decide how much information is essential in the cutline. This selection of data will depend on:

1. Is the photo floated? That is, it has no accompanying story. A photo and a cutline are run as a unit. Floaters need more information than the cutlines which are used for a photo which accompanies a story.

2. Is the photo a part of a picture story which will have a copyblock and other pictures and captions? Generally, such cutlines are terse. They do not repeat information in the copyblock. Often they add a fact or two to the overall story — information not in the copyblock — while selling the photo and referring to action in the photo to cause the reader to look back at the picture a second or third time.

3. Is the photo a 1-column mug shot which accompanies a story? Usually, the identifying name of the individual is enough. Some newspapers run a descriptive phrase or a bit of news in one line under the name.

Examples:

Jesse James	Whirl Away (a horse)
HE ROBBED BANKS	BRINGS BACON HOME

In selecting information for your caption, ask: What single fact makes this story news? Build your caption around your news hook. Answer obvious questions which would come to the reader's mind as he reads your caption. Generally, the 5 W's and the *H* and common sense are a guide in selecting pertinent information.

Usually a reader glances at a picture. If it interests him, his eye drops down to the caption. The caption has two functions: (1) It contains information which will add more meaning to the photo (2) It refers to action in the photo or to some object in the photo which might escape the attention of the reader. The reference should cause the

248

reader to look back at the picture for the second or third time, to note the object or action referred to, and to see if he agrees with the comment of the caption writer.

Summary

1. Try to get the mood of the photo and reflect this in the kicker through a twist or angle: figure speech, pun, twisted cliche, slang, title book, song, movie.

2. If a twist comes hard, then use the kicker to refer to an object or action in the photo.

3. Find the news hook — the reason for the picture — and build the caption around it. Answer obvious reader questions, usually covered by 5 *W*'s and *H*.

4. If the kicker contains a twist, then the body of the caption should contain some reference to an object in the photo which the reader might overlook or a reference to the action of the picture. Reason: to cause reader to look at photo again.

5. In checking a caption, ask: (a) Does it add more meaning to the photo? (b) Will it make the reader look back at the photo?

Other General Rules

1. Don't waste words on the obvious: The picture above portrays . . .; shown above is . . .; The pretty girl or the beautiful woman (the picture will tell).

2. Unless a name is exceptionally news worthy don't place it at the beginning of the cutline.

3. The first word or phrase (kicker or readin) should be colorful. And the first part of the caption immediately after the kicker should be a direct statement of the action in the picture.

4. In striving to be terse, some writers find themselves putting two unrelated ideas into one sentence. Don't do it.

5. A simple sentence is preferred to either compound or complex sentences. Because cutlines may be two or more columns in width, sentences should be short so they will be easy to read and understand.

6. People in pictures must be clearly identified. If more than one individual is shown, each must be identified in terms of his position in the picture. Position is usually expressed in terms of left, center, and right. If only two are in a photograph, only one position will be indicated.

When a left to right designation is meaningless, try: in the foreground, nearest the camera, wearing a sweater, standing, seated.

7. Watch verb tenses. One school holds that all cutlines belong in the present tense (present: see; past: saw; future: shall, will see). A larger school believes tense should be logical. In using the latter, take care that tenses are not shifted in the middle of a sentence.

8. Don't try writing a cutline without seeing the picture. If the photograph has to be sent to the engraver, look at the picture and make some notes for the cutline you will write later. (Publications have to meet deadlines. A photo cannot be held until a writer is ready to write a cutline.)

9. Be alert. Don't accept syndicate captions as infallible. After reading a caption, carefully check the photo content to make certain the two belong together.

10. Don't use fraudulent information in a caption. Don't use an old photograph of the President of the United States and have the cutline indicate that the picture is a recent one.

11. Give syndicates their required credit line. Also be generous with by-lines for deserving photographers. A *good* photographer works hard.

12. Be certain that the guideline on the back of the photograph, the cutline and the dummy are the same.

13. Cutlines for 2- and 3-column cuts should be 9 or 10 point type when the type line is more than 1-column in width.

Unit Count For Newspaper Heads, Overlines — Chart 38
For Caps and Lower Case Letters

All lower case letters = 1 count except	All punctuation = ½ count except
Thin letters: 1, t, f, i which = ½ count	Dash Dollar sign
Fat letters: m, w which = 1½ count	Question mark Percent sign = 1
All cap letters = 1½ = count except	All Figures = 1 count
Thin I = ½ count	All Spaces = 1 count
Fat M, W = 2 count	

Writing to Space

Caption writers must write words which will fill in a specific space. The caption cannot use more space than has been left for it in the newspaper. Therefore, the caption writer must figure out a system to know, as he writes, whether the caption will be too long or too short or fit the space.

It is possible to work out a ready-reference table. First, find the average number of newspaper type characters which fill a 1-column line under your photograph. This average may be arrived at by counting each letter and space in the line. Suppose the first line has 34 units, the second 33, the third 37, and the fourth 31. Add these four

250

figures together for a total of 135 units. Divide this total by 4, the number of lines, to find the average number of characters in one line. In this case, it would be about 33.5 units per line.

Second, type the cutline on your typewriter, using margins of 10 and 70. Note the average number of typewriter characters which will make up one printed line, 1 column in width. Record this information in your ready reference chart. Repeat the process of 1½ columns, 2 columns, 2½ columns, 3 columns. Put the information into your ready-reference table.

Newspaper body type is usually 7 or 7.5 points in size. Some papers use 8 point body type. The larger the figure, the larger the point size of the type. For example, 8 point type is bigger than 7 point or 6 point but not as big as 9 point type. Type for cutlines is usually a little larger than body type with more white space between each line and the type is bold face or blacker than body type. Larger, black type with more white space between the cutlines gives a page a visual change of pace. If the cutline type is 8 points in size, it should not be longer than 16 picas or about 2¾ inches (6 picas = 1 inch) in width. Longer lines of 8 point type are difficult to read. Nine point type can be 18 picas or 3 inches in length. And 10 point type can be 20 picas or 3-1/3 inches in length.

145. A NEWS PICTURE REQUIRES NO RELEASES WHEN RUN AS NEWS. But if this picture appeared in an advertisement, any person in it whose face was recognizable could sue for invasion of privacy. And there is a twilight zone between the two situations. When in doubt, get release! Jerry Huff, UPI.

252

CHAPTER 16

The Photographer
and The Law

News Photographs Which Don't Require the Subject's Release

Court decisions indicate that the following situations can be photographed and published without getting written permission of those involved: events in public places, news events, and public characters.

The general rule on public places: You may photograph anything so long as you do not interfere with the rights of others. People in the public place came there voluntarily, surrendering their rights of privacy. If they don't want to be photographed, they must stay home.

Because people in the United States are a self-governed people, they need information about government and office holders which will help them make wise voting decisions. The U.S. Constitution gives newspapers freedom of the press. In return for this privilege, newspapers have the responsibility of providing readers with information on vital matters — government, conduct of office holders, and other news matters. In areas of information which are vital to voters, newspapers fight vigorously against those who would withhold such news. Newspapers say that the readers have a "right to know" this information. Court decisions involving photographers tend to indicate that when they are shooting "right to know" pictures, even though they trespass on private property, photographers have the right to shoot the picture. But the courts *can* fine the photographers for trespassing. A news figure can't retreat to private property and expect to be safe from photographers. So all who are charged with a crime, or involved in a law suit, or the object of public interest, become fair game for photographers. These people are news! They fall in the "right to know" category. Their photographs may be taken and published without consent, even when they protest vigorously and threaten action. Such threats generally are empty *unless* the right of privacy has been invaded.

Public characters are people who have surrendered a part of their privacy to the public. Such people include candidates for office, office holders, authors, actors and sports participants. These all voluntarily submit their talents to the public for approval. If the public happens to disapprove, public characters must accept the disapproval with the same calmness as they would the approval. The public is free to comment on and criticize official acts of an office holder, the manner in which an actor portrays a part, or the writing and the plot of a book. But the public may not comment on or criticize the *private life* of even a public character unless the private life also overlaps with and affects his ability as an office holder, or an actor, or a writer. These principles are true for photography, too.

However a free lance should get releases of all photographed subjects who will be submitted to publications, even events occurring in public places, involving news events and public characters. Most general-interest house organs and Sunday magazine supplements will not buy your photos without such releases. No advertisement can include the photo of a person who has not given written permission for the use of the picture. But news photographers do not worry about releases for events in public places, news events, and public characters.

In theory, a person who is not in the news and who is not a public character may sue for invasion of privacy if his photo is taken and published without his consent. Invasion of privacy is an interesting legal theory which says that "each individual has the right to be left alone and not to be dragged into publicity."[1]

This theory is a fairly new one, having been discussed in 1890 in the *Harvard Law Review*. Some states have passed laws which define this right and set up punishment for violation of it. Many states have no such law. Some courts recognize the right. Other courts do not. Generally, because the invasion of privacy is a clouded issue,[2] it really is more of an ethical question than a legal question. Since many courts often do not protect this right, whether the right is recognized depends on the ethics of individual editors.

In an early New York case,[3] parents of a young girl sued a flour company for printing her photo on box containers without permission. The court agreed that one has a right to pass through this world with-

---

[1] Cooley, T. M., A Treatise on the Law of Torts, Chicago, Callaghan and Co., 1930 (3rd ed.), p. 364.

[2] Rothstein, Arthur, *Photo Journalism*, American Photographic Book Publishing Company, New York, 1956, p. 192 says the invasion theory has been recognized in 25 states either by statute or court decision.

[3] Roberson v. Rochester Folding Box Co., 171 NY 538, 64 N.E. 442, 59 L.R.A. 478, 89 Am. St. Rep. 828 (1902).

out having his photo published. But, said the court, the invasion of privacy theory is so new that no New York State laws exists on the matter. The girl's privacy was invaded, but she had no recourse at law.

An aroused New York legislature passed a law which said that the unauthorized use of a person's name or photograph for purposes of trade (in advertisements) was a misdemeanor. California and Virginia have similar laws. Eleven other states by decision have recognized this principle.[4]

From the standpoint of a free lance who wants to sell his stories to house publications and to newspaper Sunday supplements, the easiest thing to do to avoid being sued for invasion of privacy is to get releases from all persons who appear in picture stories, especially any individual in a street scene (not news and not public character) who is singled out and blown up into a photo of one person. You cannot assume that because some one poses for you and cooperates with you in the shooting of a picture that the person is giving consent for the publication of the photograph. He isn't. Nor can you assume that because some one permits you to photograph a pet dog or cat that you later have the right to sell the pet's picture without a release from the owner. You don't. In neither of these situations is consent for publication implied.

Public Places

No statute forbids photographers from taking cameras into public and semi-public places where people come and go freely: hotels, railway stations, cafes, ship piers, and office buildings. Examples: any event which occurs in public places, traffic accident in the street, Easter promenaders as they stroll along, a man chasing his hat as the wind blows it along.

Owners and managers of public places have rights. People who come and go in public places have rights. A hotel manager has the right to toss out a man with a camera who insists on popping flash lamps in the faces of people in the lobby. A restaurant owner or a night club owner can keep a photographer from photographing every one who enters a place of business.[5] If the photographer is on property belonging to the business, he is trespassing. If the photographer is on public property, the business owner can get an injunction which forbids the photographer from taking pictures. Basis for the injunction might be that the photographer was a public nuisance or that he was injuring the business by causing patrons to go to a restaurant where no pictures would be taken.

---

[4]Steigleman, Walter A., *The Newspaperman and the Law*, William C. Brown Company, Dubuque, Iowa, 1950, p. 226.

[5]Friedman v. Cincinnati Local Joint Executive Board, 6 Ohio Supp. 276 (1941).

Public buildings may be photographed and published without permission. But permission is needed before photographing private buildings such as famous hotels and sports arenas. Universal Pictures found out this truth the hard way. It made a film featuring hockey in Madison Square Garden without getting the consent of the Garden. The Garden sued and won damages for the use of its name and the publication of its pictures.[6]

An eccentric college president wore a bathing suit in summers in his office. He refused to pose for news photographers. A photographer stood on a public street and got a picture of the president on the campus (private property). The president had no basis for preventing publication. He had exposed himself to public gaze. His peculiar dress made him an object of public interest — a news item.[7]

Two company guards prevented a photographer from taking a picture of an outdoor accident on company property. The photographer complained through a newspaper lawyer to the court. The guards were indicted for assault and battery. The court said: When the occurrence is of public concern (news and right to know) it makes no difference whether the photographer is on public or private property. The basic right of the photographer should not be impeded.[8]

Exceptions

A girl was struck by a car and knocked to the pavement. Driver of the car was at fault, not the child. Her picture was published in a newspaper the next day. Since the event was news no permission was needed. No complaint was made. However, 20 months later the same photo was published in a national magazine in an article titled, "They Ask To Be Killed." The idea was that careless, thoughtless pedestrians were usually at fault in car-pedestrian accidents. Cutlines under the little girl's photo said: "Safety education in schools has reduced child accidents measurably, but unpredictable darting through traffic still takes a sobering toll."

In a box beside the child's picture was this message: "Do you invite massacre by your own carelessness? Here's how thousands have committed suicide by scorning laws that were passed to keep them alive."

Because of the passage of time between the accident and this publication, the child's parents *assumed* that the news value attached to the incident had vanished. So they sued for invasion of the child's privacy.

Actually, the use of the child's photo was not an invasion of privacy. If the magazine article had used the photo in an article about *careless*

[6]Rothstein, *op. cit.*, p. 189.
[7]Steigleman, *op. cit.*, p. 212   [8]*Ibid.*, p. 215.

motorists who endangered lives, the case would have been thrown out of court. No grounds would have existed for the suit. But the magazine used the child's photo in an article about careless pedestrians, making it appear that the child had been at fault when she was struck by a car. This was not the case. The court ruled that the child's parents should be paid a settlement by the magazine because it had misrepresented the true facts in the case, and by so doing, lost its *privilege* to use the child's photo without being subject to a law suit. No publication has the right to twist or distort the truth. The magazine article made the child seem to be a pictorial, frightful example of pedestrian carelessness, which she was not. In this instance, the editor and not the photographer was responsible for the law suit.[9]

A man and his wife were seated in their shop in the Los Angeles Farmer's Market — a *public place*. They were photographed without their knowledge or consent in an affectionate pose. The picture was published in a magazine article on marriage. The couple sued for invasion of privacy and won. The court said: Couples in amorous demonstrations should be protected from the broadcast of that most intimate relation . . . even though the display is in a public place. That they are unthinking . . . does not give consent to be photographed.[10]

Who Owns The Picture?

The person who pays for the making of the photograph owns it. A portrait photographer keeps negatives. But his customers own them. The portrait photographer who displays photographs of customers in his windows or who sells a photograph for publication off of a customer's negative without written permission is courting trouble. In both cases, the customer through the court can (1) make the photographer remove the picture from his window; (2) recover the money paid to the photographer for the picture and also damages resulting from publication, if these can be proved.

Staff photographers on newspapers and magazines do not own the pictures they shoot. The pictures belong to the employer, who paid for having them made.

A free lance who undertakes a job — hires out — will not own the pictures he shoots unless he has a written agreement with his employer about who owns what rights. If the photographer states in his written agreement that he is selling one-publication rights to the employer, and that the free lance retains all other rights and is the owner of the negatives and all other photos made from them, he is protected.

---

[9]Leverton v. Curtis Publishing Co.
[10]Rothstein, *op. cit.*, p. 184.

A free lance who offers photographs for sale to publications should stamp on the back of every picture what rights can be bought with the pictures. Silence works in favor of the picture purchaser. If no restrictions are stated in writing when the picture is sold, the entire picture and all rights pass to the purchaser.

Also unless your written sales agreement specifies a byline, the purchaser doesn't have to give you the credit line. One who buys property, even a photograph, has the right to do with it as he wishes. The purchaser of your photographs may even crop out your name in the corner of the photographs if he wishes.

Only the owner of the picture has the right to copyright it. You should copyright all photos with a market value. Free registration forms can be obtained from the Registrar of Copyrights, Library of Congress, Washington, D. C. Your protection will last for 28 years. It can be renewed once for the same period of time. Some professionals who sell regularly to publications rely on the fact that the entire publication is copyrighted. If your photograph was sold with a one-publication right, this is slim protection.

Photographs sent to salon exhibits should be copyrighted, even though most jurisdictions hold that such exhibitions do not constitute publication.

All photographs are protected by a common law copyright until they are published. After publication, unless protected by a legal copyright, pictures belong in the public domain, and can be used free by anyone. If someone appropriates one of your unpublished photographs and publishes it, under the common law copyright you have solid grounds for a suit.

Libel Is No Joke

If you make a picture of someone as a joke which holds the person up to scorn, ridicule, contempt, and hatred, and causes people to shun him, you have harmed his good reputation and libeled the individual. And if you show this photograph to a number of your friends, the photograph is published. If the subject of the photograph hears what is happening, you may find yourself in a very serious situation, facing a libel suit.

That you meant no harm to the individual will not be a defense. The law is very strict. It insists that a publisher must be responsible for what he circulates. For example, newspapers can't possibly check out all the Associated Press and United Press International stories they print. But if a newspaper uses a wire story which is libelous, the newspaper is just as guilty of the libel (it circulated it) as AP or UPI, whichever service originated the libel. In this example, the newspaper

258

certainly didn't mean to libel anyone, and had no bad motive or intent to harm the person libeled. But the paper circulated the story which harmed a reputation. So the law holds the paper guilty of the libel along with the wire service.

Five Restrictions on Photographs

Photographers must cope with five restrictions on photographs. Two restrictions concern content. The law bans content which is either libelous or obscene. Further restrictions include other photos banned by law, the invasion of privacy, and difficulties of shooting court room events.

Libel

As indicated in the last section, libel is printing, pictures, or signs which injure a person's good reputation by holding the person up to ridicule, scorn, contempt, and hatred and causing others to shun him.

The content of the photo may be libelous, an invasion of privacy, or both. Or the picture may be an innocent photograph, but the overline or the cutline libelous. The greatest trouble in libel with regard to photographs results from the writing — the overline or the cutlines. The speed with which a newspaper must be thrown together results in such errors as getting two pictures and their captions mixed. Suppose a girl commits suicide, which the law holds as a crime. The paper has the story and a 1-column mug shot. But after the paper is published, it turns out that the photo which was published is of a girl who is still alive. The reputation of the live girl is harmed by publishing that she has committed suicide. She sues and collects for libel from the newspaper.[11]

Situations which are of more concern to cameramen concern libelous photographic content and the invasion of privacy. When either of these occurs, the injured plaintff will sue the publisher because the latter has the most money. However, the suit can include all who had anything to do with the libel or the privacy invasion, especially the photographer.

Practical joke photos and photos for which models did not get compensation and give release are dangerous. Professional men — doctors, lawyers, ministers, and teachers — guard their reputations, for their livelihoods are at stake. A lawyer on a golf green with a volume by Blackstone pasted into his hand won't think it's funny. A doctor in evening dress with a glass of champagne (at your New Year's Eve

---

[11]Wandt v. Chicago American, 109 N.Y. 70.

party) pasted into a background of the operating room where he seems to be directing affairs could end a friendship and cost you a lot of money.

Any kind of publication which causes a person or a group to want to breach the peace is criminal libel, a crime against the state. A thoughtless editorial in the South on integration or a photograph which causes a riot could be prosecuted for criminal libel.

Suppose a professional model posed for photographs for a State Health Service. The male model was paid and signed releases. His photograph was used in a series of educational releases on venereal diseases. He was referred to in the release as a man with a venereal disease. If the model tried to sue for libel, a court would hold that he was paid for his services and that when he signed releases, he gave his consent for the Health Service to use the photos in the promotion of their work — the public's health. He should have suspected how a health service might use the pictures. The model would lose the case.[12]

Suppose you photograph a girl model, give her some pictures, and forget to get the release. Your agent sells one of the pictures to a national magazine. The agent made an honest mistake and furnished a release for another picture. The photograph is used in an article on prostitution. The girl isn't called a prostitute, but the implication is there. She will sue and she has an excellent chance of winning.

Obscenity

Obscenity is regarded as criminal libel by the law. Obscenity is defined by the American Legal Institute Model Penal code as that which predominantly appeals to a morbid interest in sex and nudity. Words are obscene which go substantially beyond the limits of candor in describing sex and nudity.

Most courts apply the Roth test[13] in trying to decide whether a book or a photograph is obscene. Average people (not art experts) of a community must examine the object (book or picture) and ask: Does it appeal to my base and degrading interests? Is it lewd, indecent, and a corruption of public morals? If the answer is yes, the object is obscene.

Any photographer who turns out obscene photographs or who joins a group not affiliated with a recognized college, university, or art school for a "life" class with nude models is living dangerously. Penalties for obscene photographs range from about one year in jail, or a

---

12Thayer, Frank, *Legal Control of the Press*, pp. 368-69.
13Roth v. US, 354 U.S. 476, 77 S. Ct. 1304 (1957)

fine of $150, or both, up to five years in jail, or a $5,000 fine, or both. Some states have a law which permits the confiscation of property in relation to arrest for obscene photographs. A typical statute says:

Any peace officer may seize any equipment used in photographing, filming, printing, producing or projecting of pornographic still or motion pictures and may seize any vehicle or other means of transportation . . . and such equipment or vehicle may be subject to forfeiture . . .[14]

It is illegal to sell, lend, give, show obscene photographs or to have them in your possession with the intention of selling, lending, giving, or showing them.

"Life" classes where models pose in the raw which are not conducted by recognized educational establishments invite the surprise appearance of the sheriff. All participants will be jailed. Unwelcome publicity will result.

Other Banned Photographs: Federal Regulations

In addition to avoiding libel and obscenity in photographs, photographers are not permitted to make pictures of money, stamps, securities, or citizenship papers which would be counterfeit. But photographs of one person handing another money, or a stamped letter would not run into trouble. Postal regulations forbid the mailing of obscene photographs.

Regulations of the Navy, Army, and Air Force provide authority for military officers to ban photography on military posts, installations or naval vessels. Photography may be permitted under military supervision. If so, an armed forces public relations officer has the right to review all prints before publication.

Outside of military installations, military officers have no authority to interfere with news photography reporting unless classified material is involved. If the classified material cannot be moved out of the scene, military officers have the right to request that photos not be taken. Any photographer who ignores such a request and photographs classified material faces prosecution under Title 18, Section 793 (e) of the United State Code. On conviction, the maximum penalty is a fine of $10,000 or a 10 year sentence, or both.

Generally, photographic coverage of both houses of congress is permitted. However, secret committee sessions of both houses occur occasionally and reporters and photographers are barred. Some committee sessions permit reporters and bar photographers.

---

[14]Sherwin, Robert Veit, *Legal Aspect of Photography*, Chilton Company, Philadelphia and New York, 1961, p. 17.

Invasion of Privacy

Decisions in two cases which do not involve photographs exclusively show why the right of privacy is more of an ethical than a legal right. Boris Sidis had been a child prodigy who enrolled at Harvard at the age of 11. He dropped out of sight after having amazed Harvard professors and receiving a degree. In 1937 the *New Yorker Magazine* did a profile on Sidis, over his vigorous protest. Sidis sued to prevent publication. The court denied the plea of Sidis and permitted the publication, saying:

> Regrettable or not the misfortunes and frailities of neighbors and "public figures" are subjects of considerable interest and discussion to the rest of the public. And when such are the mores of the community it would be unwise for a court to bar their expression in the newspapers, books, and magazines of the day.[15]

The Alabama Supreme Court rendered a similar decision on a suit brought by two sisters over a radio program featuring their deceased father. The suit charged the program was an invasion of family privacy.

> The court held that the broadcast was of public interest, saying: Frequently the public has an interest in an individual which transcends his right to be let alone, and freedom of speech in broadcasting, like freedom of the press, among other things, is to preserve untrammeled a vital source of public information.[16]

These cases indicate that courts often do not intervene to protect privacy, so editors must set their own standards. The code of ethics of the American Society of Newspaper Editors leaves room for individual interpretation. This code says, "A newspaper should not invade private rights or feelings without sure warrant of public right as distinguished from public curiosity."

In an early case involving publication of a photograph, the state of Washington denied the right of privacy. A news story reported the arrest of a man charged with swindling. A photograph of the defendant *and his daughter* was published. The daughter sued for invasion of privacy. As in the case of *Roberson vs. Rochester Folding Box Company,* the court admitted a wrong had been done, but said that since the state had no law on the matter, no remedy existed for the young lady.[17]

---

[15]Sidis v. F-R Publishing Corp., 113 F. (2d.) 806.

[16]Brown, Charles M., *News Editing and Display,* Harper & Brothers, New York, 1952, p. 303.

[17]Hillman v. Star Publishing Co., 64 Wash. 691, 1911.

Some states which have refused to recognize the theory of the right of privacy do afford a little protection. Where a photographer has been responsible for the publication of a picture which harmed the subject, the court has held that unless there is a release, an *implied contract* exists between the photographer and the subject that the photograph *will not be published*. Since the implied contract has been breached, the subject should be repaid by the photographer for the harm done. And if the court doesn't pursue this reasoning, then the subject has no recourse at law unless he can prove that the publication of the photo has injured him.

Clear-cut Invasions of Privacy

Court decisions indicate that the use of a person's photograph for purposes of trade (in an advertisement) without the person's permission is a violation of the person's rights. If individuals weren't afforded this protection, their photographs might be plastered wholesale in rest rooms, houses of prostitution, and bars.

Unless a medical patient gives consent in writing, no one has the right to make photographs of him, not even the operating physician. Neither the physician nor the hospital has the right to give a photographer permission to photograph the patient. A physician who took photographs of an involved operation was forced by a court to destroy the negatives.[18]

Privacy After Death

A new-born baby's heart was outside of its body. The baby died. With permission of the hospital, a photograph of the baby was made and published. The parents sued for invasion of privacy. The court said: The right of privacy for the baby ceased at the death of the baby. On appeal, a higher court said: Publishing the baby's photograph was also an invasion of the parent's privacy. So the defendants lost the suit. This decision was counter to the general rule that privacy does stop with a person's death.[19]

A later case in 1951 contradicts the previous case, tried in 1930. A photograph of a child who had died in an automobile accident was published. The parents sued for invasion of privacy. The court referred to the early case and then pointedly insisted that the general rule was a good one: The right of privacy ceases at death. So the parents lost this case.[20]

---

[18]Sherwin, *op. cit.*, p. 65.

[19]*Ibid.*, p. 61.   [21]*Ibid.*, p. 62.

[20]Steigleman, *op. cit.*, p. 217.

The risk of invading someone's right of privacy, even though you may sell the photograph for a large sum of money, will bring you little but trouble.

Privacy Suits Which Failed

A woman who wanted to sell her sofa ran the following advertisement: "Robert Mitchum (the movie star) sat here." Mitchum sued for invasion of his privacy. The court denied Mitchum's plea, saying: Movie stars make a living selling themselves to the public. They have only a very limited claim on privacy.[21]

A women committed suicide. A newspaper published her photograph with this news. Her husband sued for invasion of privacy. The court denied the claim saying: The woman was the principal in an occurrence of public interest.[22]

A husband and a wife who had been divorced were involved in a custody suit over their two children. During a court recess, a news photographer photographed the mother and the two children. Picture captions said, "Mrs. Berg, 36, comforts youngsters during break in trial," and "Bewildered, Charleen, 7, and Charles, 3-1/2, stick close to mother." A suit for invasion of privacy was filed by the father. The court denied the plea, saying that the litigation of Berg and his wife made them participants in a matter of public interest.[23] Many editors would have refused to publish this picture with the children in it. Why drag these innocent victims into the lime light?

Court Photographs

Courts were set up to dispense justice and replace physical violence between two parties having a disagreement. So that the judge could keep order in the court and be respected by all with whom the court dealt, judges were given a powerful weapon — the power to cite for contempt of court. This is the power to fine or to imprison or both anyone who is rude to the court, or who lies to the court, or who causes a court disturbance, or disobeys a judge, or ignores written court orders. Acts committed in the court room which are cited for contempt are *direct* contempt. Acts committed outside the court which are cited are *indirect* contempt.

Federal and state constitutions require criminal prosecutions to be public. But these guarantees do not give reporters and photographers an absolute right to be present at trials. A "public" trial means that

---

22Metter v. Los Angeles Examiner 95 p. (2d.), 491.

23Brown, *op. cit.,* p. 304.

others beside court officials are present. It does not mean that all who wish to attend may do so. Some cases are not fit for young people to observe because of the human depravity that is revealed. A trial is considered to be "public" if a reasonable portion of the public is suffered to attend. A public trial is for the benefit of the defendant, to make certain that elected officials deal fairly with all. Judges may exercise discretion on who and how many may attend a trial, depending upon such factors as the nature of the trial, the size of the court room, and the temper of the public. The public and reporters and photographers may be barred from trials involving divorce, obscenity, juvenile delinquency, criminal trials, and insanity hearings.

Judge Harris, New York Supreme Court, in citing a photographer for contempt, said, "A defendant in a criminal trial doesn't come into court of his own free will. His presence is required. Further, the defendant is considered to be innocent until proven guilty. The judge is the individual who must see that the defendant's rights of privacy are observed. The defendant is under the protection of the court. He is entitled to be brought into court without molestation — without having his picture taken."[24]

In the early days of photography, films were not as sensitive to light as they now are, and flash lamps had not yet appeared. Indoor photographs required flash powder which made a noise and filled the room with fumes. Pictures under these circumstances in a court were out of the question. In the 1930's after film had been improved and the flash lamp was commonly used, judges were not keen on having court events photographed. The flash was a distraction. Putting in and removing flash lamps did make noises. An occasional photographer who didn't conduct himself properly in court gave the other photographers a poor reputation with judges. Then came the kidnapping and murder of the Lindbergh baby and the subsequent trial of Bruno Hauptmann for the crime.

Lindbergh was a national hero. The public and trial officials with the aid of newspapers went on an emotional binge. Trial by newspaper took place. A week after Hauptmann's arrest in September, 1934, a newspaper headline said, "Clues Build Iron-Clad Case Against Bruno, Police Claim." Another headline proclaimed, "Bruno Guilty, But Has Aids, Says Man in Street." This head was over a story in which a reporter had selected 12 people at random and interviewed them about the case. The group was referred to by the reporter as a jury. These headlines asked the public to believe newspaper evidence before any evidence had been submitted to a court of law. Guilty or not, Hauptmann had a right to be tried only once before an unprejudiced jury.

---

[24]251 N.Y.S. 615, 1931.

Seating capacity was 260. About 275 people without passes were let into an already crowded room. Pictures were forbidden, but they were taken anyhow. A paragraph from *The Newspaperman and the Law* says:

At the trial of Bruno Richard Hauptmann for the kidnapping of the Lindbergh baby, photographers operated without much restriction. One of the best pictures was that of Charles A. Lindbergh. . . . So many flash bulbs were popping most of these pictures looked as if they were taken on a hazy morning.[25]

Trial officials acted irregularly. Some had political ambitions. Most depended on popular favor. None had the courage to get caught between advocating what was right and public emotion. The press carried stories which prevented a fair trial. Why? Editors and reporters like to compete, to get their teeth into a juicy, emotion-packed story and to feel reader response. Paper owners did not intervene. Lindbergh copy, fair or unfair, sold papers.

Deeply disturbed over this Roman carnival which took place in a court where a man's life was at stake, the American Bar Association passed Canon 35. This rule says the taking of photographs in court or during recess detracts from the proceedings and distracts witnesses and degrades the court and should not be permitted.

So you find yourself with an assignment to get some court photographs. With a 35 mm camera and fast film you can get excellent pictures without flash. You will make less noise than a reporter taking pencil notes for a word story. No longer is the photographer's equipment a disturbance in court. But TV has come along with bright lights and cables, and it wants into the court, too. There is some question of whether a defendant can do himself justice on the witness stand, knowing that millions of viewers are watching his every move.

Federal judges who are appointed for life are the most militant about keeping cameras out of courts.[26] Judges in state district courts are elected officials. Generally, they are more cooperative, and most of them do permit cameras and photographs in court. But the wise photographer will get permission in advance rather than risk a citation for contempt. Permission to take court photographs is not permission to stand in your seat, to move past the guard rail, or to disrupt proceedings.

The National Press Photographers Association has done much to educate judges and lawyers on advances which have been made in

---

[25]Steigleman, *op. cit.*, p. 165.
[26]Federal courts are governed by Rule 53, Rules of Criminal Procedure, adopted by the US Supreme Court in 1945. Rule 53 says neither the taking of photographs nor radio broadcasting will be permitted during the judicial proceedings.

photo equipment so that photos can now be taken in court without anyone, even the judge, knowing where the camera was located. Photographs have been made at state bar association meetings and mock trials to prove this point a number of times.

A judge with his power of contempt is not an opponent most photographers are equipped to joust with. It is a losing game, as the following cases indicate.

Cases

Judge O'Dunne of the Baltimore Criminal Court saw a flash and requested the negative. The photographer handed him a blank. Another photographer remained in court with a small, concealed camera and made other photographs. All were printed in either the *News* or the *American*, both under one management. The judge cited the editor and the photographers for contempt. The editor was fined $5,000 and both he and the photographers spent one day in jail.[27]

The case was affirmed by a higher court which commented:
The challenge . . . of the court's right to forbid the use of cameras in the courtroom during . . . the trial presents an issue of vital importance. If such a right should yield to an assessed privilege of the press, the authority and dignity of the courts would be seriously impaired.

A Georgia judge forbade cameras in the court house or near it during a trial. At a noon break, one of the attorneys involved in the case began some remarks from the court house steps to all who wished to listen. Soon 300 people were trying to hear him. They blocked automobile traffic in the square. Photographers took pictures of the attorney addressing the crowd. The judge cited the photographers for contempt. Under Georgia law, judges are empowered to preserve and enforce order both in the court room and as near thereto as is necessary to prevent interruption, disturbance, or hinderance of the trial.[28]

National Press Photographers Association "Canons of Courtroom Ethics"

1. In advance of the trial, have a conference with the judge. Reach an understanding on what the judge will and will not permit. Observe the judge's desires.

2. Acquaint court officers and bailiffs with the rules which the judge has agreed to. These people can be of great help to photographers.

3. Since your camera will draw attention to you, dress conservatively and inconspicuously. Your behavior should not be a source of embar-

---

[27]Ex Parte Sturm et al, 136 Atl. 312, Md. 1927.
[28]Atlanta Newspaper, Inc. v. Grimes, 216 Ga. 74, 114 S.E. 2d 421 (1960).

rassment to the paper you represent nor to the newspaper profession. Remember the judge's power of contempt.

4. Don't move about the courtroom between shots. Stay in one seat until recess. Use telephoto lenses for closeups.

5. In trials of national interest, only one or two photographers may be permitted to shoot for a large group of papers. Pooled pictures are better than no pictures at all.

6. Show your appreciation for the judge's cooperation in permitting you to shoot photos in his court by thanking him during a visit to his chambers after the case ends. This is both good manners and good public relations.

7. Use small, roll film cameras to be as inconspicuous as possible. Avoid the distraction of continued eye-level focusing. Focus once, then point the camera from waist level or from a table or railing for triggering.

8. Even if the judge will permit flash, do not use it. It distracts participants and spectators. Measure the light in the court and make tests, if needed, before the trial begins.

Photographer's Rights

The fourteenth amendment of the US Constitution says: No person may be deprived of his personal property without due process of law.

This tenet applied to photography means that no railroad detective or police chief has the right to confiscate your film and camera to prevent you from taking pictures of a train wreck or an incident involving a friend of the chief's. The railroad detective can order you off railroad property. He can prosecute you for trespassing on private property. But he doesn't have the authority to confiscate your private property.

The police chief in Newport, Kentucky, took a photographer's camera and destroyed the film during a gambling raid. After the raid the photographer was arrested and jailed. A Department of Justice investigation resulted in a $1,000 fine for the chief.[29]

Salon exhibitions and picture galleries do have the right to refuse to let you bring in cameras and photograph displays.

Employers of photographers have a responsibility for employees who are injured or who die in the pursuit of duty. A New York City newspaper photographer died while covering General Eisenhower in an American Legion parade. The day was a hot, steamy one. The photographer had chased the General's car for over a mile with a heavy load of equipment. The photographer collapsed and died. The New York State Board of Compensation ruled that the employer should pay for the funeral expenses and pay the widow a pension of $21 a week.[30]

---

[29]Rothstein, *op. cit.*, p. 194.
[30]*Ibid.*, p. 194.

Bibliography

Arnold, Edmund, *Feature Photos That Sell.* Morgan & Morgan, Inc. Hastings-On-Hudson, N. Y. 1960.

Arnold, Rus, *Advanced Flash Photography.* Little Technical Library, Crown Publishers, Inc., New York, 1953.

Carroll, John S. *Photo-Lab-Index.* 25th Edition, Morgan & Morgan, Inc. Hastings-On-Hudson, N. Y. 1966.

Costa, Joseph (ed.). *Complete Book of Press Photography.* National Press Photographers Association, Inc., 1950.

Feininger, Andreas, *Feininger on Photography.* Ziff Davis Publishing Company, Chicago, New York, 1949.

Gebbie Press House Magazine Directory. New York City 17, New York, 1954.

Haz, Nicholas. *Image Management.* Nicholas Haz Books, Cincinnati 1, Ohio, 1946.

Kalish, Stanley E. and Edom, Clifton C. *Picture Editing.* Holt, Rinehart & Winston Company, New York and Toronto, 1951.

Lootens, J. Ghislain. *Lootens on Photographic Enlarging and Print Quality.* The Camera, Baltimore, Maryland, 1946.

Luray, Howard. *"Strobe" — The Lively Light,* Camera Craft Publishing Company, San Francisco, California, 1949.

Medlin, Calvin J. *School Yearbook Editing and Management.* Kansas State College Press, Manhattan, Kansas, 1949.

Mitch and Eberman. *The Technique of the Picture Story.* New York and London, McGraw-Hill Book Company, Inc., 1945.

Morgan, Willard D., *Graphic-Graflex Photography,* 11th Edition. Morgan & Morgan, Inc., Hastings-On-Hudson, N. Y. 1958.

Morgan, Willard D. *Leica Manual.* Morgan & Morgan, Inc. Hastings-On-Hudson, N.Y. 1965.

Murphy, Don. "Edgerton and His Magic Light," *Readers Digest*, April, 1958.

Reddick, Dewitt C. *Modern Feature Writing*. Harper & Row, New York, 1949.

Rothstein, Arthur. *Photo Journalism*. American Photographic Book Publishing Co., Inc., New York, 1956.

Scacheri, Mario and Mabel. *The Fun of Photography*. Harcourt, Brace & World, Inc., New York, 1938.

Sherwin, Robert V. *Legal Aspects of Photography*. Chilton Company, Philadelphia, New York, 1957.

Steigleman, Walter A. *The Newspaperman and the Law*. Wm. C. Brown Company, Dubuque, Iowa, 1950.

Thayer, Frank. *Legal Control of the Press*. The Foundation Press, Inc., Brooklyn, 1962.

Vitray, Laura, Mills, John Jr., and Ellard, Roscoe. *Pictorial Journalism*. McGraw-Hill Book Company, Inc., New York and London, 1939.

White, Theodore H., *The Making of a President*: 1964, Atheneum Publishers, New York, 1964.

Whiting, John R. *Photography Is A Language*. Ziff Davis Publishing Company, Chicago, New York, 1946.

Index

C

Camera, angle between, and moving object, 22
closeness to subject, distortions resulting from, 151

for record shots, 126
placing, corrective portrait lighting, 101
point of view of, 153
proximity to subject, 153-54, 173
swing of, 24
Camera angle, 173
Camera-flash synchronization, strobe light, 120
checking, 121
Camera situations, changing, aperture size for, regulating, 9-11
shutter speed for, regulating, 9-11
shutter speeds and, 7-9
variable in photography, 11
Cannon, Dr. Gaine, 217-21
Canon 35, American Bar Association, 266
"Canons of Courtroom Ethics," National Press Photographers Association, 267-68
Caps, Robert, photo by, 236
Captions, writing, 247-50
to space, 250-51
unit count for headlines and overlines, 250
C cell photoflash batteries, 120
Center of interest, record shots, 172
Change of pace posing in record shots, 134
Charts, time and temperature, 44
Chemicals, photographic, buying, mixing and storing, 74-75
developer ingredients, 46
Circle of confusion, 20
Clark, Joe, photos by, 154, 204 238
Close-up shots, 153, 154 173
meter measurement, 79-80
strobe light 122
Cobb, Dick, photos by, 38, 43, 92, 94, 96, 108, 110, 114, 124, 127, 130, 133, 134, 135, 136, 137, 138
Collage, 246, 247
Color blind films, 6, 85
"Colorless" light, 87
Color sensitivity of film, 36, 86

Common law copywright, 258
Community, source of photo ideas, 202-05
Composition, action in pictures, 28
improving, to tell the message, 150-58, 162
Condenser-type enlarger, 75-76
Confusion, circle of, 20
Congress, U. S., photographic coverage of, 261
Constitution, U. S., 253
Contempt of court, 264-65
Continuous tone photos, copying, 90
Contrast, characteristic of enlarging paper, 57
of emulsion, 36
negative, *see* Negative contrast
negative and print, 60
print, changing, 59
scene contrast affects, 63
scene, negative density and print contrast affected by, 63
translating into density and transparency, 63
Contrasty light, 13
Contrasty negative, 62
Contrasty subject matter, 14
Controlled blurs, action in pictures, 28, 155
Converse, Gordon N., photos by, 16, 28, 30
Copying photos, 90-91
Copyright of photos, 212, 258
Correction filter, effect on sky, 88
Corson, Dave, photo by, 129
Courtroom photographs, law and, 264-68
Crookedness in photojournalism, 145-48
Cropping the photograph, 136, 137, 172, 239, 245
Cutline, writing, 247-51
captions 247-50
to space, 250-51
unit count for headlines and overlines, 250

D

D'Addario, Vincent, photo by, 162
Darkest object method, 82
Davis, B. G., photo by, 13
Dead space eliminating, 171
horizontal, 125, 128, 131
vertical 124, 128, 131

278

mailing, preparation for, 212
overexposed, purposely, 59
reproduction of, 235
rubber stamp for, 211
Print tongs, 70
Proportion, determining size of printed
    picture, 239-40
    scale of, using, 242-45
Public characters, definition of, 254
Public places, law and, 255-57
    exceptions, 256-57

Q

Quality and quantity of light, 24-25

R

Ray, Billy, photo by, 98
Reader interest, 182-83
Reader preference, news photos, 169-
    70, 171, 178
Reader's Digest, 202
Real action, 32, 33
Record shots, 123, 170, 171-72
    action in, 171
    cropping, 172
    dead space in, eliminating, 171
    depth of field, 172
    emotional shots vs., 149-50
    negative, exposing, 171
    posing people for, *see* Posing people
      for record shots
Reducer, developer ingredient, 46
Reducing size of photo to smaller cut,
    244
Reel, 41, 43
Reflected light, meters that measure,
    83
Reflectors, 104, 109-10
Region, source of photo ideas, 202-05
Release form, 210-11, 255, 260, 263
    news photos not requiring, 252, 253-
    55
Rtmbrandt lighting, 94
Reproduction of the print, 235
Restrictions on photographs, legal, 259-
    68
Reticulation, 50
Revolving calculator, 90
Reynolds, Paul R., 192
Reynolds Tobacco Company, R. J.,
    photo from, 153
Rights of photographers, legal, 268

Rights of privacy, 265-66
Roberson vs. *Rochester Folding Box
    Company*, 262
Roberts, Bruce, 217
    photos by, 147, 160, 218-20, 222-27
Roth test for obscenity, 260
Rozumalski, Ted, photos by, 28, 153
Rubber stamp for prints, 211
Rules, mixing and applying, 23-24

S

Saturday Evening Post, 160, 169, 185
Scale of proportions, using, 242-45
Scaling to determine size of printed
    picture, 240-45
Scanagraver, Fairchild, 124-25
Scayles, Joseph, photo by, 236
Scene contrast, negative density and
    print contrast affected by, 63
    translating into density and r tans-
      parency, 63
scharfman, Herb, photo by, 120
Schulke, Flip, photo by, 30
Schweitzer Dr. Albert, 217, 218
Script outline for photo sequence, 215
Seals, Sandy, photo by, 13
Seasonal pictures, 180, 182, 183, 184
Securities pictures of, 261
Selective focusing, emphasis by, 159
Sequences, *see* Photo sequences
Seubert, Earl, photos by, 135, 177
Sex appeal in photos, 139
Shadow, background, 108-09
Shaffer, James L., photos by, 12, 160
Sheet film tanks, 38, 39
Short focal length lenses, 18
    distortions in, 20
Shoulders, Jim, 198
Shutter speed, 7-9, 26
    changing from one speed to another,
    8
    regulating, for changing camera situ-
      ation, 9-11
    selecting, for flash exposure, 103,
      104, 105
Sidis, Boris, 262
Significant detail, 154, 160, 174
Silhouette, 174
    improving composition, 155
Silhouette halftone, 247
Silhouette lighting, 94-95
Silk, George, photo by, 147

281